The
Episcopal Church,
Homosexuality,
and the
Context of Technology

The

Episcopal Church, Homosexuality,

and the

Context of Technology

George Hobson

Foreword by
Craig G. Bartholomew

PICKWICK *Publications* · Eugene, Oregon

THE EPISCOPAL CHURCH, HOMOSEXUALITY,
AND THE CONTEXT OF TECHNOLOGY

Pickwick Publications
An Imprint of Wipf and Stock Publishers
199 W. 8th Ave., Suite 3
Eugene, OR 97401
www.wipfandstock.com

ISBN 13: 978-1-62032-261-1

Cataloguing-in-Publication data:

Hobson, George, 1940–

The Episcopal Church, homosexuality, and the context of technology /
George Hobson ; foreword by Craig G Bartholomew.

xviii + 200 pp. ; 23 cm. Includes bibliographical references.

ISBN 13: 978-1-62032-261-1

1. Episcopal Church. 2. Homosexuality—Religious aspects—Episcopal
Church. 3. Technology—Religious aspects—Christianity. I. Bartholomew, Craig G.,
1961–. II. Title.

BX5930.3 .H62 2013

Manufactured in the U.S.A.

Updated print file 7/9/2013

For John Paris and Dave Simpson:
Brothers in Christ, dear friends,
Who have revealed to me different colors
in the spectrum of our Savior

and

For Guy Bonnal, Georges Siguier, and Jacques Bossière:
Spiritual fathers, companions in the work of the Gospel,
Intrepid witnesses to the risen Christ

Contents

PART I

TECHNOLOGY AS THE MATRIX OF MODERNITY:
ITS RELATION TO THE QUESTION OF HOMOSEXUALITY

Section I

Section II

PART II

THE QUESTION OF HOMOSEXUALITY
IN THE CONTEXT OF MODERNITY

Section III

Foreword

I AM GLAD TO write a foreword to this excellent work by George Hobson. The homosexual issue is highly controversial in the Western context and is as a result one that many academics simply avoid addressing. Not so George. He rightly and courageously insists that this is a nettle that needs to be grasped since so much is at stake in how we respond to the challenge of homosexual practice in our culture today.

This work represents a fresh and comprehensive approach to homosexuality. I would describe it as *missional*. Lesslie Newbigin rightly noted that mission is done at the intersection, the crossroads, of two stories, the biblical story and our cultural story. He described the intersection of these two stories as a place of unbearable tension, the place of mission. The genius of this work is that it wrestles with the ethics of homosexual relations at this tense intersection by insisting on exploring rigorously the biblical and theological traditions *as well as* our cultural story and the intersection between the two.

Indeed, a central and persuasive thesis of this book is that we will not grasp the challenge of sexuality today unless we understand it in the context of the larger dynamic of modernity and, especially, of technology. Readers familiar with the literature on sexuality may wonder what on earth technology has to do with the subject. That is precisely the point. What is manifesting itself in sexual practices today is far more than a liberal ethic; instead sexuality, being a profound aspect of our relationality, inevitably expresses the deepest cultural dynamics of our day. And technology is a major entrance into such dynamics. Years ago Jacques Ellul noted how our Western culture was being dominated by technique and more recently in four major books on the topic Bill Vanderburg has built on Ellul's analysis.[1] George persuasively connects contemporary sexual ethics into the currents of modern culture thereby showing that far from being liberating they are part of our brokenness and a manifestation of negative aspects of our declining culture. George's analysis of Western culture is far more nuanced and richer than my brief reference to it here. What must be noted is that his cultural critique is radical and cannot simply be dismissed as "right-wing".

Just as homosexual practice cannot be separated from the cultural dynamics of our day so too it cannot be separated from the network of Christian belief. To shift from orthodoxy on this issue necessitates major reconstruction of Christian doctrine to the point where it becomes unrecognizable. George's evocative critique of "open communion," now widely practiced in Episcopal churches across America, is a case in point. Communion has become *the* place at which to express inclusivism so that any notion of the necessity of repentance in order to receive Christ has long disappeared. Christian ethics *is* theological and George rightly and in exemplary fashion insists that a Christian approach to homosexual practice must engage the biblical drama and the Christian tradition. It simply will not do to keep declaring that this is just a matter of social justice, without even carefully examining the tradition of justice with which one is working.

George is quite open about the fact that he comes down on the conservative side of the homosexual debate. In this I think he is right. However, his brand of conservatism is far from a right-wing, anti-homosexual caricature. He is deeply sensitive to the pain and oppression of homosexuals, rightly aware of the importance of civil rights for all citizens, and deeply concerned for an appropriate pastoral response to members of churches with homosexual orientations. But he rightly argues that we best serve our neighbour and culture by serving God, and thus by upholding a biblical view of marriage and sexuality.

The aim of this book is to open a dialogue. In my opinion one could not wish for a better dialogue partner. Not surprisingly – George is a published poet – the book is very well written, the style is irenic and carefully nuanced while clearly putting the central issues on the table for discussion, as should be the case in healthy dialogue. There is much here

---

1. See Bill Vanderburg, *Growth of Minds and Culture*; *The Labyrinth of Technology*; *Living in the Labyrinth of Technology: A Preventive Technology and Economic Strategy as a Way Out*; *Our War Against Ourselves: Rethinking Science, Technology and Economic Growth*; all published by the University of Toronto Press. Vanderburg did his post-doctoral work under Ellul.

for both sides to learn from in the currently polarized debate about homosexuality in the church. None of us are exempt from the disordered love that our culture is awash with and an understanding of where this is coming from should increase our compassion and pastoral integrity. At the same time it simply will not do to bypass Scripture and the tradition; our allegiance to God demands that we take these with utmost seriousness. By focusing on the homosexual issue in depth George has ended up casting a light on our present situation that extends way beyond sexuality. This is a profound book and one that calls for serious engagement. My hope is that it will receive precisely that.

Craig G. Bartholomew.
H. Evan Runner Professor of Philosophy and Professor of Religion and Theology at Redeemer University College, Ontario; Principal of the Paideia Centre for Public Theology.
Publications include *Ecclesiastes* and *Where Mortals Dwell: A Christian View of Place for Today.*

Acknowledgments

I OWE A HUGE debt of gratitude to Sylvie Botétémé, without whose technical assistance I could never have submitted a finished manuscript to the publishers. Many kind friends—I shall not even attempt to name them all, they know who they are—provided sensitive criticism and invaluable encouragement. My wife, Victoria, first-rate editor and most loving helpmeet, gave me unflagging moral support over the three years that I was engaged in this project, and tirelessly bore with me the strain of my task. I cannot express to her how grateful I am and shall always be.

Introduction

THIS ESSAY IS AN attempt to stimulate serious dialogue between the extreme positions adopted within the Protestant mainline churches, in particular the Episcopal Church, on the subject of homosexuality. I write from within the conservative camp, but my aim is to provide a new perspective on the subject that may help to promote genuine theological debate. Such debate has been largely lacking so far. The matter at issue is momentous and is dividing the churches, just at a moment when the Christian Church across the world is under major attack on every front, from without and from within. The mainline churches seem rather indifferent to this larger context, which should at the very least incite them to seek to speak with a single voice. Unity should be our aim. But this cannot be, of course, at the expense of truth. What is the truth in this matter? That is the challenging question.

The problem is that both sides in the debate so far—if "debate" is really the word to describe the hostile stand-off prevailing today—claim to "have" the truth. The "liberal" position is certain that its stance is prophetic and represents a powerful move of the Holy Spirit in our time. The "conservative", or "traditionalist", position holds that the liberal position is an arbitrary betrayal of the Gospel and of the universal Church's long-standing and well-founded tradition. Between these positions there is little common ground, which makes the quest for unity seem quixotic and futile. The concern for "truth" appears to trump unity.[2]

---

2. The majority of churchgoers in TEC and other mainline Protestant churches in America probably don't fall categorically into one or the other of these two clear-cut positions. Ambivalence, uncertainty, confusion, are the order of the day. This is probably true of many priests and pastors as well, and of the parishes they lead, who will be struggling to find some way of harmonizing the two extremes. For the purposes of this essay, however, I shall use the words "liberal" and "conservative" in broad-stroke manner to characterize the opposing perspectives on the place of homosexuality in the Church.

In an issue as fundamental as this one, it may well be that, at bottom, substantial truth is on one side and not on the other, and that substantial doctrinal unity is impossible. It may well be that "compromise" is not possible. I am inclined to believe, reluctantly, that this is the case. But that cannot be determined without ongoing and extensive dialogue, nor does it make what I might call "performative unity" impossible. "Performative unity" can be achieved by doing what the Apostle Paul calls "speaking the truth in love" (Eph 4:15), even if the positions on the substance of truth are at odds. Such "speaking" is what I mean by genuine debate, or dialogue. It involves rational exposition of the respective positions in an attitude of mutual consideration, which, under the circumstances, is the way of love. Even if substantive unity is never achieved, such debate would give glory to God by showing evidence of the Gospel's power to lift opponents above hostility into the sphere of respect and understanding.

It is this that has been largely absent in the last three decades, since the issue of homosexuality came into prominence in Western society and in the Church.[3] *Discussion* in the churches there has been, certainly, though it has focused principally on canonical or administrative points rather than on theologically substantive ones. These points are important, but they cannot go to the heart of the matter. There have been numerous declarations and resolutions emanating from authoritative sources, but scholarly or pastoral *arguments* from those same sources, taking into consideration the broad range of theological and social issues involved, have been few and far between. What has been missing, once again, has been genuine *debate*, as I have defined it above, where both sides sit down and in good faith, with patience and respect, present their case, each side taking care to respond thoughtfully, point by point, to the other's arguments. Such reasoned exchange, which would take years, would prohibit rash or peremptory conclusions.

I believe that this is what our Lord Jesus Christ, in whom we all claim to believe and whom we wish to obey, wants of us. He is the Truth, and He is Love. No side "has" the truth, even if it should be the case that

---

3. A notable exception to this general state of affairs was the publication by the Anglican Church of the *St. Andrew's Day Statement* in 1995, subtitled "An Examination of the Theological Principles Affecting the Homosexuality Debate". It was followed in 1997 by *The Way Forward?*, a volume of thirteen essays by well-known British theologians responding from a variety of perspectives to the St. Andrew's Day Statement. This volume was a loud call for, and example of, just the sort of debate this essay is intended to stimulate. A second edition was issued in 2003, followed by an American edition in 2004. To my knowledge, The Episcopal Church has produced nothing similar.

one of the sides discerns and is more faithful to God's truth than the other. He who *is* the Truth "has" *us*, and requires of us that we love each other. This is a command. He who *is* Truth is above our truths, which means that "performative unity", in obedience to the command to love one another, is possible even where there is strong disagreement. It is to this that we are called.

This short essay is intended to promote such "performative unity". My desire is to widen the field of debate and open new horizons. Writing, as I said above, from within the conservative position, I pull no punches in the essay, but I argue with respect for the liberal position and appreciation of its perspective. The motive of "love" that undergirds that position is honorable and well-intended. Enormous harm has been done by the Church over the centuries to homosexual persons because of fear, incomprehension, and simple lack of love. We have acted out of the Law, not out of grace. This does not mean that the Old Testament Law and moral injunctions in the New Testament concerning homosexual practice are not to be taken seriously—and I shall speak to this in Part II of this essay—but the Church must always situate its understanding and application of the Mosaic Law within the wider framework of grace as it has been shown us once and for all in Jesus Christ.

We must have great compassion for those who really do have a homosexual orientation and who, being *different* from the heterosexual majority, may suffer because of this. The liberal churches are to be commended for genuinely seeking to show such compassion. But their theology and methods—both—must be examined and defended more cogently than has been the case thus far. The liberal position needs to be presented with greater depth by the leaders of the liberal churches, as is fitting for a debate taking place *within* the Church, where only arguments made on theological grounds can ultimately carry conviction. Where my own arguments may be found to lack cogency, I trust that counter-arguments will be offered based on reason and not mere sentiment. Many of my points, in both Part I and Part II, will want in future to be developed more fully by others—either in defense of them or by way of critique—than I am able to do in this short work. My primary goal is to stimulate fresh reflection and exchange by opening an in-habitual perspective on the issues. I offer this contribution as a service to the Church and to its Lord, who is also the Lord of the whole world, our Savior Jesus Christ.

I must add on a personal note that this is a difficult essay for me to write. First of all, the subject as it presents itself to the contemporary

Church is extremely complex, theologically and pastorally. I have the feeling of trying to square the circle. I am encouraged in this, however, by the thought that Christ's achievement at Calvary, and the Holy Spirit's action in the Church, is indeed a supreme and eternal squaring of the circle, in that here judgment and mercy have come together in the Person of Jesus, and in such a way that by grace through faith we inherit and may enter into the miracle the Son of God's sacrifice has accomplished for us, provided we die with him to the "natural man" and allow God to raise us up into new life.

Secondly, a number of persons very close to me are among those whose position I am critiquing. I love them no less for that, and it is my dearest hope that they may be able to say the same thing about me after reading my reflections. My conviction is that this issue—this *question of homosexuality* in the form that it is taking shape in our societies today—has a much deeper significance than is generally recognized. It points to a theological/social reality that goes far beyond the particular issue itself. This is why, in the first half of the essay, I take up the *question of technology*, as providing the appropriate and overarching context for a proper analysis of the question of homosexuality itself.

The ideas presented in Part I may appear difficult, even off-putting, for some, but I would make a plea to such readers to persevere, as I honestly believe that the deeper meaning of the *question of homosexuality* in our day cannot be uncovered without a theological elucidation of matters of much wider scope, in particular the all-encompassing *question of technology*. At first blush the relation to technology of what one might call the *sexual revolution* of the last generation may seem obscure, but I am persuaded that a true grasp of the significance of this revolution requires a consideration of the technological framework in which it is taking place. This in turn, in my view, requires at least a brief theological analysis of a number of factors contributing to the rise and development of modern science-technology itself. I do not aim here to measure the length, breadth, and height of the all-enclosing edifice we call "technology", nor do I propose practical responses to the challenge of this tremendous reality. My hope is that by shedding some light on the connection of these two questions, *homosexuality* and *technology*, both of which are integral to modernity, this essay will help Christians to grasp more clearly the nature of the age we live in and, concomitantly, will open new dimensions in the current debate within the Church regarding the status and practice of homosexuality.

Part I

Technology as the Matrix of Modernity
Its Relation to the Question of Homosexuality

*"Your wisdom and knowledge mislead you when you say to your-
self, 'I am, and there is none besides me.'"*

(Isa 47:10b)

Section I

Technology-as-idol is the ultimate expression and vehicle of mankind's pursuit of autonomy; its aim of auto-salvation, of auto-construction—a New Creation—is a dehumanizing counterfeit of the Gospel that reduces subjects to objects

I.I.1

Humanity's barbarity; technology as a false panacea; the only rational ground of real hope is in Christ

WHEN PEOPLE TALK ABOUT the issue of homosexuality today, they rarely consider its wider theological and cultural setting. For Christians, debate about the issue turns on one's attitude to Scripture and individual rights, as these are construed in the context of modern democratic culture. These are vital matters, of course, but the broader question of the nature of modernity itself and the bearing this has on contemporary understandings of sexuality, is seldom addressed. The debate remains two-dimensional and often seems unconnected to deeper historical and theological currents. Undoubtedly this is one reason why it so quickly becomes polarized and ends in confrontation. Between the opposed positions, large numbers of church-goers, including many priests and pastors, sit mired in confusion. They lack maps to guide them in the rough modern terrain. The traditional coordinates no longer serve, or are no longer enough.

How, for instance, are pertinent biblical passages to be applied to the contemporary scene? "Where are we?" many people ask in bewilderment. "What in the world is going on?" These are common questions when the contentious issue of homosexuality comes up in a conversation.

3

Many Christians have no idea how to address the issue in order to make a rational decision about what position to take or how to act. They are disoriented. To make matters worse, few church leaders come forth to provide them a compass to help them find their bearings. In many parishes on both sides of the divide, the subject is taboo. As a result, parishioners either fall silent or else try to ease their anxiety by grabbing hold of one of the sides of the polarized debate, but without adequate reasons for doing so. Their inner confusion only deepens.

My desire is to dissipate at least some of that confusion, first by a succinct analysis of the cultural setting in which the issue of homosexuality is raised in our day, and second, by an examination of the phenomenon of homosexuality itself and the response to it of the mainline Protestant churches, in particular of The Episcopal Church (TEC). It may appear that my analysis of the cultural setting is excessively dark, not because I do not offer hope for modern men and women, but because the *principle* hope I offer is in Christ and God's grace rather than in human beings themselves and their capacities, prodigious—and in countless ways constructive—though these capacities may be.

I take seriously the prophetic theology of history as set forth from the beginning to the end of the Bible, a theology to which modernity and post-modernity are fundamentally opposed. The last one hundred years have cured many in the West of the common eighteenth and nineteenth century belief in mankind's general moral progress, in consonance with its scientific and material progress; but a sort of "background noise" generated by that belief persists, with the result that the biblical picture of a world gradually collapsing into chaos until Christ returns in glory and establishes order, is ignored or viscerally resisted, even by many in the Church disposed to believe in theory in the divine inspiration of Scripture and its eschatological vision. Despite having witnessed unprecedented evil, modern men and women still hold on in some way to a romantic view of our race and refuse to believe that resistance to God's being and providential order entails dire and ongoing consequences. It may be, after all, that we have lost the naïve belief that mankind in its historical ("fallen") state is "good" (whatever that is supposed to mean), but precisely our own sinfulness—our inordinate pride—prevents us from acknowledging that the human race, barring divine intervention, is trapped in violence and immorality and irremediably lost.

The veneer of benignity in materially prosperous parts of the world, created by technological innovation, democratic aspirations, cultural exchange, and rising prosperity for many—all of which phenomena are admirable in principle and to be applauded—has blinded us to the un-yielding nature of the innate selfishness hidden in the human heart, which undercuts and distorts these phenomena. Under stressful conditions, this selfishness can become barbarity, though in sophisticated societies a sheen of respectability may obscure this. We continue to believe that this barbarity will be definitively overcome—or managed—by our own efforts, through education or health or wealth . . . or *something*. Today, technological development—nothing else—drives this belief and gives it credibility. This is what we mean today when we speak of "progress". But there is really no rational ground for this belief—this *hope*—despite the spectacular technological achievements that make material life for mil-lions so much easier and more comfortable than it used to be. The hope is a longing of the human heart, not an expectation rooted in reason. Ul-timately it is a longing for God and his kingdom of peace, but idolatry of self has turned our hearts away from God, so that we look not to him but rather, in our day, to technology to rescue us from our human plight. This hope-in-man may be no more than a form of denial and self-protection in the face of the horror the world has seen and continues to see, but its force is such that even the widespread fear and confusion that grip many today cannot dislodge it.

If, in this essay, I refuse both cheap grace and illusory optimism, I am no advocate of existential *angst* or the cynical despair of Godless men and women. My aim is to exhort the Church to open its eyes and see that the inner movement of history in our time corresponds more to biblical revelation than to the liberal shibboleths of the Enlightenment, or the fuzzy spirituality of the Romantics, or post-modern relativism, or the technological projections of contemporary human beings. And I also want to appeal to those who, for one reason or another, have lost all faith in God and so inevitably in man as well, and who trust nothing and no one. I say to them: have the courage to lift your gaze beyond the closed universe, beyond the technological dream, to behold the God in whom you don't believe, and to open your hearts to the possibility that Jesus Christ is indeed the Lord of history, and that in him lies your salvation.

This is the hope I espouse: Jesus, Savior and Lord. The Gospel, I am persuaded, is the primary source of the best of what we cherish in modern society, which has to do with human dignity and rights, demo-cratic expression, and openness to the *other-than-ourselves*, in particular to other human beings, as being God's creatures made in the Creator's image and equal before him, therefore deserving, in principle, of respect and welcome. The Church, for all its many deviations in practice from this Gospel since its emergence two thousand years ago, has been the vehicle for the worldwide dissemination of the Good News in Jesus Christ: forgiveness for sins through Christ's reconciling work; the possibility of a changed heart and a new beginning in life regardless of one's past; and hope in a life beyond death in communion with the Creator of all things, in the context of a renewal of this "old earth" under Christ's sovereign Lordship. Wherever this Gospel has been proclaimed and has taken root in a manner faithful to its essence, it has acted as yeast in civil society and, over the centuries, has altered the culture for the better, in the direction of human dignity and equality, mercy, and freedom.

Humanitarian work, struggle on behalf of the poor and oppressed, efforts and advocacy for development and social justice—actions and movements such as these, which we take for granted as givens in developed modern societies, are ultimately rooted in the Christian Gospel and the call of Jesus to love the neighbor, care for the downtrodden, and act justly even to those who harm us. They flow from the Christian conviction that history is purposeful and that human beings have the power and freedom to improve society, even if they cannot redeem it or attain the harmony amongst themselves that only God, through Christ, can, and one day *will*, establish. Regrettably, the Church has not spoken out in the past as it should have done to denounce the destruction of the planet by the human race and push for ecological awareness, but a growing sensitivity to the interconnections of agrarian and social lawlessness is changing this.[1]

No pure Christian society has ever existed, and often the Gospel has been betrayed by its proponents; but this has not changed the Good News in itself, or its liberating power wherever Jesus Christ has been welcomed and followed. It is he who is the hope of those who believe: "*Christ in you, the hope of glory*" (Col 1:27). This is what I mean when I speak of Christ as our hope. With respect both to this world and to eschatological reality, the Person and work of Jesus is the source of hope. It follows that the Church, which is the Body of Christ, is at the heart of any authentic hope modern

---

1. See Davis, *Scripture, Culture*, for an outstanding example of what is coming to be known as "agrarian theology". Using critical biblical exegesis, the author analyzes the Scriptural perspective on agrarian policy and land-use, in contrast with the practices of modern industrialized agriculture. Another wide-ranging analysis of agrarian, ecological, and technological issues based on the doctrine of creation is Norman Wirzba's profound study, *Paradise of God*.

men and women may find. In our secularized age, it may seem counter-intuitive to say this, but it is the case. The Church must not be discouraged. Christ is the Light and Life of the world, and only Christian believers know this. As the clouds darken over humankind, we must shine more brightly. We must grasp with greater passion and exercise with greater wisdom our responsibility to preach, teach, and live the Gospel authentically.

Technology, in its positive dimension as *technique* used for the genuine benefit of humanity—and I do not speak here of its underside, which I shall examine later in this essay—has brought much good to the world, as anyone can see; it has often been the means of achieving some of the social benefits alluded to above. But it cannot change the heart of human beings, or bring forgiveness, or give hope of eternal life, even if, as I shall argue, rebel Man seeks to use it to do just that. Yet these are the deep issues at the heart of human meaning, where we seek truth that will give our lives joy and purpose. Only Jesus Christ can bring that truth in its fullness, for he is Truth, the revelation of a loving God as the Creator and Redeemer of all things. Therefore, only Christ can *save*. Technology cannot bring us to God our Creator or reveal his redeeming love, which is at the core of what salvation means; indeed, I shall argue in this essay that technology's *essence*, as it has evolved in the hands of our fallen race, is *opposed* to God. It is for all these reasons that I say that humanity's true hope is in Jesus Christ alone.

I.I.2

The "sexual revolution" and the progressive institutionalization of the subjective perspective on reality; the rise of the individual subject and of science-technology

What is frequently called the "sexual revolution" of 1968 swept across America and Europe with tsunami-like force, opening the way, as is well-known, to a liberalization of traditional constraints on sexual practices of all sorts. The introduction in the 1970s of revolutionary birth-control techniques and the legalization, within certain limits, of abortion "rights", abetted this movement. The rise of militant gay activism in the same decade was another expression of the new sexual openness and tolerance of behavior long deemed unacceptable by the Judeo-Christian tradition.

So far and so fast has Western society moved in forty years that we find our governments—and even our liberal churches—actually legislating on the basis of sexual "orientations", using as norms nothing more than subjective psychological tendencies and the "rights" of those with such tendencies. The Treaty of Amsterdam, for instance, established in 1997, stipulates "respect for orientations", and puts sexual *orientation* on the same plane as sexual *identity* (male and female), ethnic identity, and religious affiliation. These latter, having a universal reference, do indeed involve human rights, a truth that makes positive rights legislation on their behalf entirely legitimate.[2] But a sexual "orientation" is a psychological, subjective category that does not warrant a formal legal status being granted it. As Tony Anatrella points out, the irony here is that this effort to institutionalize the subject—apprehended *subjectively*—ends up actually de-socializing him or her, because he/she cannot be linked any more with objectively recognized universals.[3] A kind of social compartmentalization is going on here that accompanies, ironically, a flattening out of important distinctions at another level. Equality between persons, acknowledged in our democracies as a universal, is taken to imply necessarily equality of affective situations. This reductionist move, without any sound rational basis, has managed to seize the moral high ground in our post-modern society. The *subjective* perspective—reality as seen from the standpoint of the *individual-with-rights*—is henceforth in the driver's seat and is seeking, with considerable success, to overcome, or re-orient, what used to be known as the *common good*, and to discredit any appeal to a wider, more objective framework. As I shall show in Part II of this essay, gay "marriage" is a case in point.

The story of how Western civilization has come to this unprecedented state of affairs is long and complex, and a detailed account of it is beyond the scope of this essay. But I do want to focus what seems to me to be at the heart of the matter, theologically speaking. The emergence in the last four thousand years of the *individual subject*, from a position of cultural obscurity to one of pre-eminence, is central to our discussion of homosexuality; and the rise of the *individual subject* is closely related in turn to the emergence of *science-technology* as we have come to understand it in our time. The role of the Bible in these developments is crucial. The eruption into prominence of the homosexual issue in the last forty years cannot be comprehended adequately unless it is placed in this

2. Anatrella, *Narcisse*, 180.

3. Ibid., 176.

larger theological/cultural frame of reference, at the center of which is the question of science-technology.

I.1.3

The treatment of character and social distinctions in the Old and New Testaments and in Homer; the vivid sense in the Bible of the movement of momentous historical forces

Erich Auerbach, in the first chapter of his ground-breaking book *Mimesis*, contrasts Homer's view of reality, as reflected in his depiction of character and incident, with that of the Old Testament writers. In the second chapter he contrasts the "realism" of the Roman writers Petronius and Tacitus, with that of the New Testament authors, in particular Mark.[4] Auerbach stresses the multilayered character of the biblical figures, including the central figure, God. They possess "background", depth in time, and layers of consciousness, often conflicting. The figures in the Hebrew narratives all have a vertical connection with God, and move in a moral and spiritual context that has universal-historical claims. Truth, not "realism", is the objective of the authors; and truth has to do with the relation of the characters to the God of all the earth, in obedience or disobedience to his revealed will. Persons are called by God and receive promises and have destinies, so they move out of a past into a future; there is development, process, change.

The Homeric heroes, by contrast, live fully in the present; their emotions are strong but simple, and find instant expression in their words and deeds; each is like a Greek sculpture, perfectly honed in three-dimensional space but fixed in time and, in a sense, motionless. Auerbach writes:

> Odysseus on his return is exactly the same as he was when he left Ithaca two decades earlier. But what a road, what a fate . . . between David the harp player, persecuted by his lord's jealousy, and the old king, surrounded by violent intrigues, whom Abishag the Shunnamite warmed in his bed, and he knew her not! The old man, of whom we know how he has become what he is, is more of an individual than the young man; for it is only during the course of an eventful life that men are differentiated into full individuality; and it is this history of a personality which the Old Testament presents to us as the formation undergone by

4. Auerbach, *Mimesis*.

those whom God has chosen to be examples. Fraught with their development, sometimes even aged to the verge of dissolution, they show a distinct stamp of individuality entirely foreign to the Homeric heroes.[5]

The Old Testament figures are under God's hand, Auerbach affirms. They are bearers of the divine will; yet they are fallible, confused, rebellious. But God has a purpose for them and through them, so he shapes and molds them, now bringing them low, now raising them up. "Humiliation and elevation go far deeper and far higher than in Homer, and they belong basically together." And Auerbach goes on to insist that the greatness of these characters, "rising out of humiliation, is almost superhuman and an image of God's greatness."[6]

This treatment of human character, which is continued in the New Testament narratives, provides a psychological density that is far more "realistic"—true to human reality—than the realism of the Homeric narratives, marked as they are by a legendary simplification of events and character. Even material in the Old Testament that may be considered legendary has the feel of historicity to it. Again, this results from the authors' concern with *truth*, that is, with the relation of individuals to their Creator and to the purposes he has for them personally and that he is working out through them for the good of the wider world. The particular has universal-historical import because it is rooted in the divine intention and disclosure.

The *social* picture provided by the Homeric and biblical narratives is also very different. In the former, we have to do with the ruling class, a feudal aristocracy that operates according to static categories of activity and social relationships; there is no common "people", and nothing pushes up from below. In the latter, we have to do, originally, with a collection of nomadic tribes. Class distinctions are hardly felt in the same way, and issues are constantly bubbling up from across the social spectrum. The fact that Israel was a theocracy and then a theocratic monarchy whose source, *raison d'être*, and inner dynamic was the relation of all its members to their Creator, Savior, and Law-Giver God, had a democratizing effect that was manifest from the moment the people had crossed the Red Sea and found themselves in the desert. Contestation, social demands, tribal and intra-family rivalry, are everywhere present, to the

5. Ibid., 17–18.
6. Ibid., 18.

point that Auerbach can make the striking observation that "the origins of prophecy seem to lie in the irrepressible politico-religious spontaneity of the people."[7] As there was rebellion against the law-giving God who demanded holiness and reproved idolatry, so there was prophecy that called the people back to obedience and provided the divine perspective on events that combined judgment and mercy.

In the Gospel narratives, the figure of Jesus has the same centrality as the figure of Yahweh, the Lord, in the Old Testament. Moreover, Jesus's own intimate communion with his heavenly Father means therefore that every person in the New Testament, linked horizontally with Jesus, is also linked vertically, as in the Old Testament, with God. Next to this reality, class distinctions and differing social ranks in the Jewish and Roman communities have only a functional importance. Before God, everyone is on the same footing. The roles, masks, and appearances that normally define social relations and hierarchical distinctions between persons, along with the rhetorical conventions observed in classical literature to express these, are undercut in the New Testament writings, or are simply absent. This is one reason why they appear so fresh and "modern" and have such universal appeal. People appear, and act, as they are *in truth*, under God's light. The moral ambiguity of human action is portrayed frankly, without frills or "effects", and stands out in sharp relief against the luminous deeds and words of Jesus.

One has, in these pages, the feeling as of a tremendous wind blowing through the harsh realities of human life—a sense, as Auerbach puts it, "of a deep subsurface movement, the unfolding of historical forces."[8] Something profoundly new—revolutionary—is being born. History is being re-shaped before our eyes by spiritual power that comes from outside it and yet penetrates into it. Jesus, as the incarnate manifestation of God himself, opens up otherwise unimaginable horizons of human hope and transformation. There is evil and there is greatness, as in Homer and the Greek tragedians; but these find expression not in the actions of "heroes" but in those of ordinary people, and they are not the fruit of static fate but rather of dynamic personality endowed with moral freedom and responsibility. The focal presence of Jesus, whose portrait conveys astonishingly—and in each Gospel, differently—both his humanity and his divinity, gives a singular potency to every encounter, as well as a

7. Ibid., 21.
8. Ibid., 44.

universality of reference that lifts the narrative altogether beyond its local place and time. At once we are in the midst of particular, concrete history *and* transcendental truth. Face-to-face discourse, with simple, direct, un-stylized exchanges such as are almost never to be found in classical literature, provides a dramatic immediacy and a poignancy to the myriad individual figures who move across the narrative landscape. A vast, earth-shaking drama—yet of the utmost intimacy at the same time—unfolds before us, describing and portending huge upheaval and the surfacing of subterranean forces that, in interaction with divine power, will totally re-direct human history.

I.I.4

Genesis and the revelation of the universal nature and dignity of human beings, as made in God's image; inversion of the "imago Dei" by sin; its restoration in and by Christ, God's Very Image incarnate; our call to be conformed to Christ

In the Old and New Testaments we meet hundreds of persons from across the social spectrum, drawn with succinct strokes related mainly to their actions and with little external description or psychological commentary, who, in their motivations and ambitions, display the complexity, the "density" of characterization, that one expects to find in Shakespearian drama or in a great nineteenth- or twentieth-century novel. Novelistic descriptive detail is absent, but an extraordinary truthfulness to character is achieved through the attention given to the inner reality of persons, the mystery inherent in human *subjects* with moral freedom. The affinity with Elizabethan drama or the later novel is not by chance. It is in the Bible that what could be called the world-historical revelation of the nature, dignity, and worth of human beings is made known—the revelation that has served, ultimately, along with the Greco-Roman principles of reason and law, as the basis for the moral development of Western civilization. By examining closely several Scriptural texts, particularly in the book of Genesis, I want now to unpack this statement and show its relevance to my discussion of technology and homosexuality.

 The first chapter of the first book of the Bible—Genesis—speaks of man as *"created . . . in the image of God"* (Gen 1:27; and see 5:1–2 and

9:6).[9] "Man"—*Adam*—is made up of male and female: *"male and female he created them"* (Gen 1:27b). In the second creation account in the second chapter, "woman"—*Eve*, a name resembling the Hebrew word for *living*—is made from one of Adam's ribs, by which is shown both the oneness and the difference of the two genders, man and woman. Adam is made from the dust of the earth, from the ground (*adamah*), and then God breathes into his nostrils the breath of life and he becomes a living being, a creature fashioned from both earth and the very spirit—*pneuma*=spirit/wind—of God. The woman, Eve, taken from Adam's side, is his partner and helper, his wife, the one like him (as the animals are not) who is yet distinct from him, a person in her own right, equal in dignity (*"flesh of my flesh"*: 2:23), but of a different gender.

Together, in the wholeness of their complementarity, the two represent concretely and supremely the masculine and feminine principles—initiation and reception—that constitute all reality and are inherent in God the Creator and reflected in every aspect of his created order. This is one way in which we may understand the creation of man/woman as *imago Dei*. But the male and female *two-in-one-in-mutual-love* that is the true being, the *ontological identity*, of humankind, may also be understood as reflecting the Godhead that we know, through the later incarnation of the Eternal Son in Jesus, to be love—that is, *communion*, a mutual self-giving and receiving of distinct divine Persons in a perfect unity of Being.

That mankind is created in the image of God is a *revelation*—indeed, it is a *double* revelation. We cannot read off from nature that man (man/woman) is *created by God*, or that he/she is created *in the image of God*; and no philosophical argument will ever lead us to this conclusion.[10] Nor would it be wise on the part of a modern skeptic, however, to argue that the *imago Dei* is a pure speculative fantasy devised by starry-eyed "believers", since he or she would be speaking within a democratic culture of which every political benefit and right that he or she, the skeptic, enjoys could probably be traced back *ultimately* to this anthropological principle placed at the beginning of the Bible. It is on the basis of this revelation and not on any other ground that the notions of universal human dignity, equality before the law, and equal democratic

---

9. All citations from Holy Scripture are taken from the New International Version.

10. That God is Creator is itself a revelation, of course, and not the fruit of any rational speculation. Even Plato's demigod in the *Timaeus* is merely a *fashioner* who works with previously existing elements and cannot in any true sense be compared with the Creator God of the Hebrew Scriptures.

rights and justice for all, have gradually emerged in Western civilization and are now being extended, not without difficulty, across the world. No other anthropological affirmation has similar theoretical power—and *effectual* power as well, as the principle seeps into a culture—against the dark passion in human beings to subjugate, dominate, and destroy other human beings.[11] Respect for the other—the alien—and for the weak and the helpless, solely on the ontological basis of the dignity they have as human creatures made in God's image, is the only stance that can withstand, *in principle*, the ruthless drive to power, with its contempt of the powerless, that characterizes most human societies.[12] The paradox inherent in

11. In this connection, it is enlightening to note that the third mention of the *imago Dei* in the Bible is in Gen 9:6, in the post-Eden and post-Flood context of human culture, and bears directly on the question of murder, of the shedding of blood of one human by another. God requires an "accounting" for human life, precisely because *"in the image of God has God made man"*. Justice in the Old Testament requires that a murderer be punished—blood for blood—because human life, created by God, has great value: it is *imago Dei*. Of course, such a procedure, whatever its form, cannot ultimately solve the problem of sin and violence, but it serves well as a pedagogical palliative and social discipline. Only the atoning sacrifice of Jesus—the blood of the Son of God himself shed for mankind's redemption—can provide the ultimate answer to human evil and enable man/woman as *imago Dei* to be created anew and enter a new possibility of living.

12. It is clear that Nietzsche, with the strange, theoretical cruelty that shaped his vision and made him scornful of the unnatural "slave religion" of Christianity that gave honor to the weak and opposed the strong if they misused their power, knew this very well and saw in Christ the great opponent of "natural" man, that is, of man as dominator/master. And he was quite right in this assessment, albeit foolish in his seeming incapacity to grasp the reality and utter horror of *evil* as it informs and shapes the human will-to-power. Nietzsche was opposed to anti-Semitism, as his polemics against Wagner make clear; and though he is sometimes credited, perhaps correctly, with contributing—unknowingly, of course, though a philosopher's responsibility for the consequences of his theorizing should not be minimized—to the rise of Nazi ideology, I am sure he would have had only contempt for the Ottoman Sultan Abdul-Hamid and then for the Pan-Turk despots who deliberately slaughtered two million Armenians, Greeks, and Arameans between 1895 and 1922, or for Hitler and the Jewish genocide he orchestrated—which was notoriously stimulated by the "success" of the Armenian genocide a generation earlier—despite the fact that the Armenian and Jewish genocides were obviously ultimate manifestations, at the political level, of the will-to-power that Nietzsche considered to be the fundamental—and *positive*—reality of Being. It is important to see that these genocides were *logical* expressions of the will-to-power and not, basically, perversions of it. An intriguing thought–experiment is to imagine Nietzsche philosophizing in the period, say, of Stalin's purges in the 1930s in Soviet Russia or in the hay-day of Nazi totalitarianism or during Mao's Cultural Revolution. Surely the despots who ruled the Soviet Union, Germany, and China in those times were not examples of what the philosopher meant by the "overman", as

modern society, and the central theme underlying this essay, is that this respect for the other—for the free subject that he or she is regardless of ethnic or social status—is under dire threat from the very reality—all-controlling and omnipresent—of science-technology, which, at another level, is the very vehicle, ironically, for its dissemination across the globe. The biblical revelation of the true nature of man/woman that ultimately

---

they stand in singular contrast to Nietzsche's prime exemplar (along with himself) of the "overman", Goethe. Nietzsche would have despised them. Yet it was, after all, Zarathustra-Nietzsche who wrote: "'Man is evil'—thus said all the wisest to comfort me. Alas, if only it were still true today! For evil is man's best strength. 'Man must become better and more evil'—thus I teach. The greatest evil is necessary for the over-man's best. It may have been good for that preacher of the little people [Christ] that he suffered and tried to bear man's sin. But I rejoice over great sin as my great consolation." (*Thus Spake Zarathustra*, Fourth Part, Section 5).

This is irresponsible bravado of the most foolish kind, and to call it 'heroic' or 'prophetic' or 'bold' or 'profound' is adolescent prattle. The bankruptcy of nihilism, as evidenced in these remarks, is always shown by its proponents' incapacity—or un-willingness—actually to confront, or take the measure of, *real* evil, philosophically or practically. Rather, they *glorify* it, directly or indirectly, benefiting no doubt from some sheltered social or historical position that gives them immunity from evil's tremendous horror, and impunity from the consequences of their grotesque elucubrations. In acting thus, they simply do not know what they are doing. Nietzsche's hatred of the "unclean" rabble (e.g. *Thus Spake Zarathustra,* Second Part, "On the Rabble") was surely not in-tended to stoke the fires of genocide, but it fitted well with the racism rampant in late nineteenth-century Europe and undoubtedly contributed to creating the atmosphere of contempt for "lower" forms of human life that opened the way for later systematic campaigns of annihilation and "cleansing". Nihilism *justifies* evil, perhaps by designating it, approvingly, to be the "natural" way of human beings, or by denying it outright and calling for a "transvaluation of values", for a "willed creative act" that will take us "beyond good and evil", as if such a proposal—heedless that it is—solved anything or illuminated anything, which it clearly does not; or else nihilism leads its proponents, should they be faced personally with a situation of undeniable evil, into a state of inner moral contradic-tion, impotence, and, finally, madness, as conscience engages in ultimate combat with a predilection for death. Nihilism is indeed a predilection for death, even if it aspires, as in Nietzsche's case, to a higher, life-affirming vitality, which, when the smoke from Nietzsche's detonations clears, is just a glorification of paganism, minus the gods and the supra-sensory. Nihilism, whatever its form, digs its own grave—indeed, it *wills* to dig its own grave—and appears, in the face of reality, to be in the end as naïve and myopic as the attitude of benign idealism it despises. Nihilists, in this sense, are like those who crucified Jesus; as the Lord said of them from where he hung on the cross: "*Father, forgive them for they do not know what they are doing.*" (Luke 23:34a). One must resist the un-charitable temptation to imagine "creative nihilists" such as Nietzsche being subjected, say, to life as an untouchable (rabble!) in India, or being shipped to a concentration camp or a killing field under orders from some power-mad tyrant—the perversion of an "overman"—who would agree happily with Zarathustra's dictum that "the greatest evil is necessary for the overman's best."

underpins any notion we may have of the equal value of all human beings, is being deliberately set aside by the civilization to which it gave rise, thus removing the metaphysical ground for continuing to hold such a notion. Within the technological frame, we are all equal, yes, but we are equal as *objects*, not as free subjects. The modern world is trapped in a fundamental contradiction, of which the consequences can only be dire. I shall be examining this theme in the course of the essay.

After Genesis 9:6, where the value of human life and the reprobation of murder are linked to the *imago Dei*, reference to this revelation about the fundamental nature of humankind more or less disappears from the Hebrew Scriptures (Psalm 8 indirectly refers to it, however, and the whole Old Testament, concerned with God's relation to human beings, presupposes it). It re-surfaces in the New Testament, where it is applied by the Apostle Paul to Jesus himself. Jesus, the incarnation of the uncreated Son of God, is the *very* image of God (Col 1:15; 2 Cor 4:4). Those who are called by God—that is, those men and women who hear and heed God's call to aspire in their heart to know him—are destined to be *"conformed to the likeness of his Son"* (Rom 8:29)—i.e. to the Image of God. As they contemplate the Lord's glory, in this life and in the life to come, they *"are being transformed into his likeness with ever-increasing glory."* (2 Cor 3:18). This is a work of sheer grace, but we have our part to play. God accomplishes this progressive transformation by his Spirit as we *"take hold of the hope offered to us"* (Heb 6:18), as we enter by faith into the *"new creation"* that God has made us to be in Christ (Gal 6:15; 2 Cor 5:17) and begin to behave in ways appropriate to this reality: *"Do not lie to each other, since you have taken off your old self with its practices and have put on the new self, which is being renewed in knowledge in the image of its Creator. Here there is no Greek or Jew, circumcised or uncircumcised, barbarian, Scythian, slave or free, but Christ is all and is in all!"* (Col 3:10–11)[13].

13. The "new self" can be understood as *grace perfecting nature* only if the Pauline distinction between the old and the new nature, and the Johannine emphasis on the new birth, are taken seriously. The old nature—Paul's "old man"—cannot be perfected by grace. What grace can and does do is to lead the "old man" to recognize his sinfulness and to die to himself through repentance and the reception of baptism in the fullness of its sacramental meaning. This is God's justification of the sinner, who henceforth is called and enabled to be Christ-centered instead of self-centered. The progressive spiritual and moral fleshing out of this justified "new man"—the perfecting of the "new nature"—involves the life-long process of inner healing and of sanctification (the two are not the same, but they go together, and both are the work of the Holy Spirit); and sanctification involves again and again the dying to the impulses and habits of the "old man", as the "new man", constituted with a new heart and spirit

We may conjecture that the reason why explicit mention of the *imago Dei* vanishes from the Hebrew Scriptures after Genesis 9 is that earlier in the narrative the human race has defied God's Word and entered into disobedience, a development of which the narrative account is given in Genesis 3. With this event—and we shall never know how primitive human beings, coming into consciousness, turned away from communion with God instead of welcoming it—the *imago Dei* was, as it were, *inversed*; the relation of men and women to their Creator—a relation both intimate and structural—shifted from a positive to a negative mode. This ontological relation has not so much been broken as it has been turned inside out and upside down. We human beings, knowing ourselves to be guilty, hide from our Creator. We replace communion with the true God by idolatry with gods of our own making, a universal and inherently self-serving human practice. God becomes humankind's *rival* and, when the logic of this self-affirmation is taken to its end point, our *enemy*. And along with this alienation from our Creator, we are alienated, of course, from our fellow-human beings, so that the *other* becomes an enemy, and fear and jealousy replace love.

Instead, then, of a development in the Hebrew Scriptures of the blessed communion God and man/woman were intended to share, we have the narration of God's dealings with alienated humanity, of his judgment, and of his merciful plan of salvation for the disobedient human race through a chosen people, the Hebrews/Jews. This plan culminates in the coming of the Jewish Messiah, Jesus, who, by his resurrection from the dead, is revealed to be the Son of God and proclaimed Lord of all creation (Rom 1:4). At the anthropological level, what this involves is the upending by God of the primordial reversal of the relation of humanity to God occasioned by human disobedience. The *very* Image of God—Jesus Christ—who is also representative man (man/woman), the second Adam, takes upon himself the opprobrium and punishment for human sin and opens the way, by his life and passion, for man/woman to be forgiven and restored to the *positive* mode of their true nature as persons created in the image of God. Transformation into Christ's likeness, and everlasting communion with the Triune God and with his people and the whole creation in this life and in the life to come in God's Kingdom, are

---

(cf. Ezek 36:26–27), learns to know and love God better and to grow more like Christ, becoming conformed to his image and so made progressively into the person he/she was created to be.

henceforth made possible for those among the human race whose hearts desire the true God.

I.I.5

The human pretension to be the autonomous arbiter of what is good and what is evil; history as the conflict between the Creator and his creature, man/woman; humankind made for relationship, not autonomy; opposition to God entails violence between human beings

The Bible containing both the Hebrew Scriptures and the Christian Gospels and Epistles presents a cosmic/historical meta-narrative that does not fit into the philosophical and political meta-narratives that postmodern thinkers repudiate. It is a *theological* meta-narrative containing multiple genres and countless stories, written over a period of more than a thousand years, that unfolds within the framework of an historical narrative and yet that brackets this framework by an evocation of both the beginning of the cosmos and the eschatological consummation of the drama being worked out in the historical narrative itself.[14] The narrative direction is linear and moves from a commencement to an eschatological fulfillment. The transcendent, eternal God, Originator of all that is, omnipotent and glorious, is shown interacting with human beings in the mundane contingency of their daily lives. The language has nothing of the stylized, stilted diction often found in other sacred or "spiritual" writings purported to be about gods and epiphanies and revelations. This is true even of the myth-like portions of the Scriptures, such as those in the early chapters of Genesis (see *footnote 17* below). The divine Person relates to human persons in a matter-of-fact way that manages mysteriously to convey at once God's transcendence and his active presence in the midst of human life. Realism and mystery go hand in hand. The writers and

---

14. Richard Bauckham has an illuminating essay in Davis and Hays, eds., *Reading Scripture*, entitled "Reading Scripture as a Coherent Story", in which he contrasts the meta-narrative of Scripture with the rational/philosophical meta-narratives criticized by Jean-François Lyotard, such as those of Hegel and Marx, that aim "to subsume all events, all perspectives, and all forms of knowledge in a comprehensive [rational] explanation" (45). Bauckham goes on to write: "Unlike the modern meta-narratives, the biblical story accounts for history not in terms of immanent reason or human mastery but in terms of the freedom and purpose of God and of human freedom to obey or to resist God" (48).

compilers of the texts clearly saw themselves as inspired by this one true God who, for the sake ultimately of all mankind, had revealed himself to his people and who continued to do so. The purpose of this divine self-revelation, and of the texts God inspired to make this revelation known, was the redemption of humanity wandering in the maze of its spiritual and moral confusion; and the content of this redemption consisted in the restoration of humanity to a state of communion with its Creator, in which love toward God, fellow-human beings, and all other creatures would replace pride, fear, domination, and violence. The scope of the revelation was universal, but its focus was a particular people, Israel, which would be the vehicle of its accomplishment.

The beginning, middle, and end of the Bible are about *relationships*. A God who is personal and all-powerful Spirit—an authentic *Creator*, neither a demiurge nor a mere "force"—is depicted as creating a universe at the center of which is a creature with whom this Creator wishes to share his creation and enjoy eternal communion. This wish presupposes a likeness between the creature and the Creator at the same time that there is necessarily an infinite qualitative difference between them. This likeness is expressed, as we have seen, in the phrase "*imago Dei*", used first in Genesis 1:26. Communion between them would be impossible if the creature were not rational, self-conscious, and morally free to establish its own identity either by cleaving to its Creator in love and obedience or by rebelling against him and claiming its own autonomy.

At the heart of the biblical drama is the presentation of historical reality as a conflict between this created being and its Creator. The conflict is not original to the creation but arises subsequently, through the misuse by man/woman of the freedom God had granted them. They were given full run of the creation, with one exception: they were forbidden to eat of the Tree of the Knowledge of Good and Evil. This commandment may best be understood as a prohibition against humanity's setting itself up as the arbiter—indeed, as the *creator*—of what is good and of what is evil. Such an act amounts to self-determination, to a declaration of the creature's autonomy with respect to God, of his status as the equal of God. Ultimately this must lead to atheism: the denial of God's existence and his replacement by Man.

God is undivided and incapable of doing evil, that is, of doing that which is in opposition to himself. To know what is evil is to know what is in opposition to God. God is good, and his creation of a reality other than himself was/is a manifestation of the good. For a creature to destroy it or to presume to be able to create in like manner, is evil. The Creator did not want his creatures to go that way because he knew what the calamitous consequences would be. *Hubris*—acting like God, as if one were all-powerful—can only lead to destruction, because it goes against the grain of reality. We are not creators in the strict sense but *makers*, working with what God has created. The pretension to think of ourselves as creators and to act accordingly—which is the philosophy of modernity— is a recipe for disaster. The modern form of *hubris*, rooted in technology, as I shall argue, generates the odd tendency to confuse the *discovery* of physical laws with a kind of divine power, as if we ourselves were the creators of those laws and should take credit for their existence.

Humankind was not made for autonomy but for *relationship*, of which the primary one is with God. For human beings to live in opposition to God is thus necessarily for them to live, individually and collectively, in opposition to themselves, to their true nature. War, conflict, violence, have their ultimate cause in this opposition. The chaos these social phenomena represent is out of phase with the harmonious interlocking of all natural phenomena in the universe—this ecological *unity* that is the discovery of contemporary man and that provides a new way of conceiving the oneness of *Being*, so dear to Parmenides, and of which the consciousness, as Heidegger sees it, has been lost, ever since Aristotle, in the multiplicity of particular beings.[15]

Nature is not "red in tooth and claw" in a pejorative sense, as social Darwinists have disparagingly asserted, suggesting an inappropriate parallel with human cruelty and violence. The phrase is an unhelpful anthropomorphism. Killing and domination in the animal world are amoral realities, different from killing and domination among human beings. Nor, it seems to me, is it appropriate to call convulsive natural phenomena such as earthquakes, *evil*. The creative violence of natural stellar and planetary phenomena, and the mutual killing and eating of creatures in the biological sphere, take place in an evolutionary framework that

15. The Christian understanding of God the Creator as Trinity—an understanding based not on speculation but on revelation—of God as One God in Three Persons, as a single Divine Life in three Personal Expressions, provides the optimal metaphysical explanation for the astonishing unity-in-diversity and diversity-in-unity exhibited in the cosmos, non-organic and organic, of which modern science is beginning to take the measure. The inter-connectivity of all elements in a single universe, and the intelligibility of this universe to the human mind, are realities in no way to be taken for granted. Such unity-in-diversity could be expected if the universe is understood to be the creation of God-the-Trinity and as reflecting in consequence the *being* of its Creator.

requires death in order for change to emerge, and within an ecological system of stunning equilibrium; they have nothing *essentially* to do with the *moral* realities of chaotic violence and willful cruelty that make of much of human history a bloody, gruesome tale.[16] Natural cataclysms are part of the creative activity of God that has fashioned the planet and made life on it possible, and the fact that human beings, as well as other living creatures, are sometimes, tragically, victims of such events, does not make the events themselves evil, despite the ravages they cause. To apply the word "evil" to such phenomena is a category mistake. Evil, like good, is a personal and moral category. It involves a willful opposition to the good of creation, that is, to the Creator himself. It *aims*, intentionally, to destroy, efface, annihilate. It *arises out of rebellion*—the refusal of divine order—and causes *chaos*.

Eating of the forbidden Tree was the primordial transgression; thereafter, men and women would live within the realm of this newly acquired knowledge, this experience of autonomy from their Creator. They would live within the realm of perpetual conflict between good and evil, between order and chaos. Their refusal to seek after and obey the true God would become a conscious choice, informed by *knowledge*. Knowledge itself, for itself and for the power it bestows, would become—rather than the knowledge *of God*—the central human objective and source of

16. It is true that the presence in the biological world of what can properly be called *cruelty*, as distinct from the presence of killing as such, is a baffling feature in a creation that the Creator God in Genesis calls "good." It raises the rarely discussed biblical issue of Lucifer/Satan and the fallen angels—perhaps to be identified with what the Apostle Paul calls "powers and authorities" (Col 2:15), and "the powers of this dark world. . . the spiritual forces of evil in the heavenly realms" (Eph 6:12b). The Bible clearly points to Satan as a being created before the creation of man, who, with the angels that followed him in rebellion against God, will have been present in the natural world from early in its evolution. Obviously this powerful angelic being will have done what he could to distort and pervert God's unfolding creation. This essay is not the place for it, but theological consideration should be given to this neglected issue as a way of shedding some light on the aspects of biological life that seem out of phase with a good creation. The fear that many theologians in the West have of broaching the possibility that Satan, fallen angels, and demons are not mythological structures but are conscious spiritual beings who were created by God and at some point rebelled against him and set themselves to destroy his creation, must be overcome if we are to make complete sense of what we may see as deformity in the evolution of nature and also in the history of humanity. It is my conviction that a phenomenon such as genocide, for example, cannot adequately be explained by recourse to psychological and social forces alone. Dismissing out of hand the hypothesis of Satanic influence and manipulation on the basis of an *a priori* denial regarding the possible existence of conscious evil powers, has more to do with dogmatic bias than with scientific open-mindedness and method.

identity. This idolatry, as the present essay will attempt to show, is the shape human culture has given and is giving to the primal rebellion, the eating of the forbidden fruit. From the moment of that rebellion, the path was open to strive to rival and ultimately to replace God and to make unwillingness to believe in and submit to the Creator, a way of life. But this "way of life" was in fact a *way of death*, since what is set over against the Creator, who is Very Life and the source of life, must die. For the human race this penalty took the form of spiritual alienation, of history characterized by violence and suffering, of physical illness, and of death experienced with dread, humiliation, and hopelessness.[17]

17. The narrative in the first chapters of Genesis is unique in world literature in its presentation of a God who is all-powerful and personal, the *Creator*, who creates order out of primordial chaos. The story is monotheistic, no other divinities are involved; nor is there any of the violence often found in the conflict tradition of many mythological accounts about how the world came to be, such as the Babylonian *Enuma Elish*. In the space of three chapters, we are introduced to an omnipotent, absolutely transcendent God who creates the cosmos (ch. 1), *and* to a God who walks in the midst of his creation and talks with his special creature, man/woman (ch. 2)—and the two Figures are one and the same God! The omnipotent Spirit, the Mind who brings into being the universe, has an intimate and special relation with the creature made in his image, human being. While obviously outside the experience of the writer or writers, the creation account in Genesis lacks altogether the "feel" of mythology, or of fable or even of saga. It is myth-like without being myth; history-like without being history. Neither the word "myth" nor the word "symbol" is an accurate description of this narrative, though elements of each are present (Ellen Davis, in her *Scripture, Culture, and Agriculture*, 43–45, reminds us of Walter Brueggemann's characterization of Genesis 1 as a "liturgical poem", and then develops this insight in terms of poetic form as illustrating and participating in the formality of creation). The "characters" involved—God, Adam, Eve, even the snake, not to mention Cain and Abel and the other figures who appear in chapters 1–11 before Abram comes on the scene—have an uncanny verisimilitude about them. At the level of sheer *style*, it is arguable that this outstanding originality brings a kind of confirmation of the Jewish and Christian claim that these texts are *truth*, revealed by the Spirit of God to divinely inspired authors. They do not provide what we would call today a "scientific" cosmology, but the Hebrews who told and finally wrote down these stories, and who later gathered them into their canon of sacred Scripture, clearly believed that they provide a *theological* cosmology and anthropology that is *true* and *comprehensive*—an account of the origins of the universe, of man/woman, of evil, of sin and violence, and of the consequent alienation from God which made of human death a humiliation and a grief, that is deeper, richer, and more inclusive of the totality of human experience and intuition than any mythological or—if they could have carried out such a thing—*scientific* account, could possibly be. We are certainly not dealing here with history in any current understanding of that term, but the personal and dynamically creative nature of the God who is acting in these stories gives them the "feel" of history, of a drama about primordial events that reveal the metaphysical and anthropological foundations of

reality as human beings experience it. The drama is told with a kind of "naturalism", indeed of "realism". I would argue that it is the unique nature of the God we meet here, who has revealed himself to the people of Israel, that determines the unique style of the narratives in which we meet him. The "history" we have here does actually represent, with the concision and multi-layeredness of meaning that poetry makes possible, the coming-into-being of the cosmos, of the planet earth, of life, and of humanity; it does actually make manifest imaginatively the special relation of God, presented as Creator of all that is, to mankind and to the history that would unfold subsequently. That history, we are being told with stunning authority, is to be understood in the light of this account of origins.

This means that historical developments like *modern science* are to be properly comprehended—in the sense of their significance within the overarching creative project of God for mankind and for the cosmos—*within* this narrative, understood as a representation of *the way things truly are* in this conflicted and infinitely complex reality we call cosmic and human history. Here, within the framework of the creation order and of the human disorder that ensues, we are to find the ultimate basis for our theological and ethical norms. Of course, historical developments will continue to bring new hermeneutical perspectives to bear on these foundational texts, as the astonishing recent discoveries in physics and astrophysics (e.g. chaos theory, non-locality, the Anthropic Principle) and the increasingly complex debate about the mechanisms of evolution, are currently in process of doing. But it will remain the case that the metaphysical and existential *meaning* of life on earth will be found within the implications of the Genesis texts and not through the insights of science. The God revealed in this foundational narrative is the Creator who speaks space and time into being by his Word and then acts to bring into existence within this framework an infinite number of inorganic and organic creatures to which both law and contingency are granted so that they may evolve with a large measure of autonomy according to their natures.

The nature of the human being, created in God's image, was special, and ch. 3 records the catastrophic outcome of the risk God took in creating a creature like himself with a free moral will. It is clear that the transgression of God's commandment by humanity as represented by the figures of Adam and Eve, must have an historical basis of some sort, for otherwise "sin" could be understood as being simply a natural part of human nature as it appears to have evolved from pre-human being, in which case the Scriptural account both of divine judgment and of redemption would have no *raison d'être* and could be dismissed as mythological. But a fundamental affirmation of the Judeo-Christian tradition is that sin is not natural, in the sense that it is not part of the created being of man/woman. A turning away from God by primordial humanity, through deliberate choice in favor of self-assertion, must have occurred in some way over time and been reinforced by repeated social behavior. The incarnation of Christ reveals both divine and human nature as they *truly* are, and in the light of the Second Adam we can infer the godliness and goodness of the First Adam before the Fall. The judgment of death referred to in Gen 2:17 would appear to refer to alienation from the Creator, the source of life, rather than to physical death itself, which would seem necessarily to characterize all organic life as such, including human being (see Gen 2:7; 3:19,22), and to be a necessary factor in biological evolution. Debilitating sickness and plague among humans may perhaps also be understood as an alienating consequence of the Fall and of Satanic opposition to the human race, rather than as an inevitable part of evolution. They are certainly not phenomena willed by God. The human person being, for the Hebrews, an indivisible whole—an "en-spirited" body that is a "living soul" (see Gen 2:7 and e.g., 1 Thess 5:23)—a spirit/soul alienated from God through disobedience would involve the whole person, for whom crippling illness would be common and physical death would be experienced henceforth with fear, as desolation and horror, rather than as a peaceful transition into the presence of a loving Creator. Everlasting life, for human beings, can come only through integration into the life of God, and Christians believe that this possibility is offered to humanity only through the resurrected Jesus Christ, into whom, at the eschatological Judgment, will be incorporated all those whom the Father has called in the course of human history (John 6:35–40; 10:27–30), whether or not they had the possibility of hearing and believing the Gospel during their time on earth. The Judgment by Christ the Lord will reveal the state of their hearts and the inner nature of their actions, whether the core of their being was inclined towards God and whether, at least occasionally, mercy somehow characterized their actions (see Hos 6:6; Matt 9:13; 12:7; Rom 2:12–16; 14:10–12; 1 Cor 3:11–15).

Fossil discoveries of the last generation suggest, in an evolutionary perspective, that the incredibly complex hominoid brain, far bigger than that of its closest simian ancestor, evolved in the astonishingly short period of time (in terms of *geological* time) of something over two million years (see, e.g., Holmes Rolston III, *Three Big Bangs*, ch. 3). This amazingly rapid increase in biological complexity, was, like the emergence of the first living cell, a singularity inexplicable by current evolutionary theory; and, interestingly, it presents a state of affairs in which one could reasonably envisage the scenario of the Fall: a rational creature takes form, endued, by virtue of a voluminous information-gathering cranial capacity, with self-awareness, spiritual consciousness, a capacity for language, and moral freedom, and moves knowingly in the presence of his/her Creator and in spiritual communion with him, but grows proud and covetous of the divine status for himself, and so ends up by turning away in disobedience from the God who gave him life. Such a perspective illustrates how one might, in this case, coordinate putative scientific knowledge with the metaphysical blueprint of the creation order provided by the Genesis texts.

How it is that the Creator has directed or overseen or infused with his wisdom the evolutionary development from the original matter/energy of the Big Bang, of organic life, consciousness, and self-consciousness/mind, is utterly beyond our knowledge; but the singularities I have pointed out (the cell and the human brain), coupled with the astonishing fine-tuning (now called the Anthropic Principle) of the physical conditions necessary for the ultimate emergence of carbon-based life on our planet, point in the direction of a creative Mind and an ordering purpose for the cosmos like what we encounter in the creation narratives of Genesis. It is not a question here of saying, for example, that human self-consciousness/mind provides evidence of *direct intervention* by a divine Mind—the scientific and theological dimensions of reality cannot be causally joined in this way—but the increasing complexification of life and a directionality that appears to lead to the ultimate emergence of mind from what was at the beginning mere matter/energy is so astounding that it must make us pause (John Haught develops this insight cogently in his *Is Nature Enough?*). Indeed, the Genesis narrative of sequential creation by a Creator has a far wider explanatory power than the materialistic hypothesis of chance-plus-time, which provides no really plausible account of the teleological shape of the process of evolution or of the astonishing increase of

I.I.6

The ambivalence of history: idolatry and glory; hunger for the absolute, but on human terms; the drive to create our own Eden; the City of Man and the will-to-power; the way to the Tree of Life opened by Jesus, but the human race seeks auto-salvation, self-divinization, the replacement of the original creation by its own

Human history is characterized by ambiguity and moral ambivalence. The human spirit, by which men and women have the capacity to know and have communion with the true God, who is Spirit, has been darkened and can be illumined only by grace, through revelation. But man/woman is made in the image of God, even if that image is experienced in the negative mode, and the human *spirit*, though darkened, is still extant and operative. It is, negatively, open to the demonic realm and to occult spiritual powers; but, positively, it can also capture intuitions of spiritual truth and apprehend, albeit dimly, transcendent reality, even if it cannot attain *by itself* to knowledge of the true God, since the way back to Eden, where God and Man walked together, has been barred. Men and women cannot, by themselves, quench their hunger for an absolute, which even the angry atheist attests to by his clenched fist. Our rebellious hearts seek to satiate that hunger with the tasteless food of idolatry, of which the atheistic exaltation of mankind, in its twin forms of indifference to the divine and of vehement denial, is the ultimate expression; but the inner human yearning for truth and peace and life, for communion with our Source and End, is part of our ontology and cannot be annihilated. Certainly, in the very midst of the rebellion of our race, the deep heart

---

information and ordered complexity. The formula of "chance-plus-time" is a facile and purely speculative conjecture with no rational basis of the sort that can be ascribed, for example, to the Darwinian principle of natural selection.

As to the picture in Genesis of the peaceful Eden, for the primordial existence of which evolutionary theory would appear to provide no evidence to date, I suggest it may be understood within the theological parameters of these texts as being an ideal vision—a vision both *paradisiacal* and, in light of other biblical texts, notably the messianic passage in Isaiah 11, *eschatological*—of the perfection of God's creative project, of its aim of communal peace and harmony, and of its ultimate fulfillment. The correspondence of this vision to a deep and inalienable hunger and hope in the human heart, which, as this essay argues, mankind on its own, without God, is trying to satisfy through technology, provides another existential confirmation of the inherent *truth* about the essential nature of humanity that we encounter in these inspired texts.

of billions of people through the centuries and in all cultures has been turned toward the Sun of Righteousness, even if these multitudes, like the Greeks whom the Apostle Paul addressed in Acts 17, have not known the Name of the One God, Creator and Redeemer, who revealed himself to the Hebrews and became incarnate in Jesus Christ.

The tragedy of human existence is that humankind seeks to fulfill that yearning by grasping—*creating!*—that fulfillment for itself rather than by *receiving* it from God. Autonomy, not partnership with his Creator, is our objective. The central human project, shared by all human cultures, is to establish the kingdom of Man. Our fallen race's deepest desire is our own glorification, not God's. At bottom, we strive to overcome our creature-hood and alter our ontological status. We want to justify ourselves by projecting from within our fallible finitude, through religious, political, or technological means, ultimate solutions to the existential insecurity and moral ambiguity of our human predicament. We want independence more than communion. Our pride is greater than our desire for life, if that life demands obedience to the Author of life himself. Human beings equate freedom with *autonomy*, not with the mutuality, responsiveness, and liber-ating humility required by love. That equation is an illusion, a mirage, but a thousand idols *seem* to make it substantial, they give it the *appearance* of reality. Yet for all that, because we are made in the image of God, the lie inside which humanity lives and moves makes us uneasy. We sense the fragility of the mirage. And so we ache to make it *really* substantial, to make the *lie real*. The objective structures and constraints of the reality we find ourselves in and which we did not create, we wish to replace by a reality of our own making. We do not like being obliged to someone—being the recipients of a *gift*. We want to be the *origin* of what we are.

But the ambivalence remains. Human culture is undoubtedly a self-aggrandizing project, ordered to any number of self-serving idolatries; but it is also, where its excellence shines forth, the glorious achievement of human beings, God's favored creature, to whom the Creator gave the task of having dominion over his creation, caring for it and serving it: "*God blessed them [male and female], and said to them, 'Be fruitful and increase in number, fill the earth and subdue it. Rule over the fish of the sea and the birds of the air and over every living creature that moves on the ground.'*" (Gen 1:28). We are equipped to accomplish this, through our rational and intuitive powers, our mind and imagination, our art, our music, and our science, our technology and our poetry, all of these lodged in brains of incalculable complexity inside bodies of surpassing agility and beauty. Not for one moment, in my critique of the human project as it is taking shape in the modern world, do I forget this, or mean to mock or discredit the wonderful accomplishments of *tool-making man* in science, the arts, and technology, manifested in all kinds of marvelous productions within the astonishing variety of cultures that have constituted human history. I stand in wonder before them, as I stand in wonder before God's original creation. It is precisely the brilliance of these accomplishments that makes their dark side so very dark.

The *inner* nature of human culture, as a project set over against the divine project of partnership with God, is depicted in chapters 4 and 11 of Genesis. In chapter 4 we are told that Cain, the murderer of his brother Abel, *"went out from the Lord's presence and. . . .was then building a city."* (Gen 4:16a, 17b). We are told that Tubal-Cain, one of Cain's descendants, *"made all kinds of tools out of bronze and iron"* (4:22), a piece of information that is followed immediately in the text, perhaps to suggest a link between tool-power, pride, and violence, by the boast of the swaggering Lamech that he has killed a young man for wounding him and that he will be avenged seventy-sevenfold, that is, far more than the sevenfold vengeance God had promised to Cain in the event that someone should kill him. And later, after the flood, we are told that the families of Noah's sons spread out across the earth, and that some came upon a plain in the land of Shinar and settled there and said: *"Come, let us build ourselves a city, with a tower that reaches to the heavens, so that we may make a name for ourselves. . . ."* (Gen 11:4a). The Lord came down to inspect the city, and he said: *"If as one people speaking the same language they have begun to do this, then nothing they plan to do will be impossible for them. Come, let us go down, and confuse their language so they will not understand each other."* (Gen 11:6–7). Thus the city was called the Tower of Babel. Here is the very picture of technological civilization with its aspiration to be like God (*"a tower that reaches to the heavens"*); but here too is the warning that God remains in control and will bring mankind under judgment for its *hubris*.

The way back to Eden being barred, humanity set out to create its own Eden, its *counter-Eden* in the form of a *city*, a technological structure, of which the Tower of Babel *"that reaches to the heavens"* is the enduring symbol. After humankind's primal disobedience, God had said, *"'The man has now become like one of us, knowing good and evil. He must not be allowed to reach out his hand and take also from the tree of life and eat, and live forever'. So the Lord God banished him from the Garden of Eden to work the ground from which he had been taken. After he drove the man out, he placed on the east side of the Garden of Eden cherubim and a flaming sword flashing back and forth to guard the way to the tree of life."* (Gen 3:22–24).

As post-modern thought, following Nietzsche, has made clear, human beings left to themselves, alienated from the true God, have made of history an ongoing *struggle for power*. Building up, tearing down, and conflict mark every culture. Suffering, disease, death, hopelessness, have been our lot. The ethnic, tribal, racial *other* has not been welcome. Love and solidarity have been confined to *one's own*.

The way to the Tree of Life was not to be opened until Jesus the Messiah, Son of God and Second Adam, came and by his obedience unto death reconciled man to God. *"I am the way and the truth and the life,"* Jesus said to Thomas. *"No one comes to the Father except through me"* (John 14:6). Whether it be on this side of the grave or the other, through conscious faith here and now or through a life God judges somehow to be worthy, those who are graciously received into the Kingdom of God will be welcomed on the basis of the merits and passion of Jesus. *"Salvation is found in no one else,"* declared Peter, standing as a prisoner before the rulers of Jerusalem, *"for there is no other name under heaven given to men by which we must be saved"* (Acts 4:12). Jesus does not lead men and women back to Eden, but forward into his eschatological Kingdom. Human history cannot be annulled. But both in Eden and in the Kingdom of God the Father, communion in love with our Creator is the heart of the matter. This enables communion with other creatures—with the *other*. This is life and wholeness, a harmony of being, of which we see a material image in the interlinking of all things in the physical world around us. This is *shalom*, the form and meaning of salvation. Human beings—indeed, all creatures—are relational in their essence. We are free to the degree that we love. In *love*—not elsewhere—we find the true meaning of life. Inter-dependence, not autonomy, is the nature of reality. Ecological science is teaching us this today in a new way. Unconnected units do not exist. In the last two centuries we have been exploiting the natural world as if such units *did* exist, as if there were no natural, integrated (divinely instituted) order that we needed to respect—and now we are reaping the whirlwind.[18]

---

18. See Davis, op. cit., for an exegetically thorough theological discussion of land-care according to Scriptural norms. The author's agrarian approach to the Old Testament is of the greatest interest and value in our age of ecological crisis, and should be made widely known in the Church.

Human beings, as we have seen, want to construct their own reality and set out their own norms for what is good and what is evil. We have eaten of the forbidden Tree. Like Cain, we go out from the presence of the Lord. . . and *we build a city.* Like the men who tried to build a tower that reaches to the heavens, we want to establish a *counter-reality*, one that depends solely on us. Since the gift of Eden has been withdrawn from us, we will make a city to replace it. We want to be like God. That is what the serpent said to Eve in the garden: *"You will not surely die. . . .For God knows that when you eat of it* [the forbidden tree] *your eyes will be opened, and you will be like God, knowing good and evil"* (Gen 3:4).

This is what the *will-to-power* is all about down through history and, via technology, in a more and more focused and deliberate way since Nietzsche coined the phrase in the late nineteenth century. We have built marvelous cities. In many ways human culture really has carried out the creation mandate to domesticate and cultivate the earth. We have created structures of great beauty and power, including the astonishing new tool that is the Internet. We have discovered many basic structures of physical reality, such as the realm of particle physics, the human genome, and the multitudinous host of galaxies. But the City of Man is a cruel and violent place, in the image of Cain, the first builder. Underneath all its melodies, some of surpassing loveliness, sounds the pedal point of violence and death. The sprawling modern agglomerations that call themselves "cities" reveal this reality in the harshest possible way. Next to significant and praiseworthy social achievements of every kind, the daily existence of millions consists of abject poverty, ugliness, crime, drugs, human trafficking, slavery, pollution, dereliction, despair. It expresses the chaotic predicament of man-in-rebellion. The serpent *lied* to Eve. Our transgression has *cut us off from life.* In common parlance, *we are way in over our heads.*

It is just this truth that Modern Man resists. We want to deny that this really is the way things are; or, if we recognize that they really are this way, we argue that we can change them fundamentally. We have various responses to our human predicament, to what we perceive as our *imperfection*, the blame for which, in our modern age, we put on God and his defective engineering, not on ourselves. *As a race*, we insist that we have the means and power to make things "right" by ourselves, and we *will* to do just that, whatever the cost. We will do it by technological manipulation. This is an evident counterfeit of God's righteousness as portrayed in Scripture, which consists essentially in *his* faithfulness to set right those things that have been wrong, warped, or broken by *us*. As *individuals,* we do everything we can to escape the common human plight and live more or less "happily" or and more or less in denial; or else we throw up our hands and curse life and God and plummet into darkness; or else, in Nietzschean mode, we posit, in the face of Nothingness and as a kind of nihilist counterfeit of the Resurrection, a heroic affirmation of *whatever is*, chaos and evil included—and some of us, self-importantly, go on to say that we find meaning by "defying" (whatever that is supposed to mean) what we declare to be the meaninglessness of the universe. In any case, we resist God's reality and God's decrees. We refuse the commandment to love God and our neighbor as ourselves. We refuse to worship God. We do whatever we want, to the extent that we have power to do it. We resist the decree that we shall die. In the negative mode of the *imago Dei*, the project of man/woman, coming to fruition in the modern period, is not to care for the creation, but to tame, exploit, and—ultimately— *transcend* or *replace* it. What God ordained, as set forth in the opening chapters of Genesis, we seek to undo and make over. In the modern age, we simply deny that God ordained anything. We accomplish this *tour de main* by flatly denying God's very existence. We do not want to be made in the image of God; to the contrary, we want God to be made in the image of Man.

Feuerbach famously articulated this ambition in the early nineteenth century, by arguing that God is a projection of the best qualities of the human species, gathered together in a notion of perfection and attached to a virtual being called a deity. We generate God, not the opposite.[19] In our age of suspicion, such thinking has become commonplace. As Van Harvey, cited by Kevin Scott, points out, the major atheistic thinkers—Marx, Nietzsche, and Freud, along with their contemporary progeny—see themselves as liberators of the human spirit, long held down by the illusion of a divine Being. These thinkers, in their own view, are like Moses, leading his people out of slavery; or like Jesus, through whom salvation is being brought to humanity. We have here, in this Messianism, an exact reversal of the biblical picture. Salvation is deliverance from belief in God, not the gift of communion with God; the Antichrist, not the Christ, brings this salvation. It is not deliverance from sin

19. Feuerbach, *Essence*, 25. Sections 1 and 2 provide the essential outline of Feuerbach's thought. See Scott, *At Variance*, 56–58, for a pithy summation of Feuerbach's thesis, as it is set forth more amply in Van A. Harvey, *Feuerbach*. A more extended discussion is to be found in Brun, *Philosophie de l'Histoire*, ch. 14, "La Gnose Historiciste". Brun's remarkable book, from which I draw several ideas, is an illuminating exploration of the development and significance of the sequence of philosophies of history in Western thought.

through forgiveness that humankind needs, but deliverance from belief that there is such a thing as sin and that forgiveness is necessary; not God's grace through faith that will redeem us, but humankind's will-to-power through unbelief.

The dominion over his creation that God gave to humankind was to be the visible manifestation of man/woman as *imago Dei*, for man/woman would be the Creator's agent and representative on earth, his *image*, caring for and developing his original creation. The creation was God's gift to the human race for our enjoyment; we would cultivate it and offer it in turn as a gift to its Creator. But the more knowledge we have acquired, through the very gifts God has given us, the more that dominion has been exercised in the form of domination, exploitation, and appropriation for ourselves. Civilized societies are more sophisticated than primitive ones, but, at bottom, not a whit less barbarous. The harmony and equilibrium the Creator intended us to sustain and nourish, as his stewards, we have upset and undermined, to the point where the once healthy planet itself, and not just the degraded human race inhabiting it, has become sick, mutilated, and unbalanced. Nothing illustrates this better than the climate change currently coming upon the earth, due significantly to human manipulations. The catastrophes contingent upon this change, both natural and social, are already wreaking havoc on every continent. This can only continue to get worse. It is the fruit of uncontrolled technology, of the will-to-power loosed from all spiritual or moral constraint.

We do not want to be God's agents on the earth. We want to be original creators, like God himself. This is logically impossible, of course, since we necessarily start with the objective *given* of ourselves-in-a-world—but we prefer to ignore this logical truth in the interests of the mirage we so passionately pursue.[20] We not only want to extrude God from his creation by denying his existence and ignoring his Word, we want to *make over* his creation and eliminate the divine footprint altogether. Instead of being *his* image in *his* world, we want to construct a

---

20. As I said earlier, we don't like *givens*, or *gifts*, because we're not the source of them. A *gift* to us carries with it the unwelcome evidence that we are not self-sufficient, that there is someone greater than, or prior to, us. This is why we don't like God's grace, as offered to us in Christ. We are "control-freaks" who want to be the source of all initiatives and who cannot stand something that did not start with ourselves. This, as I commented earlier, is surely the explanation behind the curious tone sometimes found in commentary on the great discoveries or speculations of cosmologists and physicists, suggesting that the apprehension of cosmic laws by human intelligence is practically equivalent to the existence of the laws in the first place.

reality from which he is absent and of which we are absolute master. We will construct cities that cover the earth and put our imprint on every inch of the planet, so that nowhere will the original creation be evident, or the trace of a power greater than ours be manifest. Not the image of God will be present throughout the earth, but the image of Man. The whole earth will be instrumentalized, used for human aggrandizement, wrapped up in the twine of trillions of lines of communication, physical, electronic, and cybernetic, and knotted in limitless genetic combinations through the possibiities opened up by the process of recombinant DNA and the technique of genetic splicing—a brave new world made by humankind for our own glory.[21]

21. Jeremy Rifkin's *The Biotech Century* is a formidable attempt to set out in detail the new world being opened up through the combined power of the computer and biotechnology. He describes the content of this revolution, its foreseeable benefits, the enormous stakes involved, and the incalculable dangers. What he calls the five thousand year old "age of pyrotechnology", culminating in the industrial age, is burning out, and is being replaced by the "age of biotechnology". Pyrotechnology involved the manipulation of fire/heat to "melt down the *inanimate* world and reshape it into a world of pure utility" (7); the new "operating matrix" that is enabled by the *conjunction* of information and life science, of computer power and genetic re-combination—both grounded in cybernetic systems of information and feedback—aims to reshape the *organic, living* world (32). Rifkin speaks of "algeny" as a new philosophical framework and metaphor for the biotech age, replacing that of "alchemy", with its vision of refining all metals into gold, that is, of perfecting *inanimate* nature by hurrying it along to a more perfect state, as represented by gold. The same vision of perfecting nature inspires algeny, but its range, dealing as it does with *living* matter, is much greater, and its potential is virtually unlimited. This quality of open-ended *limitlessness*, the perpetual construction and recombination of elements, an endless 'becoming' of entities with no fixed essence or 'being', is a fundamental characteristic of modernity and the one I am concerned to highlight in this essay. Rifkin writes (33–35):

> Algeny means to exchange the essence of a living thing. The algenic arts are dedicated to the 'improvement' of existing organisms and the design of wholly new ones with the intent of 'perfecting' their performance. . . . For the algenist, species boundaries are just convenient labels for identifying a familiar biological condition or relationship, but are in no way regarded as impenetrable walls separating various plants and animals. . . . The algenist contends that all living things are reducible to a base biological material, DNA, which can be extracted, manipulated, recombined, and programmed into an infinite number of combinations by a series of elaborate laboratory procedures. By engineering biological material, the algenist can create 'imitations' of existing biological organisms that to his mind are of a superior nature to the original being copied. The final goal of the algenist is to engineer the perfect organism. . . . His task is to 'accelerate' the natural process by programming new creations that he believes are more 'efficient' than those that exist in the state of nature.

And this human-made world, we tell ourselves, will be *better* than the first one created by God. We will have ironed out the "flaws", such as disease, moral evil, even death. Science and its outworking as technology will perfect and ultimately re-configure the world that God's fiat brought into being in the beginning (Gen 1). Natural forces will be understood and then mastered for the benefit of humanity; the wild planet will be ordered and monitored like a greenhouse; grains, plants, and edible animals will be modified and enhanced artificially through genetic manipulation and cloning, solving the problem of adequate food production for the world's growing population;[22] human passions and behavior will be controlled and channeled by behavioral scientists and genetic engineers for the well-being and productivity of all. Disease will be circumscribed and finally overcome through biological, chemical, and genetic manipulations; intelligence will be increased through eugenic selection and the electronic and genetic enhancement of natural faculties; human bodies will be improved by organ transplants and by artificial implants more durable and less vulnerable than natural organs; robots operating with "artificial intelligence" will multiply our merely human intelligence and do spectacular "intellectual" feats, and will also, like slaves, do the world's drudgery, so that humans—or *post-humans*—can be freed to enjoy themselves. Aging will be held at bay, and eventually even death will be defeated. All the limitations of our finitude, and all the defects resulting from our fallen condition, will have been overcome. We will long since have left behind this notion of a "fallen condition", of course, since that implies the biblical picture we recoil from, but the evident imperfections of the "natural" state of things with which historical humankind has found itself confronted, will have been analyzed and corrected. We will have saved ourselves and created our own Eden. Through technology, humanity will have accomplished for itself what God accomplished for it in Christ, of which we still await the eschatological fulfillment.

This trans-humanist "techno-utopia"—this technological "new creation"—is the dream of an "elite", of course, made up of futuristic thinkers,

22. It should be noted here that a tremendous market drive, in a subtle and insidious version of neo-colonialism, accompanies this "utopian" ambition. Rifkin, *Biotech Century*, 107–15, underscores the corporate drive to control, among other things, the world's seed-stock through the imposition of transgenic crops supposed to supplement, improve, and make more uniform and efficient the planet's agricultural production; and he observes that in fact this economic opportunism threatens to wipe out local centers of crop variety and erode the world's genetic reservoirs, gravely compromising the earth's biological diversity and ecological balance.

scientists, engineers, and, at the cutting edge of biotechnology, bioengineering firms and leading transnational chemical, pharmaceutical, and agribusiness corporations that are pouring money into biotech research. The majority of our populations would repudiate this dream, perhaps, if they understood its more extreme implications.[23] The dream, I believe, is vain, a mirage, an illusion born of *hubris*; yet its ideological—indeed, its *spiritual*—momentum, fueled as it is by the totalitarian sway and power of the scientific/technological enterprise that encompasses and orients everything, including, of course, the commercial/financial network of the global market, is great enough to cause overwhelming disruption before its ultimate collapse into physical and social chaos, of which the unstable conditions in the world today are already a harbinger. Such a dream, while articulated and shaped only by a privileged intelligentsia, describes the inner thrust of the human will-to-power—the will to be *master*, as Nietzsche puts it.

This will-to-power has taken and takes many political and economic forms, of course. Recently, on a global scale, the form was the colonial empires of the nineteenth century that extended their tentacles into every corner of the world; then, for much of the twentieth century, the form was the Soviet Communist system, controlled by the *party*; and for the last forty years, underpinned by the military might of America, the form has been unbridled free-market capitalism, led by a moneyed *elite* made up of vastly wealthy multi-national corporations, banks, financial networks, and monetary institutions, that has manipulated the world economy. What is important to note here for my purposes is that the *motor* of all these hegemonies, enabling their conception and implementation, was and is *technology*—propelled henceforth, in every department of human culture, by the epoch-changing development of computer power coupled with a vision of reality determined by the information/feedback dynamic of cybernetics.

---

23. Keith Ward, *The Big Questions*, 41, writes that the World Transhumanist Association, founded in 1998, is devoted to the development of "transhuman" forms of life superior to human beings, who will ultimately create "a virtual reality of pure knowledge and bliss, located in an intergalactic cloud far beyond the Milky Way." This vision of a technological utopia is generated by a kind of Gnostic mind-set that would wish to transcend materiality, considered to be an inferior form of reality; it is clearly a counterfeit of the biblical Holy City of Jerusalem coming down out of heaven from God (Rev 21:10).

I.I.7

Technology—Humanity's "fiat"—as the ultimate means to human mastery and auto-salvation; the revolutionary dynamic of the Gospel; the human appropriation of this dynamic and the rising up of man-as-subject; nihilism as the denial of transcendence; social and political counterfeits of the Gospel

The scientific/technological enterprise is the vehicle of this thrust-to-be-master as it enters its culminating phase. We need now to scrutinize more closely this complex question of technology, with reference at points to Heidegger's reflections on that subject. This will open a fresh perspective on the phenomenon of homosexual ideology as it has emerged in the last generation.

The natural world is being altogether appropriated and invested by mankind and transformed by technology. I am arguing that the human race, led by a messianic, technologically-minded elite, is colonizing God's creation, the planet Earth, intent on transforming it into a human-made City, a substitute for Eden and a counterfeit of the Holy City of Jerusalem that comes down from heaven and is the center of God's Kingdom, of which the final book in the Bible speaks so movingly (Rev 21). This is the City of Man we seek to build. We want neither to go back into God's Eden nor forward into his Kingdom, but to create our own Eden and our own Kingdom. Technology, inseparable from the science that undergirds it, is mankind's Word, our *fiat*. It is the spearhead of our *knowledge*, by which we intend to eradicate what God called our original transgression and to vindicate the wisdom of our choice to become our own masters. Most people are hardly conscious of what is happening around them, or of its meaning, but many scientists and engineers are entirely aware of what they are envisioning: a new creation, a new Man, a universal utopia brought into being not by religious belief or by political ideology but by applied "technique" (including "spiritual" techniques) at every level of human life.

This "technique", *as applied in this manner and with this objective*, is a new form of *gnosis*, a modern expression of magic, an updated version of the alchemist's quest to turn base metals into gold. Like all such quests to re-make reality, to transmute it into something deemed "purer", it is a *counterfeit* of the Christian Gospel. The new creation we seek to make is a *counterfeit* of the new creation that Christ brought—and brings—into being through his death and resurrection. The Gospel proclaims that humanity is enslaved by our rebellion against God's Law and subjected to the rule of might-makes-right; that this lamentable predicament cannot be alleviated by men and women themselves because we are its cause; and that God, in his mercy, has taken matters into his own hands and done through Christ what is necessary to open a new possibility for humankind—the possibility of redemption from sin and its disastrous consequences of violence, corruption, and death. This possibility—this gracious offer—involves the coming into being of a new reality, a redeemed people with new hearts and a spiritual and moral disposition *fundamentally different* from that of the fallen race of Adam. This new man-in-Christ is oriented *away* from self-aggrandizement and *to* the truth of the *Holy Trinity*, of the Three-Person God who is *love-in-communion* and who came to live amongst us in the person of Jesus of Nazareth.

This Gospel—the Good News of the incarnation, life, death, and resurrection of the Son of God—was/is the Great Revolution of human history. It brought to its point of culmination the profoundly subversive action of the God of the Hebrews as recorded in the Old Testament, who, in order to save the human race, called his people, Israel, and established a colony in the enemy territory of this world. God, not humanity, is the Revolution's author. The Great Revolutionary is *Jesus*. Through this divine action there entered into the *human* bloodstream the idea—the *vision*—of changing/improving/perfecting the human lot. A new dynamic was injected into history. Where this revolution has been true to its origins, it has created slowly, as its yeast has spread through those parts of the world where the Gospel gained an effectual foothold, a disposition to alter human behavior in the direction of mercy, justice, and respect of human dignity—expressions of love—as against cruelty and oppression. For centuries this revolutionary disposition, with what Robert Jenson, echoing other writers, calls "the church's mandated preferential options for the poor and oppressed"[24], was strikingly evident in the early Church and carried forward in particular by the monastic movements and the quiet, steady influence of the Christian liturgy. In the late medieval period, hospices to care for the sick, as well as universities to increase learning, were established throughout Europe. Then, first by the Christian humanism of the Renaissance and the democratizing effects of the Reformation in the

---

24. See Robert Jenson's perceptive essay, "How the World Lost its Story", in *First Things*, October 1993. This formulation about the poor is not a coinage of Jenson, but is found frequently in works of liberation theology, starting with Gustavo Gutiérrez's *A Theology of Liberation*. See also Juan Luis Segundo, *Theology and the Church*.

West, and later, in secularized form, by the Enlightenment, the ideals of charity, justice, and freedom passed into the wider culture, where they are still operative today.

The political and social revolutions of Western history were/are secular manifestations of this new dynamic, and have led, on the *positive* side, to the development over centuries of our modern democracies and to improvements in the daily lot of great numbers of mankind. Moreover, it can be argued that the mental disposition underlying the creation of modern science and technology, with its determination to master the forces of nature in the interests of understanding material reality and improving the human condition, was itself the fruit of this revolutionary dynamic. At its best, the scientific/technological enterprise is clearly an expression of the divine mandate to care for the earth and make it flourish, and its travesty in the form of *technologism*, as discussed in this essay, must not be seen as a denial of this.

The *favorable* historical consequences of the Gospel dynamic—that in it which has led to greater material, social, and political freedom and comfort for many in the human race—can be seen as God's *grace* flowing into history through the people of Israel and the Jewish Messiah, Jesus, and working itself out ever since in the fabric of human society through the proclamation of the Gospel by the Church. This has produced a series of social explosions in the last two thousand years, as free human individuals created in God's image, building—for the most part unconsciously—on this Judeo-Christian anthropology, have struggled to discover and lay hold of their freedom for themselves personally, in different dimensions of their lives. One example of many illustrating this was the movement from medieval feudal society, where everyone had a fixed place in the social hierarchy, into the rough and tumble of the Renaissance and the early modern world of the late sixteenth century, where the rise of a middle class and a worldwide expansion of trade and economic competitiveness transformed social relationships and expectations. Individual *subjects* were taking hold of their lives, in a movement of self-construction that represented a new maturity in human development. Unfortunately, for reasons I am suggesting in this essay, the "maturity" has gone awry because of *hubris*, and the "self-construction" has reached a point in our day, through the power of technology, where the individual is "objectifying" himself—indeed, *transmogrifying* himself—into a creature who questions and seeks to modify the very nature of his human identity.

In the case of the revolutionary explosion that we call modern science, while it is certainly true to say that in one sense science is the ultimate fruit of Greek philosophy,[25] one must immediately add that without the conditions created by the biblical view of reality—viz., that the world, as created, is not divine in itself; that it is good, orderly, and contingent (i.e., it could have been otherwise, it is dependent on something else); and that it is apprehensible by the inquiring human mind—modern science, as it came into being in Europe in the seventeenth century (not before, or anywhere else), could not have happened.[26] Greek philosophy developed the inquiring mind-set and analytical tools with which to question and explore the nature of material reality, but the leap from that intellectual disposition to the theoretical and experimental enterprise we call modern science could not have occurred without the rise and spread of the Judeo-Christian worldview that slowly took hold throughout the region that came to be known as Europe.

The *negative* consequences of the revolutionary dynamic—the bloodshed, the terror, the new modes of oppression, the ruthless, and also the *soft*, forms of totalitarianism—are the result of the human appropriation of God's act, in an effort to do by force what only God can do, that is, reconstruct humanity and liberate it from the moral and social consequences of its condition and make of it a *new creation*. The French and Russian Revolutions, the Maoist revolution in China, and the Cambodian genocide, are the most extreme political examples in the modern age of what I am talking about, all of them aiming at the creation of a "New Man", a new humanity.[27] Other examples are to be found in the sociological (Positiv-

25. For a persuasive development of this point, see Barrett, *Illusion*, ch. 10.

26. It is beyond the scope of my essay to discuss this issue at length, but a wealth of research has been done in the last three generations to back up my point. The ten volumes by Pierre Duhem, *Le Système du Monde*, published in the 1930s, were the massive opening guns of this discussion. A. N. Whitehead's *Science and the Modern World* (1946), provides a seminal discussion of the topic. More recently, Stanley Jaki's Gifford Lectures, *The Road of Science and the Ways to God* (1978), as well as his *Science and Creation* (1974) and his *Cosmos and Creator* (1980), are a major contribution. Another noteworthy work is Claude Tresmontant's *Sciences de l'Univers et Problèmes Métaphysiques* (1976). An excellent short discussion is provided by Peter Hodgson in Occasional Papers No. 4, published by The Farmington Institute for Christian Studies. Most recently, Peter Harrison, in *The Bible, Protestantism, and the Rise of Modern Science* (1998) has shown the major impact on the development of science of Protestant interpretations of the Bible.

27. There is still a tendency, especially in France, to romanticize the French Revolution, on the strength of its admirable motto, "Liberté, Egalité, Fraternité". Anyone familiar

ism), the philosophical (Hegel, Marx, Nietzsche), and now, definitively, in the scientific-technological spheres. For reasons I shall discuss below, these massive upheavals and "utopian" visions have only become possible in the modern scientific age, even if the underlying revolutionary dynamic has been there since the beginning of the Christian era.

These revolutionary ideologies may be understood as forms of *gnosis*—hitherto hidden "knowledge" now revealed to privileged thinkers—in which the incarnation of Christ, the Son of God who became Man, is reversed by a philosophical sleight of hand and turned into the doctrine of Man who becomes God. We are dealing here, I repeat, with *counterfeits* of the Gospel of the new creation in Christ. These take the form on the one hand of totalitarian, nihilist ideologies rooted in the outright *denial* of transcendence, or, on the other hand, with Hegel, in the doctrine of *absorption* of transcendence into history and the rationalization of the Christian Gospel. We find ourselves back again with the post-Edenic human enterprise of replacing God's creation with mankind's, by way of some sort of human-made "redemption" in imitation of what Christ has done. In these cases, philosophy/science—that is to say, *knowledge*—discloses an *ersatz* truth that promises to lead the way forward to a new humanity.

Nietzsche's proclamation that "God is dead and we have killed him" (*The Gay Science*, "The Madman", Section 125), and his call for a devaluation of all values having a transcendent, Platonic/Christian reference, and for a positing of altogether new values on the basis of the principle of the will-to-power, is understood by him, according to Heidegger's insight, as being the completion of the nihilistic tide running through the history of the West (and history *tout court*, I would add). Nihilism, in its essence, is understood here as the denial of the existence of any supra-sensory reality, truth, ideal, ethic, purpose or goal. Heidegger writes:

> Nihilism, thought in its essence, is, rather, the fundamental movement of the history of the West. It shows such great profundity that its unfolding can have nothing but world catastrophes as its consequence. Nihilism is the world-historical movement of the peoples of the earth who have been drawn into the power realm of the modern age. . ..The flight from the

---

with the details of the Terror that quickly replaced the idealism of the early months, will know, however, that what we would today call "crimes against humanity" were commonplace all over the country for years, and that what we might name a "proto-genocide" was committed against the royalist Vendéans in 1793 by the republican troops. For an exhaustive account of this event, see Secher, *French Genocide*.

world into the supra-sensory is replaced by historical progress. The otherworldly goal of everlasting bliss is transformed into the earthly happiness of the greatest number. The careful maintenance of the cult of religion is relaxed through enthusiasm for the creating of a culture or the spreading of civilization. Creativity, previously the unique property of the biblical god, becomes the distinctive mark of human activity. Human creativity finally passes over into business enterprise.[28]

According to Heidegger's analysis of Nietzsche's "overman", understood here not as Zarathustra himself or as those like him but as a generic term for humanity, what is happening in the present age is that Man is rising up into "the subjectivity of his essence".[29] "The earth itself," writes Heidegger, "can show itself only as the object of assault, an assault that, in human willing, establishes itself as unconditional objectification. Nature appears everywhere—because willed from out of the essence of Being—as the object of technology.... With the beginning of the struggle for dominion over the earth, the age of subjectness is driving toward its consummation."[30] What we have here is mankind as *subject*, the world as *object*—indeed, as *objectified* object. There *is* only what *is materially*, and our mastery of it. There is no supernatural, supra-sensory realm. The lie that God exists, is dead. For Nietzsche, it is not so much that we have replaced God as that we have come out from under the illusion that there *is* a God. This is the real meaning of the madman's proclamation in *The Gay Science* that "we have killed him". Nietzsche—who, ironically, was to go mad himself toward the end of his life—speaks under the guise of the madman and proclaims, in effect, the end of metaphysics, the end of belief in anything higher than human being. Consequently, all the former values rooted in norms and purposes linked with the "divine"—now known to be non-existent—must be set aside and new values posited, of which the essence is the will-to-power and its attendant non-moral code, "beyond good and evil". The *overman*, in this sense, is humanity living in accordance with this new reality and code.

We have here the fulfillment of the Adamic transgression: mankind will posit what is good and what is evil; indeed, in doing so, we will not even take into account any longer these terms of "good" and "evil", for these notions, in this perspective, belong to the former age of belief in a

28. See Heidegger, *Question*, 62–64.

29. Ibid., 100–101.

30. Ibid.

supra-sensory realm. We will "go beyond" these categories, beyond the categories of Genesis and of all subsequent moral reflection, and will understand ourselves in terms solely of what is declared to be our essence—and also *Being's* essence—that is, the will-to-power. Humankind will construct its own reality, according to its own will.

I.I.8

The biblical revelation of man/woman's dignity as the basis of the emergence of "subjectivity," in both its true and its perverted forms; technology: the distinction of "essence" and "technique"; the objectification of everything as "standing reserve," including humankind itself, as Man-the-Subject increases his technical mastery

In saying that "Man rises up into the subjectivity of his essence", and that "The world changes into object", Heidegger, explicating Nietzsche, is pointing to a movement of human culture of which we already found the possibility and the beginnings in our earlier discussion of the portrayal of character in biblical narrative. The figures who move through the Bible show a rounded three-dimensionality, a stunningly modern *subjectivity*. They display a moral freedom and a range of decision and action unequalled, to my knowledge, in any other ancient literature. This is precisely because, in the framework of the creation narrative in Genesis, they are creatures made in God's image, that is, in the image of the personal Creator God who, as infinite Spirit, is absolutely free of all external constraints and so cannot be constrained from outside himself to be or to do anything contrary to his nature, which is perfect Righteousness, Goodness, and Love.

This is not to say, of course, that the biblical characters are also, like God, free of external constraints—this is impossible, since they are finite creatures, unlike their Creator. Precisely because they are finite, they are vulnerable both to inner and to outside forces pushing them to do evil, that is, to go against God's commandments. They can choose to obey God or not to obey him. But, though finite and surrounded by constraints, they are *not fated* to go this way or that, in the manner of puppets. They are not the playthings of God, in contrast to the Homeric figures, who are depicted as being, in some basic sense, subject to the Olympic pantheon and their whims. The biblical characters are fully *subjects* in their own right. In this lies their dignity and three-dimensionality, and the inner truth of what it means that they are created in the image of God. They have not only rational souls but also freedom, the moral freedom to make ethical choices in whatever direction they will. They are responsible to their Creator, and they will come under judgment if they go against his order, but they are free to do so if they wish. And his order is not the fanciful whim of a tyrant, but the moral and physical law established by the Creator of all that is, with universal validity and the power, if obeyed, to hold the universe as well as human society in a just and harmonious equilibrium. The biblical figures are fully human persons, both free and responsible, having an intimate affinity and covenanted relation with the divine Power without for one moment being equal to it or considering themselves as on the same level as it; they know themselves to be subject to commandments from their Creator—albeit free to disobey these—but not to any metaphysical manipulation.

This truth about the essential identity of human beings—free rational subjects created by a free and sovereign rational Subject *to whom they are responsible*—is the basis for the subsequent evolution of historical— i.e., human/cultural—reality toward increasing subjectivity, that is, toward awareness of the self as the center of power as over against objective nature. The ambiguity of history arises from the doubleness of mankind: while being made in the divine image and called to care for God's world, we have rebelled against our Creator and turned the truth of our own being inside out, with the subterranean but increasingly conscious intent of making God in our own image and appropriating the world altogether for our own use. Heidegger's phrase about "rising up into the subjectivity of his own essence" is pertinent in just this double sense. The problem—and tragedy—of this "rising up" is that it is not into our essence that we are now rising up, but into the *travesty* of that essence; not into the responsible and mature communion with the divine of which we are essentially capable and which defines the fulfillment of human freedom, but into a determined stance of irresponsible autonomy and self-divinization that cannot but lead our race into ever greater bondage.

In its modern form, this bondage is very subtle, because it appears in the guise of *liberation*. As an expression of humankind's God-given rational power and a means to exercise dominion over the earth in accordance with the divine mandate, technology—understood here not in its essence but at the level of "technique", as the *web of scientifically-based technical control over all aspects of human life* and a consummate manifestation of the tool-making capacity of man/woman—has great power to improve the material condition of the human race. Most of us alive today enjoy and should be grateful for many of these improvements. But at a deeper level—the level of *essence*—this web of control is enslaving, for it turns *everything* into what Heidegger calls "standing reserve". "Modern science's way of representing," writes the philosopher, "pursues and entraps nature as a calculable coherence of forces."[31] As human subjectivity gains coercive power over nature, everything is "objectified" and becomes an object of research, to be analyzed and used for human purposes. Underneath all these purposes is the human will-to-power, the will-to-mastery. Objects lose their significance-in-themselves and become simply what we make of them. They become mere material. As such, they effectively lose their objectness. We no longer "let them be" in their objective presence; we force them to *yield* something, to *give up* something. In effect, we force them to give up themselves for our benefit, for our use. We subjugate them. All God's creatures become our slaves. Everything, as Heidegger puts it, "disappears into the objectlessness of standing-reserve."[32] This is not the dominion that God gave to humankind as a mandate; it is self-serving domination, of which the consequences can only be disastrous for our race and for the planet.

This process is what Heidegger calls "Enframing", and it entails, in his phrase, "the supreme danger". His remarks in this connection bear a striking resemblance to my own theological analysis, and they deserve to be quoted at length:

> This danger attests itself to us in two ways. As soon as what is unconcealed no longer concerns man even as object, but does so, rather, exclusively as standing-reserve, and man in the midst of objectlessness is nothing but the orderer of the standing-reserve, then he comes to the very brink of a precipitous fall; that is, he comes to the point where he himself will have to be taken as standing-reserve.[33] Meanwhile man, precisely as the one so

31. Ibid., 21.

32. Ibid., 19.

33. A striking example of this is to be found in economic technology as it is practiced today in free market capitalism. John Gray writes in *False Dawn*, 82–83:

> The argument against unrestricted global freedom in trade and capital movements is not primarily an economic one. It is rather that the economy should serve the needs of society, not society the imperatives of the market. In terms that are strictly and narrowly economic it is true that a global free market is incredibly productive. . . . There is not much doubt that the free market is the most *economically efficient*

threatened, exalts himself to the posture of lord of the earth. In this way the impression comes to prevail that everything man encounters exists only insofar as it is his construct. This illusion gives rise in turn to one final delusion: it seems as though man everywhere and always encounters only himself. . . . *In truth, however, precisely nowhere does man today any longer encounter himself, i.e., his essence.*[34]

My own understanding of humanity's essence is very different from Heidegger's,as it is based on my Judeo-Christian conviction that mankind is created in God's image. But his and my understanding of the essence of technology as that which turns men and women themselves, and not just the objects around them, into mere material, is very similar. This *essence* of technology, *thus understood*, is, I believe, the ultimate manifestation of the human project to set God aside and build a human Eden that will absolutely "humanize" and "perfect" nature (God's creation), perceived as defective in itself and in need of a total overhaul. *As such,* this essence is *evil,* the mature fruit of the primal transgression. The "humanization" of the creation entails, in truth, a "dehumanization" of humankind. The paradox here, at the heart of the human tragedy, is that technique—our tool-making power—is at once the means of fulfilling our God-given mandate and *creating* culture, *and* the means of distorting that mandate into Promethean self-aggrandizement and *destroying* culture. I shall consider this more lengthily in Section I.II.3.

This *essence* of technology is not itself technical, but it permeates and informs the "technique" by which, in every sphere of life, men and

---

type of capitalism. . . . As some economists have always recognized, the pursuit of economic efficiency without regard to social costs is itself unreasonable and in effect ranks the demands of the economy over the needs of society. That is precisely what drives competition in a global free market. The neglect of social costs, which is a professional deformation of economists, has become an imperative of the entire system.

The human being and his/her needs, such as social cohesion, employment, and a decent wage, are of no interest to an economic system of which productivity is the aim and efficiency the means. In all matters technical, efficiency will always trump every other consideration. In Heidegger's terminology, the human being has simply become "standing reserve". The market capitalist system *can* be structured differently through regulation and tax policy, or according as the State has a greater or lesser role, but whatever structure may be determined in a given cultural setting, the system must be geared primarily to the supreme technological requirement of efficiency.

34. Heidegger, *Question,* 26–28.

women seek total control. The irony, and the supreme danger, is, as I've suggested, that it is we ourselves who end up being controlled and *de-humanized*. We will apply to ourselves the same engineering that we are applying to the environment, including manipulation of our human DNA in order to "create" a more perfect humanity. Already we see the functioning of the brain and processes of thought being altered by the electronic/digital revolution. We are becoming more like machines. Indeed, precisely such "mechanization" is seen by some to be humankind's auto-salvation. Yet we must add, as always, that there are real benefits, medical and other, to be derived from applications of genetic research and neuroscience. These are positive spin-offs, and to be welcomed. But the point I am making is at a deeper level and has to do with our understanding of who we are, of what humanity is and is to become.

With regard to the particular issue of genetic and neurological manipulation to "achieve" a "better" species—an issue that actually symbolizes the all-compassing project of technology which I am discussing—we must ask by what criteria this perfected man/woman—this counterfeit of the new-man-in-Christ—is to be produced? What will be the relation of the billions who are not so "perfected", or who have no say as to what such "perfecting" involves, to the relatively few—the new elite, the new humanity!—who have the means and will to manipulate themselves—and selected others—into technicized creatures? Such questions—and there are many—are moral and elude technical answers. "Technique" here is helpless. The blind are leading the blind.[35] Denial by behavioral technicians that this is the case, or that there is even a problem, cannot change the reality.[36] Everyone is simply caught up willy-nilly in this ineluctable

35. In his chapter on a laboratory-conceived Second Genesis (Rifkin, *Biotech Century*, ch. 3), Jeremy Rifkin writes (115):

> While the genetic technologies we've invented to recolonize the biology of the planet are formidable, our utter lack of knowledge of the intricate workings of the biosphere we're experimenting on poses an even more formidable constraint. . . . the new colonization. . . . is without a compass. There is no predictive ecology to help guide this journey. . . . as nature is far too alive, complex, and variable to ever be predictably modeled by scientists. We may, in the end, find ourselves lost and cast adrift in this artificial new world we're creating for ourselves in the Biotech Century.

36. Current issues and debates in bioethics, among other things, well illustrate a basic tension between technique and morality. In any area on which technique impinges, it imposes—or pushes to impose—its own solution. This solution is a technical one, determined ultimately, always in the interest of efficiency, by physical laws and

movement of history. The "elite", whoever they are, have few references

objective mathematical parameters. For any given problem at a given point, there is a best solution—only one—and it is *technical*. Morality is irrelevant to technical problems *as such*. Technical problems are autonomous, self-reflexive, dependent for their solution only on their own coordinates. Non-technical factors are necessarily extraneous. Ethical considerations inhibit this drive because they involve subjective notions and arise from another sphere intrinsically different from the technical. The tension between them is inevitable. Nine times out of ten, the technical will determine the end result, often by indirection, very much in the manner that it deals with physical and biological laws, over which it cannot prevail *directly*. But in these cases it will seek to prevail *indirectly*, by *dominating* the laws. Jacques Ellul writes in this regard: "Whenever technique collides with a natural obstacle [e.g., a physical or biological entity], it tends to get around it either by replacing the living organism by a machine, or by modifying the organism so that it no longer presents any specifically organic reaction." (Ellul, *Technological Society*, 135). Technology, Ellul suggests, is developing a new morality, of which it itself is the judge. "Modifying the organism" is a key phrase. Technology modifies *everything*, conforms *everything* to itself. In this sense it is beyond good and evil, beyond the reach of morality as it has been understood in the past. It is beyond *nature* and beyond all that is *natural*—and this includes the pre-conventional moral sense that is innate in humankind, as well as its various cultural expressions. A "specific organic reaction", as Ellul puts it, is not tolerable. Technology makes its own all-encompassing reality. Its "total" nature provides one explanation for the fact that the words "moral" or "immoral", or even "wrong", rarely appear in public discourse today, even in cases of egregious fraud, corruption, flagrant dishonesty, abuse, or cruelty. An instance of such misbehavior will be reported "factually", in terms of contexts and causes, in terms of "what happened" and "why?"; there may be *analysis*—of a psychological or sociological or economic sort—in an effort to make sense of what occurred—but a *moral* reflection or judgment will almost never be made. The closest one comes to such a thing, normally, is to hear it said that the person at fault acted "irresponsibly". But even this is quite rare, and is usually spoken with more of a functional than a moral aim: there is disorder here and somebody needs to be blamed, but the problem, at bottom, it is suggested, must be viewed from a systemic or cultural or educational perspective rather than in terms of personal moral choice, because omni-prevalent technique with its autonomous functionality has created conditions and a general state of affairs in which personal responsibility for misdoing or for anything else appears spread so thinly that it virtually disappears. Like "fate" in the classical age, technology in all its forms—mechanical, administrative, bureaucratic, educational, juridical, penal, military, economic, commercial, psychological, etc.—operates like a monster machine, like an automaton or a multitude of integrated automata, overruling and undercutting all individual initiatives or perspectives that might be in tension with technical necessities. The word "evil" may occasionally be used in reporting some horrible event and its perpetrator, as describing something too terrible to be "scientifically" circumscribed—but the word "sin", never. This is increasingly the case even within the Church, in all denominations. "Error" or "mistake" are words often used, as a way of avoiding moral liability and any assumption of real guilt, and as being evidence of human "frailty", for which, of course, one cannot be condemned or held personally responsible. It is the all-pervasive technical milieu of the modern world that points to the reason for attitudes and discourse like these—a milieu that to lead them except . . . *science/technique!* The enslaver of the earth is becoming the slave of his own "creation". This is the fruit of idolatry.

I.I.9

The paradox of being entrapped in the framework of technology while also enjoying new freedoms technology brings; the soft totalitarianism under which we live; replacement of divine order by human control, via science/technique; the advances brought by this control, and the incipient chaos

As I suggested above, the technological heteronomy that directs modernity—what we might call *technologism*—is a diabolically *subtle* form of bondage. It appears as an "angel of light" (2 Cor 11:14), so that its constraints seem, at first, like forms of liberation. And indeed they *are* such, at certain levels. Their dehumanizing dimension is hardly noticed, because technical progress is potent and does bring countless benefits, not least in the area of medicine and physical health (access to medical care in developing countries, for example, is improving rapidly because of advances in wireless communication) and, as we have been seeing in recent years, in the sphere of politics and the quest for democratic reform. Indeed, "freedom" is one of technology's rallying cries: freedom from want, from penury, from strenuous labor and exploitation, from political domination. Without question, in all these domains technology has enabled large portions of humankind to make strides towards material and political freedom. Even the automatic use of violence and military force as the natural response to crisis is coming under increasing scrutiny and disapproval (but the irony should not be missed that at the same time, military technology is becoming ever more sophisticated, and arms are being manufactured, sold, and disseminated more and more widely among the populations of the world, fueling violence and anarchy). New kinds of connection between persons, enabling new kinds of creative action and political protest, are sweeping across the world. Many young people, and in particular women from every culture and country, are mobilizing to improve their lot and the lot of the downtrodden.

---

neutralizes morality as traditionally applied, by simply rendering it irrelevant, in its traditional form, as a possible source of either an explanation or a solution for a given event or problem.

Idealism among the young has by no means disappeared, even if it is in short supply and severely challenged. Here, on the positive side, the human heart's irrepressible hunger for freedom—for *life*—is finding new energy and hope through the powerful tools made available by technological innovation. I personally have no doubt that God's gracious Spirit, moving on the waters of our human confusion and chaos, is working providentially through humankind's marvelous tool-making powers to bring blessing to the human race, despite our rebellious passion to set God aside and achieve "freedom" and "salvation" on our own.

But, as I am arguing, there is a dark side to the technological heteronomy, deeper and much less visible. It is this that I mean when I refer to technology's *essence*. Increasingly, modern life is like confinement—one might even say *imprisonment*—in a supermarket. The goods available to us, at our disposal, are almost infinite, and, as Heidegger puts it, we exult in them and exalt ourselves to the posture of lord of the earth. We take our technological wizardry to be the expression of quasi-divine power and the guarantor of freedom—"freedom" being understood here as open-ended possibility and unlimited choice. But at bottom we delude ourselves, for we are *trapped* in the supermarket, ensnared in its labyrinthine aisles. Its walls and ceiling enclose us, and there are no exits. In terms of the society we are constructing, we have *no choice* but to be there. Every day we enlarge the building and add to its contents, making more and more entangling networks, and our existence depends totally on our ability to keep doing this indefinitely. There are *no alternatives* and there is *no elsewhere*, for Technological Man has demonstrated to his satisfaction that there is no metaphysical realm. Everything in the whole world, everything in reality as Technological Man understands reality, is inside the supermarket, along with ourselves; nothing, including ourselves, has intrinsic value any longer, it is there *only as material*. The objects exist only to be consumed in one way or another; the subjects—ourselves—exist *only to consume*. Finally, the subjects themselves, progressively depersonalized, become like *objects* and finish by consuming each other, like sharks or crocodiles in a feeding frenzy.

Such is the "soft" totalitarianism under which we in the modern world are living, whether we are conscious of it or not. Because creativity, the accumulation of wealth, and authentic advances in freedom and individual rights, are all involved in the invention and deployment of the technological wizardry, and because huge benefits and pleasures are available for those with means, much of the world population, mesmerized by the sensory gratification they are constantly experiencing or seeking to experience, is oblivious to its state of confinement. The *inner reality* of this state is below our normal radar.

It bears repeating that what makes the question of technology so complex and ambiguous is, as I said above, that technological advancement has truly brought so many benefits to the world—and this continues to be the case, undoubtedly. Yet this does not change either what might be called the "possession" or "enslavement" of humankind by its own creation, or the many obvious misuses of technology and its patently addictive nature. It would be foolish, even for those who begin to glimpse what is happening underneath the surface, to be "against" technology, because that would mean being against ourselves in our present historical existence; it would be no less foolish than for a fish to declare that it was against water. "Ludditeism" is not the point of my argument, nor is it an option. Every aspect of existence today has become technical and is subject actually or potentially to analysis, systematization, and instrumentalization. As both the means to every end and the end of every means, the technical is ubiquitous. The American philosopher William Barrett writes of this "framework" of technology: "It lays down the horizon within which our human future has to be planned. Almost invisibly it becomes our mode of Being in this historical epoch. The question looms whether we shall shortly be able to see around it or through it to grasp any other mode of Being."[37]

What is going on here has to do fundamentally with the question of *order*. The biblical picture of creation presents God's order, his systematic structuring of *being* as he creates it over against non-being, chaos, the void, and so gives form and coherence to *beings*. Kevin Scott, commenting on Genesis 1, writes:

> . . . it is clear that God's creating work was not conceived as a haphazard collection of disparate acts but a concerted action through which not only were things created, but they were created with a definite relationship one to another. There were *orders* of creation, things terrestrial and things celestial, things of land and things of sea, there were orders of plants and of animals, of man and beast, of male and female. Moreover, all these orders bore a definite relationship with each other, thus giving the creation an internal logic and meaning, and an intrinsic

37. Barrett, *Illusion*, 208.

order, sharply differentiated from the void and formless chaos from which it was resolved.[38]

This order, of which, as I said earlier, the discovery in our day of ecological unity gives manifest evidence at the physical level, provides the basis and possibility of life; to oppose or disregard it is necessarily to move toward dissolution and death—back toward chaos.

That humanity is moving in this direction is beginning to become evident in our day. The potentially catastrophic loss of biological diversity, the ineluctable rise of CO_2 in the atmosphere and the oceans, global warming and the worldwide melting of snow-packs and glaciers, the overuse of nitrogen fertilizer leading to the pollution of water systems and coastal areas, the depletion of aquifers, the destruction of tropical forests, and the growing number of natural disasters and meteorological disruptions that are shaking the planet and causing intense suffering and economic loss, are only the most obvious examples at the ecological level of the widespread global crisis that mankind is experiencing in every sphere.[39]

But again, that the world is in such a crisis is not necessarily evident to everyone at first glance. Our modern situation is extremely complex. The form that the mounting human opposition to God's moral and ecological order takes is not, and never has been, willful anarchy. Far from it. It is *our own form of order*—our *control*. As far as the *essence* of technology is concerned, as I have construed it, human *control*—through technology—is set over against divine *order* (this is not necessarily the case for "technique" in itself, where divine order and human control often coincide). The movement of history, which, I am arguing, has found its definitive focus in the modern scientific/technological age, is a matter of imposing human order/control on every aspect of the world. This order—the *human* order—is not a matter of engaging caringly and carefully with the objects of the world, but of dominating and exploiting them, of requiring them to yield up to us that which is useful to our enterprise of gaining mastery over everything. It is our human *construction* and, as such, finds itself on a collision course with the original order of creation, which it wishes not only to understand, but to remodel and replace. In the long run, only fundamental *dis*order—*chaos*—can result from this.

---

38. Scott, *At Variance*, 12–13.

39. See McKibben, *Eaarth*, for an informed and passionate warning about where our already degraded planet is headed if our exploitative and consumerist patterns of living do not change radically in the near future.

This, I believe, is what we are seeing today. What was there primor-dially in man-the-rebel, as depicted in Genesis, chapters 3–11, is coming into full blossom in the modern age. We, as self-determining *subjects*, are imposing our own order on nature and on our modern societies, in the form of technological exploitation and manipulation—and what we are beginning to experience as a result is moral, social, and ecological breakdown that is manifestly moving in the direction of chaos. To speak in the biblical terms I shall discuss in Part II, God has "given us up" to our sin, our self-aggrandizement, and we are reaping the consequences. Of course, it is in the nature of modernity to oppose this deteriorating state of affairs with more and more technological force, in the expectation that "science/technique" can overcome it and solve all our problems, moral, social, and ecological. This is the quintessential form of the modern will-to-power. As I argued above, our secular society has no other recourse; this is the only "language" modern men/women speak. Even religious discourse, *unless* we are speaking of God's eschatological power breaking into history through the crucified and risen Christ—and I shall discuss this shortly—takes place *within* this framework. We have boxed ourselves in, at the very moment, paradoxically, when the world-changing "elite" imagines the future to be open to infinite possibilities. There are indeed many possibilities open to us—but they are all *inside the supermarket*.

In pre-modern times, in the face of natural forces, suffering, disease, and the disordered human condition, recourse to philosophy or religion was a common response as people took flight from the world's pain and transience into some imagined shelter (e.g., Platonism, Stoicism, Gnosti-cism, Buddhism, occultism, esoteric sects, "mystery" religions, and, of course, Christianity, which understands itself as the redemptive God-given response to humanity's plight and cry for salvation as expressed variously in other philosophies and religions such as these mentioned). For a political, social, religious, or military elite, some form of despotic control—through specialized organizational techniques—provided a semblance of security, and military conquest, of course, provided an ap-pearance of all-powerfulness. This has been as true of the post-Christian empires as of the ancient Near Eastern and Oriental empires. But in the modern age, beginning in the seventeenth century, the scientific revolu-tion has turned the tables, and since the end of the eighteenth century, with the rise of industrial power and all that has followed, technological development has enabled mankind, initially in the West and now world-wide, to mount an offensive against the natural human condition instead simply of submitting to it or fleeing it or appearing to conquer it by decimating or dominating weaker peoples.

Since the Enlightenment, there has been a radical will to change our condition for what is perceived to be—and often *is*, materially and politically speaking—the *better*. This is what the scientific/technological age is all about, with the ambivalence and the features, good and bad, that I have discussed. As technology gains overwhelming momentum in our own day, its inner *spiritual essence*—the drive for human control over *everything*—is coinciding more and more with its actual *technical power*, thus giving rise to the *technological ideology* I have been describing, with its goal of ushering in a New Age and a New Man. In a titanic effort to overcome the disordered human condition by themselves—no causal explanation for this condition is offered, it is simply seen as the way the human animal has evolved—modern human beings, asserting their autonomy and taking their future evolution in hand, are bypassing the question of sin and their own spiritual and moral responsibility for the way things are, and are aiming to alter—through scientific analysis and "technique" applied in every sphere of existence—not only what Christians would call the "fallen" state of the world but, beyond that, the original, pre-fall divine order itself as revealed in the Judeo-Christian Scriptures—which Scriptures, of course, they have altogether cast aside.

I.I.10

The impact of the seventeenth-century scientific revolution on the understanding of the human subject in its relation to reality; philosophical considerations from Descartes to Kant; intrinsic link of science and technology; accelerating expansion of technology

I want now to give more attention to the question of subjectivity and the *self*, and to highlight the work of several philosophers who have contributed significantly since the seventeenth entury to this central movement of modern thought. My reflections, except where I resort to generalities to forward the argument, will be succinct but somewhat technical, and I ask my readers to bear with me. I am obliged to make only cursory reference to major thinkers and leave others out altogether. A thorough treatment of this hugely important theme is out of the question in this short essay, but a few comments are needed in order to bring more into focus the philosophical background of the homosexual question as it has emerged in our day, which I shall be discussing in Part II.

Many thinkers are currently working to understand the phenomenon of modernity and the reign of technology that lies at its heart.[40] The place of the "self" in this investigation is central. I am developing in this essay my own understanding of the matter from a theological perspective, using as a primary reference the early chapters in Genesis about the divine order of creation and human transgression. My remarks about the dignity of the biblical characters, and, by extension, of all human beings, are based on the revelation in Gen 1:26 that man/woman is created in the image of God and has a divine mandate to care for, shape, and refine God's world. I have suggested that the modern preeminence of the "subject", the "self", for good and for ill, is ultimately rooted in that biblically revealed truth about the human being and is central to an understanding of the complex and ambivalent question of the meaning of the reality at the heart of modernity, i.e., technology. But how did we get to this point that the "subject" on the one hand, and technology on the other, should join together to define the core of what we call the modern world?

Copernicus, Kepler, and Galileo were the three leading scientists at the end of the sixteenth and the early part of the seventeenth centuries. In his lucid analysis of the significance of their achievements, William Barrett points out that they made the giant step of moving beyond the classical approach toward the acquisition of knowledge of the natural world, and in doing so took rationalism to an altogether new level.[41] The classi-

---

40. The literature on this subject is vast, and I am familiar with only a small portion of it. Heidegger and Jacques Ellul are the seminal figures who, along with Siegfried Giedion, Lewis Mumford, Paul Tillich, Nicholas Berdyaev, Jacques Maritain, Romano Guardini, and Gabriel Marcel, among others, began in the years following World War II to discern and discuss the "problem" and challenge of technology. Other leading thinkers who have broached this subject in various ways include Alfred North Whitehead, C. S. Lewis, George Orwell, Aldous Huxley, William Barrett, Charles Taylor, Alasdair MacIntyre, George Grant, Stephen Toulmin, Wendell Berry, Jeremy Rifkin, Neil Postman, Andrew Giddens, Jeremy Begbie, Sherry Turkle, Norman Wirzba, and George Pattison. Among German theorists, in addition to Heidegger, Max Weber, Hans Jonas and Jürgen Habermas have made notable philosophical contributions. In France, along with the writers already mentioned, there is the pioneering work of Jean Fourastié and the singular contribution of Jean Brun. And there are surely many more thinkers who have written on the subject from one angle or another with whose work I am unfamiliar. Three whom I have learned of only after this book was completed are Albert Borgmann, Erazim Kohák, and Bill Vanderburg.

41. Barrett, *Illusion*, ch. 10.

cal method, going back to the Greeks and in particular to Aristotle, was to assume the "phenomenological congruence between ourselves and the things of nature."[42] Truth about the way things were in the natural world was revealed by direct observation of the phenomena. Late medieval scholasticism had sharpened the tools of rational analysis in general as it sought to coordinate Aristotelian philosophy with Scriptural revelation, and the Renaissance period from the mid-fifteenth to the late sixteenth centuries had vastly increased the range of interest in and observation of the natural world; but the correspondence theory of knowledge behind these developments had not been questioned. The work of Copernicus, Kepler, and Galileo changed this fundamentally by introducing a new method into the realm of reason.

It was not the brute facts of observation that determined their method, but theoretical concepts mathematically expressed. Experience and further observation later *confirmed* the validity of these concepts. Naked experience cannot tell us that the earth and the other planets revolve around the sun; as long as human beings relied on simple observation of planetary movements, they could not come to accurate astronomical knowledge. It required, as William Barrett writes, "the audacious step of positing conditions contrary to [observed] fact." These facts are then measured "in the light of these contra-factual conditions."[43] Galileo, for his part, "sets up an artificial concept, one that the mind does not find in nature but in itself, and he sets this up over against nature as the measure of it. The mind, out of its own powers, provides its own standards of exactness."[44] The exactness this new conceptual method attained in the understanding of phenomena went far beyond any methods of calculation or measurement achieved by human beings up till then.

Parallel to this revolutionary discovery of a new scientific method, René Descartes was laying the grounds for a new epistemological method in philosophy. He lived in an age of tremendous social and intellectual upheaval, characterized by European-wide religious conflict, the rise of the nation-state, and the terrible calamities of the Thirty Years War. Europeans were laboring to find a new basis for social order, stability, and, in the realm of knowledge, certainty. As Stephen Toulmin makes clear in an illuminating discussion of the impact of social and cultural circumstances

42. Ibid., 181.

43. Ibid.

44. Ibid., 191.

on scientific and philosophical theory, Descartes' drive for intellectual certainty was motivated in part by his reaction to the chaotic conditions of his age.[45] As a mathematician, he thought in *a priori* terms. Against Thomism, which proceeds *a posteriori* from things to ideas, Descartes moves from what he calls "clear and distinct ideas" to things. This was revolutionary. His desire to extend mathematical explication to the whole of reality led him inevitably to substitute the point of view of the *subject* for that of the object.[46] This move was analogous to that of political thinkers of the age like John Locke, who, in quest of political stability, laid the foundation for what Roger Ruston calls the "liberal paradigm" of human rights, based on a social contract between the State and the *individual*, considered henceforth to be the "fundamental building block of society".[47]

As is well known, Descartes inaugurated a form of philosophical dualism by radically separating body and mind. His skepticism regarding the reliability of the senses in the quest for knowledge led him to his famous *method of doubt*, by which he was able to call into question the existence of everything except *himself-as-thinking*: "*cogito ergo sum*"= "I think, therefore I am". An individual's mental activity is seen here as his/her primary identity. The mind/subject, now divorced from the body and the unreliable senses, becomes the sole source of epistemological certainty. This was counterintuitive and reversed the whole tradition of classical and Christian thought.

The notion of discounting the evidence of the senses and using the intellectual device of doubting in order to establish truth, went entirely against the natural human way of understanding reality, the more so as the *will* now took on a new prominence—the will to swim against the natural current in coming to a knowledge of things, by starting with ideas in the mind rather than sensory data and presuming thereby to establish the truth about the objective world. Furthermore, the notion that certain knowledge could only be determined by starting with innate ideas in the mind of the thinker deconstructed the intuitive way of knowing that had

45. Toulmin, *Cosmopolis*, especially ch. 2.

46. See Descartes, *Principles of Philosophy*, LXVI–LXXII, in *The Philosophical Works*, vol. I; and Gilson, *Études*, especially Part II. David Hart ("Philosopher in the Twilight", 46), commenting on Heidegger's assessment of Descartes' method, writes: "Whereas almost all earlier philosophers had assumed that the ground of truth lay outside themselves, and so had believed philosophy to be the art of making their concepts and words conform to the many ways in which being bore witness to itself, Descartes' method gave priority to a moment of radical doubt about everything outside the self."

47. Ruston, *Human Rights*, 9.

always been based on the apparent correspondence of sensory data and the knowledge of objects that these assimilated data seemed to produce.

One of the many problems that Cartesian dualism gave rise to was the challenge of how the disconnected mind/self could remake contact with the external world "out there"—how mind and nature could be re-integrated. More than a century after Descartes, Immanuel Kant sought to do this even while retaining the subjective standpoint that placed the source of knowledge in the sovereign subject. He developed the notion of *a priori* synthetic judgments generated by a "synthetical unity of consciousness" that was able to conceptualize and impose coherence on the stream of impressions that flowed into the brain. In this way, he overcame the sensationalism of Hume, even though he never repudiated Hume's equivalence of sensation and perception. But he did resist Hume's very odd notion that our representations of reality, such as the category of causality, were arbitrary constructs resulting from habit rather than from necessary reason, and that as a consequence they could not give us true knowledge. He went beyond the Scottish philosopher by seeing that the mind generated this coherence by virtue of synthetic *a priori* categories—causality and substance being two of these—through which the *unity of consciousness*, operating within the framework of space and time, imposed cognitive order on external reality. This discovery of the power of theoretical reason—the power of mind—to, in a sense, establish the reality of the objective world, enabled Kant to escape the Humean assertion that our *conceptions* of things were not specifically different from our *impressions/perceptions* of them, an assertion that, if true, would have made it impossible to have true, objective knowledge of things. No, affirmed Kant: we *could* have knowledge of "things-out-there".

Yet even so, the breach of self and world was not fully overcome. Having accepted the equivalence of impression and perception—which meant that perception did not involve an act of reasoning but was the same as mere sensation—Kant felt himself obliged to affirm that the "things-out-there" were no more than *appearances*, i.e., *representations* of things, and did not correspond to "things-in-themselves". Otherwise, while the apparent causal connectedness of our representations would be the work of the thinking ego, as Kant argued, the objects in fact would have no more certain objective reference than do Hume's contiguous successive impressions, which mere habit, not rational necessity, sets in "causal" association. The result, for Kant, was that our true knowledge of *things-out-there* was not the same as knowledge of *things-in-themselves*. These were unknowable.

Nature and the thinking subject thus remained separated from each other, as must necessarily be the case if, in one way or another, the subject posits the object. Although the doctrine of the unknowability of the "thing-in-itself" lost credibility in the next century, the subject/object division intensified. If the epistemological starting point is the self rather than a prior bond of *being* that exists between man and his milieu/world, as the biblical and classical traditions affirmed in different ways, no bridge can lead back to objective reality as such. In the biblical tradition, God has created both mankind and the rest of the world, and his mandate to the Adam-made-in-his-image to care for the world presupposes an ontological relationship both between God and man/woman and between man/woman and the other creatures. In the Greek tradition, as Kevin Scott points out, "the observer and the observed are related by the world-logos which informs and governs both."[48] The split of philosophy from natural science that began in the seventeenth century, and the subsequent split in the nineteenth century of ethics, religion, and art from the sphere of theoretical reason—a split rooted in Cartesianism and that led directly to the reductionist dualism of "subjective values" and "objective facts"—opened the way for materialist positivism and the denial of the possibility and/or the meaningfulness of metaphysics, at least as understood in the classical sense as referring to realities beyond the material. This in turn led straight to Nietzschean nihilism.

This being so, *alienation* of men and women *within* and *from* nature inevitably followed, since nature now did not include all those feelings and yearnings and spiritual intuitions that make actual life meaningful. It had become "objectified" and was on its way to becoming Heidegger's "standing reserve," of which the inner meaning is the absorption of objective reality into human "subjectness," the transformation of nature from "things-in-themselves" into "objects for us." Nature was seen henceforth as being over against the human subject, a material reality "out there," to be known, mastered, and manipulated (science and technology) or idolized (the Romantic movement), but not to be experienced any longer as Adam's home and "fellow-creature," his garden to be tilled and tended in a "natural" relationship of which the Source was indeed metaphysical,

---

48. Kevin Scott, in private correspondence.

beyond the subject-object nexus itself—that is, God, the Creator of both nature and man/woman in nature.

Kant's rational analysis of the process of understanding greatly contributed to the expanding authority of the human subject with respect to the objective world. In another register, his antimonies, in which he shows how the traditional rational arguments for the existence of God can be countered by equally rational arguments in the other direction, also confirm the determinant power of the human mind, even if here the point of Kant's case is to show the limits of theoretical reason in making metaphysical arguments.

In his analysis of the operations of theoretical reason, Kant is concerned to apply to philosophy his own penetrating insight into the constructive nature of modern science. A quotation from the Preface to the Second Edition of his *Critique of Pure Reason* that appeared in 1786, reveals this:

> Galileo . . . learned that reason has insight only into that which it produces after a plan of its own, and that it must not allow itself to be kept, as it were, in nature's leading-strings, but must itself show the way with principles of judgment based upon fixed laws, constraining nature to give answer to questions of reason's own determining. . . . while reason must seek in nature, not fictitiously ascribe to it, whatever as not being knowable through reason's own resources has to be learnt, if learnt at all, only from nature, it must adopt as its guide, in so seeking, that which it has itself put into nature. It is thus that the study of nature has entered on the secure path of a science after having for so many centuries been nothing but a process of merely random groping."[49]

The intrinsic link of science and technology now becomes clear. Science is not a "copy" of nature, just as a landscape painting or a portrait are not "copies" of nature. They are human constructs, conceptualizations, products of human artifice. Both science and art are intrinsically matters of "technique", although the one, as Francis Bacon, the sixteenth-century theorist of modern science, famously wrote, "puts nature to the wrack"[50] and is bent on control and manipulation, while the other has the contrary aim of bringing into *presence* the "being" of the objects it is portraying. "Here science is technological at its very source, in the formation of basic

49. Kant, preface to the second edition, *Critique of Pure Reason*, quoted in Barrett, *Illusion*, 71–72.

50. Barrett, op. cit., 74.

concepts," as Barrett concludes. "The hyphen in the compound expression 'science-technology' . . . expresses a single historical reality of which the two names denote merely differing aspects."[51]

During the century that followed, humanity's appropriation of the material world as the sphere of his revolutionary thrust to realize his utopian dream, construct his own ongoing evolution, and deliver himself definitively from the divine apron-strings, took a variety of forms, all of them holding to the same presupposition enunciated by Feuerbach that we looked at earlier: Hegelian Idealism, Auguste Comte's Positivism, Darwinism, Marxism. The *essence* of technology, as described earlier, developed momentum, even as, in parallel, technology itself—*technique*—extended its tentacles into more and more regions of human activity. Scientists analyzed more and more phenomena; industrialists, engineers, military personnel, politicians, bureaucrats, scholars, doctors, lawyers, etc., developed more and more instruments to organize, control, and administer every dimension of human life. Humankind was *taking over*.

Technology *as such* was not yet seen, in the nineteenth century, as the ultimate means to constructing a human Eden.[52] Philosophical, eco-

---

51. Ibid., 73.

52. Neil Postman, in his incisive critique of technology entitled *Technopoly*, notes the gradual development in culture from "tool-making" to "technocracy" to "technopoly". The nineteenth century, in his view, was still at the technocratic stage of development. He observes on 45–46:

> Technocracy did not entirely destroy the traditions of the social and symbolic worlds. Technocracy subordinated these worlds—yes, even humiliated them—but it did not render them totally ineffectual. In nineteenth-century America, there still existed holy men and the concept of sin. There still existed regional pride, and it was possible to conform to traditional notions of family life. It was possible to respect tradition itself and to find sustenance in ritual and myth. It was possible to believe in social responsibility and the practicality of individual action. It was even possible to believe in common sense and the wisdom of the elderly. It was not easy, but it was possible.

Postman goes on (51–52) to point to Frederick Taylor's *Principles of Scientific Management* (1911) as containing:

> . . . the first explicit and formal outline of the assumptions of the thought-world of Technopoly. These include the beliefs that the primary, if not the only goal of human labor and thought is efficiency; that technical calculation is in all respects superior to human judgment; that in fact human judgment cannot be trusted, because it is plagued by laxity, ambiguity, and unnecessary complexity; that subjectivity is

nomic, and political means to bring into being the new—man-made—world still held the field and had to run their disastrous course in the twentieth century, before the inner dynamic that made all of them even conceivable—*technological progress*—emerged clearly into the light by the middle of the twentieth century. By that time, prescient minds saw that Communism and racially-based Fascism, not to mention all the other *isms* and ideologies that jostled for influence or had fallen by the wayside, were undergirded, no less than is Market Capitalism, by technology and the instrumentalization of nature. Below the surface of variable cultures, as history moves forward, is the all-enveloping global underpinning of technology, sustaining world civilization. The Darwinian theory of evolution, perverted into doctrinaire *evolutionism*, had provided the warrant for free thinkers to cut once and for all the umbilical cord with a Creator God and declare the human being to be the result of chance-plus-time; from now on, human beings, through technology, would operate their own evolution and "create" themselves.

As the nineteenth century progressed, space and time were being invested by Technological Man. Industrialization created complex machines and systems to exploit the earth's resources, build cities, create new types of locomotion and networks of communication. Increased velocity in output and travel came to be seen as a desirable goal. Indeed, it soon became a *necessity*, as technology itself began to drive humanity forward and the notions of "efficiency", "productivity", and "immediacy"—requiring *speed*—became watchwords. The human experience of *space* was being fundamentally altered, and with it the experience of *time*.

---

an obstacle to clear thinking; that what cannot be measured either does not exist or is of no value; and that the affairs of citizens are best guided and conducted by experts. . . . Technocracies are concerned to invent machinery. That people's lives are changed by machinery is taken as a matter of course, and that people must sometimes be treated as if they were machinery is considered a necessary and unfortunate condition of technological development. But in technocracies, such a condition is not held to be a philosophy of culture. Technocracy does not have as its aim a grand reductionism in which human life must find its meaning in machinery and technique. Technopoly does. In the work of Frederick Taylor we have, I believe, the first clear statement of the idea that society is best served when human beings are placed at the disposal of their techniques and technology, that human beings are, in a sense, worth less than their machinery. He and his followers described exactly what this means, and hailed their discovery as the beginnings of a brave new world.

The *past*, too, came under scientific scrutiny in all sorts of domains, as the searchlight of "analysis" swept its beam across ever wider swathes of human experience. Much of the new knowledge was beneficial and greatly expanded human self-understanding. Numerous "ologies" were refined or came into being that delved into the past in order to "know" it and, in a sense, to bring it under human control: geology, archaeology, anthropology, ethnology, etc. In area after area, new disciplines and methodologies emerged, yielding huge quantities of knowledge totally unimagined up till then.

Comparative religion became a serious field of study in the nineteenth century, benefiting from new knowledge of oriental religions and anthropological study of primitive peoples. On the one hand, the rationalistic analysis of the history of religions tended to take over from earlier concentration on natural theology, in a traditional scholastic form or in the deistic form inherited from the Enlightenment; on the other hand, towards the end of the century and under the influence of thinkers like William James, investigation of religious experience and the deeper realms of the unconscious opened up by Freud and Jung undermined the positivistic approach of the History of Religions school and led to an overlap of psychology and the study of religious phenomena.[53] All these dimensions of *technique* uncovered new fields that contributed to the focus of modern men and women on themselves-as-subjects and as the source—in the place of God—of religious phenomena and spiritual intuition.

In the area of Christian theology, a new breed of "biblical theologian" began to put the Scriptures under the microscope, writing not so much about God and revelation as about the composition and historical development of texts and what possible meaning "revelation" could have in a world being divested rapidly of any real belief in a supernatural realm or in the very idea of divine intervention into historical reality. Miracles were denied, and writers like D.F. Strauss and Ernest Renan "demythologized" the Old Testament and the Gospels. Analytical methods seeking to be "scientific" were used to investigate what could or could not be considered historically true in the Scriptures. In all fields, that which was considered to be authoritative moved progressively away from the sphere of tradition to that of scientific investigation and validation. The past as a whole was no longer merely the sphere of tradition or an area of

---

53. See Dawson, *Religion and Culture*, especially ch. 1. These Gifford Lectures of 1947 probe the relation of religion and culture across the spectrum of historical cultures.

antiquarian interest for a few specialists, but the *object*, in area after area, of extensive scientific analysis.

I.I.11

*The rise of historical consciousness; "history" and "becoming" ab-
sorb "nature" and "being"; post-modernism, the loss of "narrative",
and the meaninglessness of history; the inflation and concomitant
de-substantialization of the subject/self*

The study of history itself was rationalized. Indeed, the idea of "history" or "historicity", began, under the pervasive influence of German
philosophers like Herder, Hegel, Marx, Dilthey, and Nietzsche, to be the
all-comprehensive concept for thought about the meaning and destiny
of mankind, absorbing into itself the idea of "nature". Historical consciousness and the notions of "development" and "becoming" became
pervasive in every region of thought. The Darwinian theory of evolution exemplified and symbolized this modern perspective, and had the
added attraction, for unreflective atheists, of appearing to make of God
an unnecessary illusion. This tendency to think in evolutionary terms
was accentuated in the twentieth century with the discovery by astrono-
mers and theoretical physicists that the universe itself had a beginning
and was evolving. Ironically, this later discovery, by concretely raising
the question of the origin of the universe, has forced cosmologists to face
the "God-issue", since the puzzle of how what exists *came to be*, when,
"earlier" (whatever "earlier" means, since *time* itself came into being with
the universe), it *was not*, can no longer be dismissed by saying simply
that it always was. An origin, according to the Law of Sufficient Reason
(Leibniz), requires a cause and points beyond itself. What is the nature
of that "beyond"? *Something* cannot come out of *nothing*. On what—or
Whom—does the *something* we call the cosmos, depend?

The significance of this "historicalization" of all reality, including
the cosmos itself, cannot be overestimated. Man (man/woman) is not just
a rational animal (Aristotle), he is an *historical* animal. His fulfillment, it
was increasingly believed, will come *within* history, not beyond it in some
sort of timeless state, as a Platonist might have imagined, or in a future
beyond this present age, as Christians have always believed. The Kingdom
of God, realized by divine power and consummated eschatologically in

a manner inconceivable to the human mind, was replaced by the notion of earthly *progress*, realized by humanity itself within history by means of the progressive mastery of nature. This revised vision of mastery was perfectly symbolized by the replacement of "nature" by "history" as the primary reference for elucidating *human being* and *human destiny*. The concept of "nature" could not fail to carry an echo of "creation", hence of God; the concept of "history" did *not*, at least not in the same way. History was *humanity's* domain. The "subjectivity" of the human race—the race as "Absolute Subject"—was gathering into itself the "objectivity" of reality.

The notion of the "historicity" of everything tends to eliminate the notion of ontology. If everything, including the human race, is constantly *becoming*, then its *being* is unfixed, always changing, and essentially relative. It has no definable nature. Clearly, then, the Judeo-Christian revelation of the *imago Dei* is ruled out as being nothing more than humankind's vain desire to believe that there is some unifying purpose, finality, and value to human existence. Henceforth, there can be no *meaning* to human life other than what we ourselves determine. Our race is a surd; we make of it what we will. There are no permanent moral values given us. The very notion of "gift", as from the hands of a Creator, is excluded *a priori*. The ultimate "value", therefore, is the "will-to-power"; in the Godless world of modernity, there can be no other.

As transcendence and any kind of supernatural realm gradually faded from the forefront, even from the background, of human preoccupation, Christian faith contracted drastically.[54] God was banished by the intellectual avant-garde both from nature and from history, both from space and from time: past, present, and future. Daily life took on a livid cast, as mystery was "deconstructed", joy reduced to pleasure, celebration commercialized. The self-revelation of God in the history of the Hebrews; the incarnation of God in Christ; the redemptive significance for the human race of Christ's death, resurrection, and ascension; the expectation of his return in glory at some point in time—all these essential features of biblical faith were relegated to the category of myth or symbol, with the result that God's saving Word, as manifest in the Law (Torah), the Prophets, and the Messiah (Jesus), was no longer heard or heeded, at first by the "progressive"

---

54. One is reminded of the words of Jesus in his parable of the unjust judge: *"And will not God bring about justice for his chosen ones who cry out to him day and night? Will he keep putting them off? I tell you, he will see that they get justice, and quickly. However, when the Son of Man comes, will he find faith on the earth?"* (Luke 18:7–8).

elite, then gradually by the population at large. A residue of faith has remained in the West, of course, and in remnants of the Church it is still potent (God will not leave himself without an authentic witness); but the bulk of Western society—and, it could be argued, of human society as a whole, given time—has been radically secularized. The human race has taken over its own evolution, its *becoming*; it has taken over its destiny. We are busy, very busy, "managing" this destiny, busy extending our scientific-technological mastery, busy trying to overcome our finite human condition. And God has *given us over* to our busyness and fallen silent.

God will not impose his presence upon us. He *is*. Modernity's proclamation that he *is not*, changes nothing, obviously, as to the Being of God. But it does remove from the sphere of history any possibility for Secular Man of finding by himself, or even intuiting, some form of ultimate truth or meaning. As our race, being sinful, cannot save itself, so, being finite, it cannot by itself attain to Absolute Truth, that is, to the Truth, Unity, and Purpose of *being* as known through the self-revelation of the Creator, which alone can provide coherence to the apparent chaos of human history. The *ersatz* meaning afforded by the notion of "progress" must fall before the hammer blows of sin, time, and death, as happened definitively in the twentieth century. As Robert Jenson has observed, if there is no Narrator of the world's story, that story is not narratable, it can have no order or aim.[55] The biblical source of coherence in time and, more profoundly, of the coherence *of* time itself, is lost, with the result that both the past and the future, both history and eschatology, ungrounded in any ultimate and fixed reality, become pointless. *Narrativity*, which presupposes some kind of sense and purpose, is henceforth impossible. The collapse—in the current and late phase of modernity that is called "post-modernity"—into absolutized relativism, subjectivism, and incoherence in every area of life, is consequently inevitable.

Our brains feed now on rapid-fire images, sound-bites, and short-hand text messages blitzing us from everywhere. As with fast food, we feel stuffed and stimulated on the moment; but fast food, like the billion bites and bits that cram our brains, is just filler and carries few nutrients, and we quickly grow hungry again. Humanity today suffers, physically and symbolically, from obesity, but is spiritually anorexic. We are, actually, starving to death. We are emaciated. Only truth, love, and beauty nourish, and these are not highly valued by modern culture. Since

55. Jenson, op. cit.

post-modern ideology denies Truth, it follows that there can be no truths. All is relative, perspectival, subjective, culturally constructed. "Objectivity" and "authority" are not merely *limited*—a principle that historians trained in the early modernist methodology of history-writing readily admit—they are taken to be arbitrary notions, generated by the coercive power structures of class or race or gender.

Indeed, from a post-modern perspective, even the *writing* of history, as the *story* of the past, becomes an arbitrary enterprise dependent not on "facts", which are taken by some post-modern historians to be coercive interpretations of events made by dominating interests, but on the disposition and inventiveness of the historian. Gertrude Himmelfarb, characterizing and criticizing the attitude of such authors, writes:

> Narrative history . . . is the primary culprit, not only because
> it depends upon such arbitrary conventions as chronology,
> causality, and collectivity, but also because it takes the form
> of a logical, orderly structure of discourse that is presumed to
> correspond, at least in some measure, to the reality of the past,
> and thus communicates, again in some measure, a truth about
> the past. This is the illusion that the postmodernist seeks to
> expose: that the narratives of history are anything more than
> the rhetorical, literary, aesthetic creations of the historian.[56]

A great irony hangs over modernity. The grand enterprise of science, supremely illustrating the power of the human mind, has both inflated mankind and broken us down. Modern materialism—philosophical and consumerist—vaunts and displays the immense power over nature that human beings have gained in the last four centuries. But it has also *reduced* man, denigrated him, and separated him from nature. It treats him/her, at bottom, as a thing or a machine. He/she is seen to be the nexus of forces, the result of chance, the object of exhaustive analysis, a self-conscious being without a soul, a solitary unit lost in a vast and purposeless cosmos. The extraordinary achievement of landing a man on the moon and viewing the blue orb of earth from outside itself, is accompanied at once by an ever greater and more poignant awareness of the earth's tininess in the unimaginable expanse of space, and by the terrifying perception of impending nuclear or ecological disaster for that very orb that human genius has now made it possible to behold from afar. The Christian vision affirms that human persons are *subjects* with

---

56. Himmelfarb, *On Looking into the Abyss*, 139.

metaphysical dimensions, marvelous creatures created by God; yet, pathetically, we have shrunk the soul to such a point that we deny the very existence of metaphysical reality—indeed, of soul itself—and find ourselves alienated even from the tangible earth on which we live.

We have split our own being down the middle. On the one hand, we have assumed *promethean* proportions: through the potency of our reason we have turned everything else in the world into material to be devoured or transformed by our will-to-power, and we have made of the claims and rights of the individual *self* a veritable religion of which we are the god. But on the other hand, this same proud, rational self/subject, forsaking reason and indulging in irrational covetousness, has become more and more insubstantial, abstract, fragmented, and powerless, even as the world he/she inhabits becomes more corrupt and polluted.

Having "conquered", in a sense, space and time through their technology, modern men/women, at the level of the individual, have *exchanged* rootedness in a place, providing stability and identity, for the dizzying experience of perpetual mobility and constant displacement, both in physical space and in cyberspace; and they have *exchanged* their past as a subjective force providing them, through cultural tradition and family narrative, a rootedness in history and a sense of personal identity, for a cultural past analyzed and catalogued—*objectified*—through the labor of thousands of specialized scientists, historians, and technicians, and set before them like a series of files displayed on an office shelf. Thus with respect to both space and time, our sense of *identity*, of who we actually *are*, is shrinking. We are becoming spectral.

The contemporary individual, unquestionably, has had many thrilling experiences traveling all over the place physically and virtually, and has acquired a great deal of fascinating and enriching information about millions of things; but at the same time he/she finds him- or herself increasingly cut off from any strong sense of belonging somewhere in *particular* and from any organic link with his/her own personal and cultural past. Paradoxically, having "historicized" all reality and "objectified" the past, the modern individual is fast losing the sense of his/her own embeddedness within the stream of history. Solidarity with others, both with figures in the past and with those in the present, is giving way to a desperate and alienating individualism, sometimes coupled with some form of what one might call tribalism or *ersatz* community (e.g., gangs, gated "communities," internet "friends," inward-looking ethnic, religious, political, nationalist, or sexual groupings). Driven by *potentiality*, by the open horizon of endless becoming provided by the infinite possibilities of technology, we are losing touch with the *actuality* of our own being. This loss gives rise, commonly, to a self-defensive posture, accompanied by deep insecurity and *angst* and a feeling of victimization, and this engenders in turn an ever more aggressive drive for some form of power. The drive may be channeled into positive social and political change, but generally it tends to produce hardheartedness and reduce the sense of social solidarity.

Homeless and restless, the modern individual lives abstracted from the very self he/she is constantly seeking to fulfill. He walks beside himself, like his own shadow. The *virtual* replaces the *actual*—quite literally in the case of the millions of lonely people, especially among the young, who, often estranged from their families, live their lives in front of screens playing "games" with themselves or with virtual partners, or "chatting" with fleshless "pals." Authentic conversation, which, ideally, involves face-to-face presence, unhurried time, and a genuine focus on one's interlocutor and the subject under discussion, is being submerged or sidelined by "texting" and by ubiquitous digital devices of one sort or another that replace personal interaction with what is often little more than self-indulgent "messages" without real purpose or point.[57] Narcissism is replacing self-reflectiveness. I have observed above that there are some real personal gains, especially political, economic, and medical, from the new global inter-connectivity via the net, but the negative aspect of "virtuality"—its capacity to dissolve tangible reality and depersonalize relationships by substituting "connection" for conversation—is undeniable. Online "everything"—shopping, dating, meeting, talking— is crowding out personal life and genuine intimacy.

On the one hand, as I argued, the *past* has been aestheticized by post-modernist attitudes and reduced to subjectivist constructions; on the other hand, it has been hardened by the scientific mind-set into data—so-called "knowledge"—a vast store of information "out there", and seems, for many, increasingly irrelevant, except as it may be *useful* as "standing reserve." The *future*, under the lens of both phases of modernity, the modernist and the post-modernist, has melted into a hazy

---

57. Sherry Turkle makes a penetrating and profoundly disturbing analysis of this growing phenomenon in a piece in the International Herald Tribune, April 24, 2012, entitled "The Flight from Conversation". "As we get used to being shortchanged on conversation and to getting by with less," Turkle writes, "we seem almost willing to dispense with people altogether. . . . We seem increasingly drawn to technologies that provide the illusion of companionship without the demands of relationship."

mirage of endless technological change leading no one knows where. The orphaned *present* has contracted to become like a point suspended in the void. We have no purchase any longer either on time or on space. All-encompassing technology is reducing the human being to a shadow, or a skeleton, struggling to create *meaning* where there is no ground on which to find it. This imposes on modern persons an intolerable existential burden that many cannot bear, leading to social disaffection, rising suicide rates, and the pervasive recourse to more technology (including countless therapeutic techniques), in an effort either to escape the real world or to transform it. We are being stripped of our flesh. I shall consider shortly the pertinence of this to the question of homosexuality and the obsession with sex in contemporary society.

Again, I hasten to reiterate that within this modern framework, this supermarket, this teeming City of Man that both enriches and impoverishes, admirable things are being done to enhance human life, to improve the material lot of billions, to liberate more and more people from want and tyranny. Technological advances, without question, are contributing here and there to genuine advances in democracy, personal freedom, enlightenment, mutual understanding and tolerance, and material well-being. Not for a moment would I think to deny this. But that is not the point of what I am arguing in this essay. Man (man/woman) is a creature of greatness, he is made in God's image, he has wonderful capacities. *Of course* our power to construct, build, wield tools and techniques, will lead—in part—to enhancement of our existential condition. We have been equipped by our Creator to do just this. The problem is, we are also rebels, proud upstarts who want to be more, and other, than we are. And the extraordinary power of technology is actually putting this possibility within our reach. But as we use this power for our own glory and to liberate ourselves from the chains of our creature-hood, we are in fact becoming *less* than we are. Modern man (man/woman) is reifying his own person along with everything else in the world; he is shrinking his heart, even as he begins to tinker with his genes; he is acting like a magician, a demiurge, expanding his power instead of applying himself to the harder work of love, which, in all circumstances, necessarily involves a contemplative appreciation of the autonomous existence and mystery of the other, the vis-à-vis, and a *renunciation* of power when viewed as a means for self-promotion. But it is this renunciation which, by ourselves, we cannot achieve nor wish to achieve. This is why we need salvation from outside ourselves—yet precisely this is what we cannot naturally accept. Humankind does not want to *be saved*; it wants to *save itself*.

I.I.12

The illusion of self-construction, as the contemporary version of the will-to-power; gnostic self-hatred and the flight from matter; nihilism and the erosion of identity and authentic subjectivity

The illusion behind the enterprise of radical self-construction is the idea that human beings can make of themselves whatever they want. We can will to *be* this or that, to *do* this or that. We are free to become anything. This is one of the central tenets of the post-World War II movement called existentialism, as formulated by Jean-Paul Sartre. Man, for Sartre, "has no definite human nature or fixed individual character."[58] What Sartre calls man's freedom is, we are told, total and absolute. A fixed human nature or character, he contends, would limit our freedom. Indeed, man *is* his freedom; he is "nothing but his own project," and "all is permitted to him."[59] This is another version of the will-to-power, of the human pretension to omnipotence, carried to an extreme theoretical point. We can choose to be other than we are because we are not anything in particular. The possibilities before us are limitless. The substantial particular ties us down and must be overcome by choosing another and then another, and so on. In fact, however, the "anything" that, according to Sartre, we can *be*, translates an underlying conviction that at bottom we are *nothing*.

This is nihilistic nonsense masquerading as *liberation*. Yet it captures a central belief at the very heart of modernism. In our pagan pantheon, *choice* is one of the chief gods. We are, as I suggested earlier, in the supermarket, where choice is infinite. To have infinite choice as to what we are and will be, defines our freedom, according to Sartre's existentialist perspective. We are what we will to choose, what we will to decide. The problem is, *there is no substantial self behind the choices*. Therefore, there can be no point or purpose to them. The whole operation is meaningless.

---

58. Barrett, *Death of the Soul*, 135.

59. Sartre, *L'existentialisme est un humanisme*, 33, cited in Jonas, *Phenomenon of Life*, 225–26. Chapter 9 of Jonas' book provides an incisive philosophical critique of the nihilism—resembling a modern form of Gnosticism—that underlies Existentialist philosophy.

Choice has become a self-serving *idol*, rather than being, as God made it to be, at the moral heart of the *imago Dei*, man/woman-made-in-God's-image. Wandering thus aimlessly in the supermarket, picking things at random off the shelves—this or that belief, this or that product to en-hance, define, or beautify one's "self"—modern people are in fact *prison-ers*, prisoners of the consumer society that technology makes possible. To claim that such a state of things is freedom, is fraudulent. People who "buy" this sort of "philosophy" and "life-style", are being had.

There is ferocious self-hatred here, a destructive drive that sits para-doxically with the vacuous self-construction that Sartre is proposing. Even those who do not share the understanding of human nature that, as a Christian, I have set forth in this essay, recognize that we are constrained in our actions by heredity, upbringing, gifting, circumstances, and other people. Sartre dislikes other people—"Hell is others", he has a character say in his play, *No Exit*—and in *Nausea* he makes it plain that he dislikes most things in the material world.[60] They limit him, obviously. They constrict his

60. See Stern, *Flight from Women*, ch. 7, for an analysis of Sartre's alienation. Stern provides a stunning account, through an examination of major writers, of the de-humanization and de-feminization of society in the West—the loss of the femi-nine values of intuition and *sophia*—resulting from the extension of the scientific/ analytic manner of conceiving of reality that has led to the technological structure and mind-set of the modern world. It is to be hoped that the current *rise* of women in all areas of society—due in no small measure, paradoxically, to possibilities opened up by technological advances—will somewhat offset this development, but it must not be forgotten that this rise itself is happening within the overall technological "Enframing" that I have been analyzing, there being no other context imaginable. It is one of the strangest ironies of modernity that, under the pressure of technology, the world is becoming more and more "masculinized" and power-obsessed, *even as*, in the West, the male's sense of his own masculine identity weakens and grows more confused, and as homosexuality becomes more prominent. This is why some social analysts like Stern can also speak of the "feminization" of contemporary society, while underlining, in a different frame of reference and with another connotation, its "de-feminization". We see today not uncommonly an emasculated maleness on the one hand and a kind of two-dimensional, functional maleness on the other hand, increasingly patterned on the machine and displaying an *ersatz* machismo shaped by the ambient culture of violence. Parallel to this, the danger is great that modernity will continue to "de-feminize" and harden the authentically feminine, as the negative expression of the feminist movement—feminism as ideology—has already managed to do (there is also a *positive* expression, of course, that seeks full recognition of women's dignity and full equality of civil and legal rights, of opportunity, and of pay scale in the workplace). What I call the "authentically feminine" inclines towards a sensitivity that is intuitive more than analytical, receptive more than aggressive, communal/familial more than individualist/independent. It remains to be seen whether a *genuinely* feminine influ-ence, such as we can unquestionably discern in many social, educational, political, and

"freedom". Sartre has a classical *gnostic* loathing for matter. Consequently, his protean "self" floats in a void of potentiality, a perfectly unreal abstraction. It is a pure construct of the philosophical imagination with no links to the concrete person whose choices and actions in daily life are in fact oriented, if not determined, by all kinds of forces.

The modern literary movement called "deconstruction" is another example of the same reductionist, anti-substantialist drive that, paradoxically, is the pendant to modernity's exaltation of the individual self. I have already discussed this type of thinking as it has affected the writing of history. Everything is reduced to "texts", to what one might call *reports* of experience, past and present. These "texts" are just systems of linguistic "signs" that are open to infinite interpretation. The text's "meaning" is whatever the reader wishes it to be, and the author's "intention" is either unknowable or merely a rhetorical convention within a particular reading community.[61] Here, relativism is absolute. Anything goes. Objective reality has totally disappeared. With it, of course—and this is perhaps less evident—subjective reality has disappeared too. What remains is "subjectivism", the self as shadow, a spectral being, appearing—as the dispenser of limitless interpretations—to be sovereign, yet in truth lacking substantial existence.

Under Sartre's spell and the sorcerer's wand of the deconstructionists, the human self has become an insubstantial phantasm and has disintegrated. How far we are, with this bloodless nihilism, from the vibrant, concrete subjectivity depicted a century earlier by the Christian philosopher Kierkegaard, known as the *founder* of existentialism, who analyzed, with compassion and profound insight, the real self in the midst of life— the "fallen" self in the Christian sense, solid but fragile, who, faced with death, is stalked by anxiety and tempted to flee the truth of his earthly destiny and preserve himself by taking flight into aesthetic refinements, or grandiose philosophical abstractions, or the acquisition of power. This is a *sinful* self, a *weak* self in many ways—yet *substantial* and not lacking in dignity. And this self, Kierkegaard argues, is called to exercise *true*

---

humanitarian movements in our day, can survive and flourish in the harsh modern climate, perhaps even attenuating the force and modifying the tenor of the technological drive, or whether modernity's steamroller will succeed ultimately in flattening gender distinctiveness and, in effect, neutering human sexual identity.

61. I owe to Richard Hays this succinct formulation. For a devastating assessment of what Roger Scruton calls the "incantatory" nature of "deconstructionist theology" and its "Real Presence of Nothing," see Scruton, *Intelligent Person's Guide*, ch. 12.

choice, *metaphysical* choice: he must choose either Christ or the world. Grandiosity of any sort is a vain lure. Humility—a totally different thing from the proud negation of the very existence of a human nature, as proposed by Sartre—is a pre-requisite for genuine selfhood. The movement of faith, of "death-to-self" in the biblical sense—that is, in the sense of the putting to death, on Christ's Cross, of the egocentric rebel self and the receiving, as *gift*, of Jesus as Lord and Savior—is the source of *life*.

The subjectivity developed by Kierkegaard goes in the opposite direction from the inflation of the subject that I have been describing in this essay. It is a subjectivity rooted in the *imago Dei*, man/woman created in the image of God. In *Christ* is where the *new* creation—the authentic one—comes into being. Here alone is true freedom, for here alone wayward men and women no longer need to waste their energy justifying themselves or trying vainly to "redeem" themselves; here, having repented and been forgiven their sin, having received a new heart and spirit, they again enjoy communion with their Creator and find themselves aligned with reality and in harmony with their fellow creatures and the rest of creation.

Section II

*Technological hegemony and the notion of limitless develop-
ment provide the context for understanding the post-modern
challenge—epitomized by gender theory—to the traditional
view of sexuality*

I.II.1

Anthropological confusion and Modern Man's identity crisis

THE CRISIS MANKIND IS facing today is a crisis of identity. This crisis is as
old as the human race, as I have suggested in this essay, but modernity is
bringing it to a head. Man (man/woman) as made in God's image wants
to renounce God and make himself in his *own* image. Science-technology
has become the all-pervasive tool and means to achieve this, replacing
and going potentially far beyond all previous philosophical, religious, or
political human "solutions" to the "problem" of the human condition.
This condition is rightly perceived to be dire, and by this powerful new
means that human beings now have at their disposition, they will to
change it fundamentally, either by concocting a new humanoid altogether or else, with Nietzsche, by making, in a post-religious world, the pagan
"values" of "natural" man, driven by egotism and the will-to-power, to be
the norm—beyond good and evil—for human behavior. It is *we* who will
determine what is good and what is evil, without reference to God, whom
we have consigned to the status of non-existence. As a race, in general, we
human beings don't want the help—the salvation—God has offered us in
Christ. We want to save ourselves by ourselves, and we mean to do this
by *re-designing* ourselves—by fabricating a New Man and a New World.
As a race, in general, we refuse the Second Adam given us by our Creator

73

in the form of the incarnate Son of God, Jesus the Messiah; we *ourselves* want to be the Second Adam, our own Messiah.

But we have come inevitably to an impasse. The problem, which is fundamentally spiritual, can also be construed in logical terms. It is not possible for a creature to create, or to re-create, him/herself, just as it is impossible for a sinner to save himself. A leopard cannot change its spots. A human "leopard", having the powers of reason, *can* attempt to do such a thing, but in doing so he/she will be acting against the very reason he is using to achieve his irrational goal, and he will destroy himself. He may remove his spots by technical manipulations, but in the process he will dehumanize himself. He will not have made himself into his own image, he will have invented a monster. He will have undone the order of creation and brought down upon himself chaos. There will be no "new leopard", no new spotless creation—only ruin.

The anthropological confusion in which we find ourselves today is overwhelming. This is inevitable, because the culture that received and developed the Judeo-Christian revelation has repudiated the God who gave it. This being so, this culture must necessarily repudiate the creature made in the image of that God, namely itself, *human* being. Both the suicidal tendency in Western culture, and man's drive to make of him/herself a new being, are the result of this self-repudiation. One could argue that these two thrusts of modern culture amount to the same thing, under different guises. On the one hand we are *de-constructing* ourselves; on the other hand we are *constructing* ourselves. Self-rejection and self-aggrandizement go together. Both movements are willful, both are willed. Man (man/woman) is in flight from his true being, as this being is revealed in the Judeo-Christian revelation.

I.II.2

The challenge to the traditional understanding of sexuality; individual "rights" and the flattening out of distinctions; the rejection of God and current civil turmoil

This is where we approach the question of homosexuality, which we shall examine more specifically in Part II. We are becoming more conscious in our day of the wide gamut of human sexual expression. We are also becoming more tolerant of the various forms of this expression. In keeping with this tolerance, we find currently in the West a drive to validate and normalize homosexual practice in human society, and this may be seen as part of a broader movement, epitomized by gender theory, to alter fundamentally the traditional human understanding of sexuality. What has always been understood as a given in human nature—namely, that there are two genders and that their complementarity is the source of love, procreation, family, and social stability—is being challenged. It is the technologically created social context of this development that enables us to make sense of it.

From the *social* perspective, the traditional human understanding of sexuality is being challenged by an ideology combining individualism and egalitarianism. A drive to assert the unlimited claims of the individual goes hand in hand with a drive to assert the absolute parity/equality of everyone. Individualism and what we might call "massism" operate together. Differentiation, distinctiveness, even between the two sexes, is being squashed, while a no-holds-barred assertion of individual rights is being pushed at the same time. This attitude of "political correctness" gives rise to an odd paradox. It splinters society into discrete cultural elements—ethnic, national, racial, religious, sexual—all of which have their own perspective on reality; but at the same time, each perspective is declared to be equal to every other perspective. They all have the same intrinsic worth, with the result that comparisons are perceived as invidious, moral judgment of their value is rejected, and what they have in common is discounted. *Rational* criticism is ruled out, because each perspective is as "good" as every other. Rather than highlighting the peculiarity of the perspectives, this approach *in effect* levels them and eliminates their distinctiveness. The validity, or invalidity, of each is vitiated by being made in principle equal to that of every other. Real dialogue across cultural dividing lines is made practically impossible because there are no objectively recognized standards outside the various subjective points of view by which to judge different positions and arguments. Mass-man (man/woman) and atomistic man are the same man. Neither is interested in community or the common weal.

Everything today is being "de-structured" and "de-regulated". Boundaries are being erased, and self-assertion is on the throne. The common good is neglected or warped to pander to subjectivist, interest-driven, psychologically based demands in favor of individual rights and a self-interested definition of "freedom". No publicly recognized anthropological or ethical basis for these "rights" is put forward apart from the bogus insistence on the part of lobbies, large numbers of academics, the media, governments, and even some churches, that these demands are basically a matter of "justice". It is true, obviously, that issues of justice may sometimes be present in these demands, and I shall consider this question more carefully in Part II of this essay; but the insistence that what the demands are all about is a matter of justice is an ideologically-driven travesty. We are dealing here with an unbridled form of idolatry.

The object of the idolatry is humanity itself. From the *theological* perspective, it is Man-as-god who is challenging the age-old understanding of sexuality, gender, and, at bottom, human identity. God's existence having been denied, men and women are now free to deny his Word at every level, both the biblical Word and the incarnate Word, Jesus Christ, and to claim that all things human, including sexuality, are merely relations of power. There is nothing given, nothing fixed; everything in human life is socially constructed, a deployment of *interests*. What we are given as divine revelation in Genesis about who man (man/woman) is and how he is to live—on the basis of which much that we value in the world today, including the notion of human dignity and rights, has come into social existence slowly over the centuries—is being deconstructed and revised—often, scandalously, with the help of naive sectors of the Western Church.

Western civilization, which is fast becoming *world* civilization on account of its technological reach, is cutting off the branch it has been sitting on. Social and environmental disorder is resulting, and can only increase. We see this on every hand, not just in the area of sexuality. It is important to point this out, because this wider disorder is the *context* in which the sexual revolution is occurring. Populations are becoming more divided and polarized. At the very time that the ideals of "equality" and "justice" are being trumpeted in Western society—sometimes honestly, at other times simply as a means to gain power—in other sectors economic inequalities and corruption are growing; a plutocratic so-called "neo-liberalism" with fascist overtones is on the rise, notably in America, undermining democracy; the military-political complex, in the context of the so-called "war on terror", now authorizes and justifies torture and extreme measures of surveillance of private citizens, overriding fundamental principles of the American Republic; racism and oppression of minorities are gaining ground, as economic uncertainty drives many to fear for their security and livelihood, even their identity; the poor, the disadvantaged, the sick, and the unemployed young are being marginalized and manipulated by market- and media-driven forces and treated like disposable waste; children in the prosperous nations are being manipulated shamelessly by commercial interests, while in many developing nations they are being ruthlessly exploited by political, sexual, or military interests. The experience of childhood is vanishing from the world.

Statistics show that suicide is more and more common in developed countries, and it is important to note, in the context of this essay, that in America a portion of these suicides is due to hatred and bullying, especially in schools, of young persons who consider themselves to be gay—a fact that reveals the deep-seated prejudice in our society that I stigmatize in this essay, and that still lingers in some of our churches.[1] Civic and domestic violence is also on the rise, to which the outrageous response of the American political right is to commercialize the prison system and build more and more profit-making prisons in order to incarcerate more and more people, of whom a majority are black. Across the world, as communities break down under the pressure of economic exploitation, rapacious leaders, religious violence, or natural calamities, millions are on the move, fleeing war, persecution, poverty, or the consequences of ecological destruction, often caused by mismanaged technological interventions. Arms sales that include more and more lethal weapons are on the rise everywhere and at every level of society, creating perilous conditions for future generations. Respect for law and concern for the common good are decreasing, leading in the direction of despotism or anarchy.

---

1. To accept and respect gay and lesbian persons does not mean to condone homosexual practice. "*Show proper respect to everyone*", says the Apostle Peter in 1 Pet 2:17. It is only by showing others honor—which is a form of love—that Christians will draw people to Jesus Christ. "Everyone", as used here, obviously must include members of the homosexual community. Christ died for us all, we are all sinners before a holy God. Christians who condemn or reject gay persons are falling far short of the standard of Jesus, who went among the marginalized of his day and forgave or healed those who received his word. He did not say to the adulteress in John 8 that she had not sinned—he said, "*Neither do I condemn you*" (John 8:11). She *knew* she had acted in a disorderly way and broken the Law. Her guilty conscience was her punishment. What she needed was to be made whole, and this Jesus accomplished through his wisdom and mercy. As to gay persons who are Christian, our honoring them will enable them to take seriously Christ's call to new life and transformation. The Christian community must act in such a way that the Holy Spirit can draw people, including gay persons, to Christ, through whom "*the law of the Spirit of life*" sets us free from "*the law of sin and of death*" (Rom 8:2). It is not up to us to strive to do the Spirit's work for him. "*Who are you to judge someone else's servant?*" writes Paul to the Christians in Rome. "*To his own master he stands or falls. And he will stand, for the Lord is able to make him stand. . .. Therefore let us stop passing judgment on one another. Instead make up your mind not to put any stumbling-block or obstacle in your brother's way*" (Rom 14:4, 13).

One positive and exciting contemporary development that is clearly the fruit of new technological capabilities such as the internet, is the eruption in many parts of the world of rebellions and popular protests against tyranny, greed, and the corruption of political leaders that, for decades, have combined to hold down local populations, suck dry national economies in favor of the ruling classes, and close off the future to upcoming generations. We must hope that these upheavals will lead to the authentic democratic liberalization that many among those who are rising up, in particular the younger generations, so passionately seek. It would be a mistake, however, to draw the conclusion that the new technology, which, in part, is what has enabled the trend to emerge, gives confirmation to the thesis that technological advance for human society yields fundamentally beneficent effects. The reality, as I am arguing in this essay, is immensely more complex. It should be obvious that the same technology can be used by dictatorial forces in any culture to squash resistance to their power and the status quo.[2]

In the democracies, legislation is increasingly manipulated by corporate power structures and the media they largely control. Greed and the thirst for power are eroding the constitutional underpinnings of these democracies, making a mockery of the example of just governance that Western nations, in particular America, used to pride themselves on providing. In some market-capitalist countries, including the United States, a veritable class warfare is erupting, and the middle class is being hollowed out. The number of people living below the poverty line is growing each year, as are the incomes of the wealthy. A super-rich global elite, feeding off profits from financial speculation and exploitative multinational corporations, is seemingly responsible to no one and connected less with any single country than with other members of its own international "club";

---

2. A recent example of this was described in an Editorial Opinion by Evgeny Morozov in the International Herald Tribune of September 3–4, 2011. He reports that spying gear of the most sophisticated sort was sold to the Qaddafi regime in Libya by technology companies in France and South Africa. Western surveillance technology developed by German and British companies has also turned up in Bahrain and Egypt. Morozov reports: "A March report of OpenNet Initiative, an academic group that monitors Internet censorship, revealed that Netsweeper, based in Canada, together with the American companies Websense and McAfee (now owned by Intel), have developed programs to meet most of the censorship needs of governments in the Middle East and North Africa—in Websense's case, despite promises not to supply its technology to repressive governments."

it exercises more and more sway over the politics, economies, media, and even the educational establishments of the nations of the world.

Large segments of the populations of these Western nations, with few or no spiritual pointers beyond themselves and little moral guidance, are thrown back on their own resources and obliged to cobble together from a hodgepodge of references some sort of ethical structure for their lives. This leaves them vulnerable to media seduction, to consumerism as a way of life and *ersatz* source of "meaning", and to propaganda and every kind of deception. Furthermore, what is labeled "Christian", especially in America, is sometimes little more than materialism with a religious veneer, and many people claiming Jesus Christ as Savior are no less caught up in the individualist/consumerist lifestyle than people professing no belief in God at all. Such self-aggrandizing "believers"—often merciless in their attitude toward the poor—are the more culpable, precisely because they claim Jesus Christ and the Gospel as their reference and judge *un*believers for their want of faith. They do thus a disservice to the one they call their Lord by providing fodder for those who consider Christians to be sanctimonious hypocrites and the Christian faith to be irrelevant or pernicious.

People everywhere struggle today to find footing in the growing civil turmoil, trampling their neighbors and the environment in the process. The very notions of community, civic duty, and the common good are vanishing from whole sectors of modern life, in parallel with the melting of glaciers and the polar icecaps, and the disappearance of hundreds of animal species and eco-systems, such as rainforests, coral reefs, and wilderness areas. The oceans are becoming polluted, as is civil discourse.[3] Slander, accusation, blame-shifting, fraud, deception, dishonesty, and out and out bald-faced lying are now common currency in Western societies that once honored decency and moral behavior. Cupidity, loosed from ethical constraints by an ideology of radical capitalism, is abetting social hatreds across the world and tearing civil society apart. The intellectual elites of societies formerly Christian in culture, followed in time by many in the population, have in the majority chosen to mock, cast off, even vilify, the Judeo-Christian spiritual and moral heritage that for centuries, in spite of the Church's faults, excesses, and occasional aberrations,

---

3. Ellen Davis, *Scripture, Culture*, ch. 1, draws on Jer 4:23–26 to show that ecological and social destruction go together. She writes: "So when Jeremiah sees the fruitful land become barren, the mountains undone, the birds of heaven fled—these are sure signs of radical social failure; there is no justice in the seat of power" (12).

provided hope and purpose for day-to-day life and a stabilizing transcendent orientation for ethical behavior in both the private and public spheres. To denounce that heritage by pointing a finger at its failures while overlooking its incalculable benefits for Western and world civilization, and at the same time ignoring or glamorizing the rising moral and societal decadence of Western culture, is not only shamefully ignorant and hypocritical, it is the bad fruit of our modern drive to take possession of our destiny. The fatuous self-righteousness of modern man/woman is equaled only by the nihilistic self-contempt hovering always just below the surface of contemporary life.

I.II.3

The enslaver enslaved; the notion of limitless development; the conjunction of moral anarchy and technical control; law blurs into process and procedure

I have argued that technology—the ever-thickening medium in which humanity is now living—is the framework for mankind's idolatry and self-divinization, and the all-invasive context for the colossal disruptions now overtaking human society throughout the world. The unconscionable evisceration of American democracy in the last thirty years by rapacious neo-capitalist interests, which have turned the media and the governing class into a money-hungry oligarchy seemingly indifferent to social solidarity, cannot be adequately understood apart from the reign of technology and the consumerism and avidity it generates. Likewise, the collapse of any coherent sexual and social ethics is simply part of an overall technocratic hegemony that is tightening its hold on every facet of human behavior.

Technology as we know it today is the culmination—ever evolving—of tool-making, by which, along with our capacity to make art, we were given the power to master the earth and care for all the creatures in it. But its *essence*, as I have maintained, has become co-extensive with our primordial transgression and our will-to-power, which can best be described as that thrust in the human soul to be as free and omnipotent as the Creator whom the human creature seeks to replace. Consequently, "technique" itself has become a double-edged sword and is subjugating its master, even while bringing mankind countless genuine advantages.

I reiterate this because it is a paradox of truly tragic dimensions, as I observed above near the end of Section I.I.8. The human race, thinking to "liberate" itself by technology, has in fact become the slave of technology's totalitarian control, yet remains blind to what is happening.

Having become the very air we breathe, technology—or rather, the *significance* of technology—is invisible. Our lives are being *taken over*, even as we imagine that *we* are taking over reality. Sheer quantity of information is drying out our minds, casting down our hearts. We are being *crushed*. As was reported recently in an article in Newsweek, "twittering" and "tweeting" and "texting" and "surfing", by overloading our brains, are reducing our capacity to make sound decisions and actually changing our cognitive behavior.[4] Our souls are being *numbed*. Mountains of data, generated by our stupendous inventions, are squeezing out of daily existence the simple pleasures of conviviality that, down through history, have given taste and joy and meaning to man's brief passage on earth. Yet most of us are oblivious to the negative effects of all this "communication" and are simply swept along on the tide. The benefits and excitement of technological progress are mesmerizing us. It is as if we were *enchanted*. Drunk with the power at our disposal, the human race has become *absolutely dependent* on technology, as once it was absolutely dependent on divine beneficence. Far from being masters, we have in fact become the mastered ones. Our power has made us powerless.

Scientific analysis and technological development being in principle *limitless*, it becomes possible to argue not only that we can *construct* human and social being in the future, but also that what has hitherto always in the past been taken as normative anthropological and social reality has likewise been just a human construct and can therefore be questioned, modified, and altered at will. This concept is now being applied to human sexuality. I will consider this issue shortly.

The point to be made first is that liberation from divine norms and control by "technique" are the two sides of one coin. Technology, as I wrote earlier, is the concrete means by which human control is replacing divine order. In place of law, undergirded traditionally by moral norms, mankind is turning to technology and law-conceived-as-technique to achieve the control of human behavior that it seeks. As the grip of technology on all aspects of human life on earth, and in all areas of the globe (globalization), increases, so will lawlessness and (unintentional)

4. Begley, "I Can't Think!" 22–27.

technologically-generated calamities; and as these increase, so—to contain them—will the dominion of technology. Growing social discontent and disorder will provoke from governments and academic authorities technological responses offered as "solutions", there being no longer any other universal reference to which to turn. But simultaneously, lawmakers will tend to go along with the demands of lobbies and special interest groups for more legislation to extend and protect their "rights", and they will do this even if the demands go contrary to the common good, are bound to destabilize social relations, and have no social justification other than the specious claim that they are contributing to greater justice, equality, and security for the whole of society. It would be naive to suggest that democracy and human rights constitute a political reference of potentially universal reach that could offset technology as the all-controlling power of our time, because these political entities, like the forces opposing them both from without and from within the democratic nations themselves, ride on technological development and are themselves technologically shaped. It cannot be a question of one or the other.[5]

This curious mixture of moral anarchy and control-through-technique is a mark of the present stage of modernity. The "moral anarchy", of course, masquerades as a new "morality" (without using the word, which remains taboo), a libertarian ethos aimed at the goal of "freedom". Law and technique are already blurring into a massive all-inclusive technological system. The growing complexity of modern society is evidence of this. Bureaucratic "process" and "procedure" are ubiquitous, strangling spontaneity and inhibiting natural relationships. The goals of production and efficiency, basic to the technological enterprise, tend inevitably to turn human beings into numbers and "cogs". Technical constructions, which are devised to solve problems, increase productivity and consumption, and control every aspect of life, are gradually replacing law understood in the traditional sense as positive legislation—ultimately based on transcendental moral norms—that is promulgated to maintain

5. The most exhaustive analysis of the all-encompassing, universal reach of technology in the modern age remains Jacques Ellul's prophetic work, *Technological Society*, first published in France in 1954. Technique and the economy, the State, agriculture, education, law, sport, art, amusement, medicine, etc., are explored in detail, after introductory chapters that define what the author means by the phenomenon of "technique", and that place this phenomenon in its historical setting. Ellul's work is indispensable for understanding what technology, as it impacts and takes over every sphere of life, is really all about.

and extend the conditions needed for the stability of civil society and the security of all its members.

More and more complicated rules, manuals, and bureaucratic formulations invade every sphere of our daily existence. Agriculture, at the very heart of human existence and well-being, is being hijacked by the agro-business industry. The commodification and inhumane treatment of animals in the interest of ever greater production and profit is a shameful perversion of the authority over other creatures given by God to humanity (Gen 1:28b, 2:19–20). Among numerous deleterious impacts of agricultural technology on the long-range health of land on the planet, we are seeing an irreparable loss of plant and crop diversity and the massive expansion of genetic modification of plants and animals and of the use of health-destroying herbicides and pesticides. Some of these techniques are surely beneficial, and increase our food-production capacity without causing harm. In the case of others, however, unforeseen ramifications are likely to prove far less beneficent. Lastly to be noted, and more sinister still, is the increase of scientific research devoted to the discovery of techniques to contain or eliminate disruptive and problematical human behavior through the neurosciences and chemical, surgical, or genetic manipulation.

I.II.4

The sexual revolution as a response to the abstractness of modern life; its deeper theological significance as a manifestation of nihilism; gender theory and the alleged social construction of gender and sexuality; "causing no harm to others" as a disingenuous ethical criterion; the co-option of reason by technique

There are also *conceptual* manipulations, in keeping with man's drive to clear the human slate of all divine traces and write on it a new set of commandments. The sexual revolution in our day, including the rise of unbridled homosexuality, is a chief instance of this. This revolution is not just a matter of self-indulgence and increased experimentation and promiscuity, in a consumerist quest for pleasure and sensation—*freedom!*—to offset the tedium and mechanization of modern life. It is that, to be sure. Underneath the febrile surface of technological society, there is terrible boredom, and human energy and aspiration desperately seek outlets, excitement, stimulation. But the rejection of constraints, if and when aimed at sexual norms, is misdirected, because the real "oppressor" is not social norms and limits on sexual behavior but the domination of every aspect of life by technical standards of efficiency and performance that subtly and imperceptibly de-nature daily existence.

The sexual revolution is also, as I suggested earlier, a search for substance, for *flesh*, in an age of abstraction and virtuality, when the individual self, for all that it is the chief object of idolatry in the modern age, has become a kind of insubstantial figment, a moving blur impossible to get hold of, like images in TV advertisements. The saturation of everything today by sex translates a hunger for physical contact in a world peopled by solitary shades, a search for love and affirmation in an age when all our familiar landmarks are being destroyed and of which the artistic symbols that resonate most with us are the isolated stick figures of Giacometti's sculptures and the dead-end characters in Samuel Beckett's plays and novels.

All this is true. But the sexual revolution in our day is much more than that. At the profoundest level, it is a refusal of the creation order, a refusal of the basic structure of humanity: two sexes, a man and a woman, who come together to join their lives and bodies and engender children, children who will then be raised by a father and a mother in a family that will be, with other families, the fundamental units of human communities and the source of personal identity and social stability. This is the meaning of Gen 2:24, at the end of the narrative about the creation of Eve from Adam's rib: "*For this reason a man will leave his father and his mother and be united to his wife, and they will become one flesh.*" Jesus cites this passage in Matt 19:6, and adds: "*So they are no longer two, but one. Therefore what God has joined together, let man not separate.*" The cosmic significance of this text is later conveyed by the Apostle Paul in his letter to the Ephesians, when he writes that the union of woman and man is an image of the union of Christ and the Church, the People of God drawn from among the Jews first and then from all Gentile tribes and nations in time and space.

Modern men and women refuse all this. They have emancipated themselves from both the creation narrative and the redemption narrative, from both the Creator of Genesis and the Messiah of the Gospels. No God created us; no Son of God redeemed us. We are the product of chance-plus-time, responsible to no one—"totally free". We are a cosmic accident, a contingent blip. But now we have the power to control and direct this haphazard evolution. Gone is our subservience to nature. We have the means to reconstruct our human condition and our very being. Indeed, it is now argued, this is *always* what we have done without being conscious of it, for the two genders themselves, and the family unit as traditionally understood, are merely social constructs, the fruit of contingent cultural notions with no permanent ontological status. The notion of human nature itself is a socio-religious construct that has had its day. No fundamental anthropological principles exist, just as no moral universals exist. Good and evil themselves are cultural constructs. All is relative, in perpetual flux, in constant becoming. We can do, and we will do, whatever we *will* to do.

This is our revenge on the God who expelled us from Eden because we ate of the Tree of the Knowledge of Good and Evil. *Gender theory* is the theoretical expression of this revenge in the area of sexuality; at the *concrete* level, its most obvious manifestation is the drive to make homo-sexuality common practice, the equal of heterosexuality. The banner held aloft by the theorists of gender theory is, as with the homosexual agenda, justice and equality. Everything must be done to make men and women equal in every way, including sexually. The divine order and "orders" of Genesis must be abolished. The implications of gender theory go in many directions, but technology, in the sense of manipulative "technique", coupled with egalitarian ideology, governs all of them.

Men and women, it is argued, are not fixed in their gender. There are no laws. They *may* do—and new surgical techniques *enable* them to do—whatever they want with their bodies. Their bodies are objects that they can manipulate for their pleasure; their sex is something they can invent.[6] The complementarity of the sexes is a myth that must be

---

6. This manipulation of the body-as-object, which shows a contempt for the body as a given in nature, corresponds to the modern consumerist ethos of capitalist society, where advertising is a form of seductive commercial propaganda that manipulates imagery of the body for sheer profit. Gender theory is an expression of this ethos, not its subversion. It is a perfect manifestation of the supermarket mentality, where *choice* is the only "value" that counts and the satisfaction of our *desires*, at the crudest level, is seen to be the aim of our existence. Technology is what enables and justifies this mentality. Such an attitude is at the opposite pole from the biblical respect for the body, created by God and redeemed by Christ. Paul writes to the Corinthian church: *"The body is not meant for sexual immorality, but for the Lord, and the Lord for the body. By his power God raised the Lord from the dead, and he will raise us also. Do you not know that your bodies are members of Christ himself?. . . ..Do you not know that your body is a temple of the Holy Spirit, who is in you, whom you have received from God? You are not your own; you were bought at a price. Therefore honor God with your body."* (1 Cor 6:13b–15a, 19–20). The bodily resurrection of Jesus was the ultimate affirmation of the value of the human body, as his incarnation was the ultimate affirmation of the goodness of God's material creation. The Word of God, in and through whom all

dismantled because it inhibits our freedom to be whatever we want and leads to prejudicial treatment, especially of women. Countless sexual combinations can be invented. Men can be turned into women, women into men. The hermaphroditic condition is desirable, perhaps even possible. Children can be produced by mechanical conjunctions of sperms and eggs, without sexual intercourse. Fathers will become unnecessary, an option among others for producing offspring. Surrogate mothers will become common, and children may never know whose genes they are carrying. Perhaps ways will be found for nurturing fetuses outside the womb. Alternate methods of reproduction, independent of any biological "constraint", will be sought, providing ways for gay couples to have a family. Children engendered in the old-fashioned way can be raised by two men or two women—it doesn't make any difference. There *are* no essential differences. Boundaries are "social constructions" that constrain "freedom", and they must be eradicated[7]. Everything is equally possible and acceptable, as long as it "causes no harm to society". There are numerous possible sexual orientations, each as good as the others. Sexual license is desirable and healthy. Homosexuality is *good*, lesbianism is *good*, bi-sexuality and trans-sexuality are *good*. They should be encouraged, even promoted. No doubt the time will come when defenders of pedophilia, even of incest, will clamor for their rights; and down the line we may expect that there will be groups demanding that persons with a predilection for intercourse with animals be granted recognition and approval by society. In any case, it is human beings who define what is good, not the Creator.

Underneath this moral anarchy is something very sinister, rarely noticed. Gender theory is a tacit denial of the goodness of creation. The traditional affirmation at the heart of natural law theory, that the creation

---

things were made (Col 1:16; cf. Gen 1), became *flesh* for mankind's sake and, through mankind, for the sake of the whole created cosmos (Rom 8:18–23).

7. It is interesting to note that the eminent French philosopher Chantal Delsol, in a piece in Le Figaro, "Non au Mariage Homosexuel," 18, argues that the demand for homosexual marriage is a *nihilist* project essentially because of its implicit refusal to consider *limits* as to what the *individual* can and should demand. This refusal, she argues, is made on the basis not of any moral value, but of the sole criterion of subjective desire and the avoidance of self-privation and suffering, and this within a context of a fierce neo-pagan rejection of Christian morality. The simple claim, "We love each other," is deemed enough to overturn all traditional, objective notions of sexual ethics and the common good.

is good and expresses the goodness and wisdom of God, is flouted. The world is *not* good, we are being told. God, even if he exists, is *not* good. Indeed, he is evil. This is a new form of Gnosticism, like that which arose in the second century and that surfaced again in the twelfth and thirteenth centuries. The world is evil. But modern gender theory, undergirded and sustained by the manipulative power of technology, puts a new twist on this ancient Gnostic doctrine. Instead of fleeing the world and barricading ourselves against it, we must overturn it, declare the new Gnostics. We must completely revamp human nature by denying that there is such a thing. And to do this, we must start at the ground level, with gender, sexuality, and procreation. We must assert that these are not givens, that sexuality is whatever we want it to be, that procreation is by no means the chief purpose of sexuality or even necessarily connected to it, and that marriage as the proper context for procreation, is not an essential good of society.

Natural law, as developed by scholastic thought in the late Middle Ages, affirms the goodness of nature and of procreation in the context of marriage, and it understands procreation to include both biological and social reproduction.[8] Gender theory's insistence that all such notions are merely cultural constructions and can—indeed *should*—be de-constructed and replaced by sheer *license*, reveals its servitude to technology. Its license is no real freedom, but enslavement. Repudiating natural law, it comes under the ruthless hegemony of *technological* law. The two are opposites, as Jacques Ellul pointedly observes:

> The second obvious characteristic of the technical phenomenon is artificiality. Technique [in the sense of *technology*] is opposed to nature. . . . The world that is being created by the accumulation of technical means is an artificial world and hence radically

8. See Porter, *Natural and Divine Law*, 212–24, for her discussion of marriage and sexual ethics in scholastic thought. While insisting that there are pre-conventional givens, such as an intrinsic link—in both animals and humans—of sex and reproductive physiology, natural law theory does not argue that convention plays no part in the social expression of sexuality. As rational beings, we are *conscious* of our sexual impulses and of their connection to reproduction and to a variety of erotic desires and attitudes. Porter insists that this knowledge and the feelings associated with it "inform our sexual activities and give rise to social structures within which sexuality is channeled" (219). But this is a far cry from the absolute constructivism of gender theory, and presupposes a pre-conventional natural state of affairs that human rationality orders and shapes within a given culture, for the perpetuation of the race and the stability of the society. Gender theory seems to have no concern whatsoever with the stability of society or with any form of order.

different from the natural world. It destroys, eliminates, or sub-ordinates the natural world, and does not allow this world to re-store itself or even to enter into a symbiotic relation with it. The two worlds obey different imperatives, different directives, and different laws which have nothing in common. . . . the technical milieu absorbs the natural. We are rapidly approaching the time when there will be no longer any natural environment at all.[9]

The gender theorists are throwing themselves off a cliff and calling their free fall "liberty". Their theory epitomizes the self-destructive willfulness of contemporary Western civilization.

All the sexual permutations and "orientations" promoted by gender theory are permissible, we are urged to believe, provided they affect only those engaging in them and "cause no harm to others". "Harm" is never defined, of course. This liberal criterion, ultimately going back to John Stuart Mill,[10] is entirely subjective and self-serving and takes no account of the inevitable knock-on effect in the wider society of "private" actions committed by individuals—this fact alone shows the idolatrous focus in our society on the "private individual" and the relative disregard, even contempt, for the public sphere and the common good. The criterion, as set forth in our day, is also hypocritical, since the groups arguing this way are all currently engaged in fierce lobbying to have their agendas supported by government legislation and incorporated into academic curricula.

Private acts, in any case, always generate incalculable social ripples because the persons doing them are members of society; what they do in private inevitably affects who they are in the public sphere, and it is disin-genuous in the extreme to suggest the contrary. When it comes to sexual promiscuity as such, of whatever sort it is, there is the added danger of dis-ease, as has been devastatingly evidenced in the worldwide scourge of HIV/AIDS. We are confronted once again with the inherent deceit and heedless self-will that characterizes our age of narcissistic individualism, in which the *self* so entirely fills the screen of consciousness that people are losing any genuine awareness of, or responsibility to and for, the *other*, becoming in the process, ironically, more like objects themselves than subjects.

Gender theory, with its arrogant defiance of the natural order and its insistence on the fluidity and manipulability of gender and sexual "ori-entation," is a telling expression of our modern culture, which is losing

9. Ellul, *Technological Society*, 79.

10. John Stuart Mill, "On Liberty," in Everyman edition (London, 1910) 65, 72–73. Cited in Himmelfarb, *On Looking into the Abyss*, 83.

all sense of fixed bearings, purpose, and objective moral law. Language itself is being manipulated to eliminate conventional descriptive words that carry moral valuations and any suggestion that one state is better or more desirable than another. Gertrude Himmelfarb writes in this connection: "Divorce and illegitimacy, once seen as betokening the breakdown of the family, are now viewed benignly as 'alternative life styles'; illegitimacy has been officially re-baptized as 'non-marital childbearing'; and divorced and unmarried mothers are lumped together in the category of 'single parent families'".[11] New words such as "parentality" and "monoparentality" are being coined to describe the multiple new possible sexual and marital arrangements and expressions. Everything is being blurred, equalized, liquidified (to use Zygmunt Bauman's evocative word to describe our current society).[12] There are no boundaries or limits. Reason, rather than being the means to the formation of virtue and the *good* of *man-in-society*, has been co-opted by an ideological agenda and the demand by *individuals* for their own gratification, becoming little more than the tool of technique and the means to enhanced power.

Power for what? The answer is simple: *power to gain more power*, through the manipulation of language, through the ideological use of concepts like "freedom", "rights", and "equality", and through control, by means of money and intimidation, of the political and judicial processes. With the biblical God consigned to the dustbin of history, and his Law, calling man to love God and neighbor, trampled underfoot, there can be no other aim. Nietzsche, who predicted this, was—in this case—right. If the biblical God has been buried, biblical morality will soon be buried too.[13] Henceforth there can be no value other than power.

The experience of *being* is being replaced by that of *becoming*, permanence by the ephemeral. *Becoming*, of course, is at the heart of the biblical revelation, with its movement from creation to eschatological fulfillment; but it is a becoming rooted in ontology, in the *being* of God and of his creation. Undeniably there is a sort of dynamism in the modern frenzy of becoming, but the dynamism is swirling us down faster and faster into a narrowing vortex. The virtues traditionally associated with moral character, marriage, and a stable society, such as covenant, trust, obligation, commitment, loyalty, and fidelity, are disappearing from view.

11. Himmelfarb, op. cit., 235.

12. See Bauman, *Liquid Modernity*.

13. Nietzsche, *Twilight of the Idols*, "Skirmishes of an Untimely Man," no. 5, in *Portable Nietzsche*, 515–16.

Relationships grow shallower and of shorter duration. The ties of friendship grow weaker, replaced by functional *networks*. We have no time or will to cultivate communion. At best we have ever-changing contacts and sensations. And out of all this we are striving to construct a New Man, a robotic sort of creature, a hybrid, who will save us and lift us from the quagmire of our chaotic history.

I.II.5

Nominalism and doubt about the intelligibility of the link between God and the world; the modern project and the imposition of meaning on reality; the challenge to faith of the disorder in the world; the irrationality and folly of materialism and the nihilist denial of transcendence; the rationality and coherence of the biblical position; the closed circle of technology and the lack of a perspective from which to critique itself

Louis Dupré, in an analysis of the intellectual foundations of modern culture, makes the significant observation that the fourteenth century movement called Nominalism began to attribute the origin of all things to the inscrutable will of God. In doing this, Nominalist thought nullified the intelligibility of the link connecting the source of reality with its created effect.[14] The fourteenth century was a time of plague, disruption, and instability in Europe, not dissimilar from the early seventeenth century and from the twentieth. Not surprisingly, each of these periods witnessed a questioning of divine providence and an accelerating quest for certainty and new forms of security. This questioning led ultimately, as we have seen, to the widespread denial in the modern world of providence and of the very existence of God, and to a quest for certainty and security that makes no reference to transcendent reality at all.

The Christian consensus that had taken shape over the first thirteen hundred years of the Church's existence and that had generated a dynamic new vision of reality, was founded on the biblical conviction that a rational and good God had created the world and placed at its center a rational creature made in his image and responsible to him. The world therefore was the product of a free act of God and was not the fateful

14. Dupré, *Enlightenment*, 2.

result of inscrutable forces. It was not ruled by an imminent necessity, as the Greeks had thought, but by the will and intelligible purposes of its beneficent Creator.

Moreover, when human beings rebelled against their Creator, God had not abandoned them. The divine beneficence, as well as the essential goodness of the material creation, were confirmed by the incarnation of the Son of God, who came into history as a human being in order to redeem the fallen race and save it from its self-inflicted chaos. This was the supreme expression of God's righteousness, that is, of his faithfulness to his covenant with mankind, as shown first in the covenant with Noah, whereby God promised not to destroy the human race again because of its sinfulness, and, secondly, in the covenant with Abraham, whereby God promised to bless the nations of the world through Abraham and his descendants (Gen 12:3; 22:18; 26:4; Galatians 3, 4; Romans 4). This promise, Christians believe, was fulfilled by the Jewish Messiah, Jesus, through whose atoning sacrifice the possibility of salvation from sin, demonic oppression, and death was made available, by grace through faith, not only to the Jews but to all mankind. The coherence and value of the world and the intelligibility of its relation to its righteous Creator were taken for granted by the Christian consensus, and proved, as principles of faith, to be strong enough to withstand and finally to assimilate the tremendous stresses, strains, and pressures of the long centuries after the collapse of the Roman Empire.

But disorder in the Church, disease, and constant political strife in the fourteenth century, erupting unexpectedly in the wake of the signal achievements of what might be called the Medieval Renaissance of the previous two centuries, created widespread disillusionment and caused thoughtful people to call these principles into doubt. Hence a kind of fatalism crept into the Western mind that opened the way for the Nominalist doubt with respect to the existence of universals and the general intelligibility that the existence of such universals implied. If only particulars existed, as Nominalist thought supposed, the uncertainties and dangers of relativism could not be far off. The fatalistic notion that the divine will at the origin of all things was inscrutable—a notion unquestionably owing something to the Islamic influence that was widespread at the time—created anxiety about God's beneficence and a new distance between him and his world. The rationality of the link between the transcendent realm and the material world began to be questioned.

"Henceforth," as Dupré writes, "meaning was no longer embedded in the nature of things: it had to be imposed by the human mind."[15]

In this last sentence, we see already the adumbration of the modern project as I have been discussing it in this essay. I have tried to point out the ambivalence of this project, as being both the fruit, in its positive aspects, of the divine mandate given to mankind that we find expressed in Genesis, and the product, in its negative aspects, of our fundamental rebellion against our Creator. I will not reiterate my arguments, by which I have attempted to sketch the broad theological and cultural context in which the emergence of homosexuality as a central issue in modern society finds its setting. But I do want to make one last point about the irrationality of the nihilism that characterizes this society and that is spreading, via the power of technology, like a toxic gas across the world.

This irrationality consists essentially in nihilism's denial of the transcendent, supra-sensory realm. The nihilist position, of course, being materialist and empirically based, sees, on the contrary, *itself* to be rational, and a position like the Christian one, to be irrational. Now, it is true that Christian faith, as developed doctrinally, is difficult, though when actually *practiced* by believers and not just acknowledged intellectually, its truth is confirmed so powerfully by the Holy Spirit, and is found to illuminate and enhance human experience so brilliantly, that the words of Jesus become self-evident and utterly convincing: "*Come to me, all you that are weary and burdened, and I will give you rest. Take my yoke upon you and learn from me, for I am humble and gentle in heart, and you will find rest for your souls. For my yoke is easy and my burden is light.*" (Matt 11:28–30). The Truth at the heart of Christian faith is simple: it is Jesus himself, God present to us in redemptive love. The Truth is not an Idea or a Concept, but a Person, a Person who manifests and reveals to us the Personal nature of the Godhead. All human beings know deep down, that what counts most in life, what gives life meaning, is other persons, is *love*. Behind and underneath the love between human persons is the love of God. It is this love, knitting together all things, that lies at the heart of the glorious complexity of the universe. Christ reveals to us this love and opens the way for us to participate in it. No affirmation is more rational or profound than this.

In the face of suffering, evil, and death, however, we are all tempted to adopt a position different from the hopeful Christian one, such as fatalism, stoicism, materialism, atheism, and so forth. On the basis simply

15. Ibid., 3.

of what one can read off the natural world, it is true that a transcendent realm, if it exists, does appear inscrutable, and God, if he/it exists, does not appear beneficent. This is due chiefly, of course, to the fact that human beings are inclined to blame God for human evil, rather than themselves. It is almost amusing, if it were not so sad, to note that, with telling inconsistency, secular society denies God's existence when things appear to be going well, and blames the same non-existent God when things go badly. Human sin as the cause of most of the world's suffering is deliberately overlooked, as eyes and fists are raised accusingly toward God—the God whose Messianic intervention into history to save us from our own sinfulness is refused or denied, even while we condemn him for not reaching down and pulling us out of our miserable predicaments when things go desperately wrong. We want God on our own terms, not on his. This is idolatry.

For secularists, however, a major puzzle remains, as Kant saw so lucidly: how is it that in the midst of the unpredictability, misery, and apparent pointlessness of life in this world as we know it, there is lawful order to an astonishing degree in the universe, inexpressible beauty, a moral imperative in the heart of man that is universal and inextinguishable, a phenomenal human power to shape the given creation through art and science, and an experience we call love that goes out from itself toward the other-than-itself, and cherishes it?

How is it that all of this co-exists with the chaotic human condition with which history confronts us? Is the only rational answer to this question to declare that existence is absurd and meaningless? The whole biblical revelation is there to declare the contrary.

What the nihilist has difficulty acknowledging is that none of the existential harshness of human life logically excludes the possibility of divine revelation. It is true to say that neither metaphysical arguments nor inferences from the natural world can lead us *upward* to *knowledge* of a personal, loving Creator, though the rational arguments of natural theology may reassure us at the theological level of the *existence* of God. We must immediately add, however, that it is logically possible that such a Creator, if he exists, might move *downward* toward us and *reveal* both his existence and his nature to human beings. The Jew and the Christian both claim that he has done just this in the Mosaic Law and the Prophets, and the Christian adds that he has done it supremely through the incarnation of the Son of God, Jesus of Nazareth, the Christ. These revelations are recorded, it is said, in the Old and New Testament Scriptures.

It is thus perfectly rational to claim that there is a God and that he has revealed himself, though empirical proof of this cannot be offered. The accusation of the materialist that because such proof cannot be offered, the claim is irrational, is *false*. It is the materialist who has a problem with the rationality of his position. Reality, it is evident, is a *given*. Man did not make it, but rather finds it as it is, and himself within it and a part of it. This means that from the start, there is something—the world—altogether outside of man's mind and prior to his existence. How it got there, he doesn't know—but there it is. When, then, the materialist comes to claim that there is no reality outside the reach of his own empirical perspective, he is actually speaking from inside a contradiction, since the world itself is already, as a given that precedes him, outside his perspective. Its own existence is empirically verifiable, yes, but its cause is not. It does not depend on man for its existence. What caused it is transcendent to it. The nihilist is thus irrational in claiming to be able to deny, from within his own perspective, the existence of another reality—a reality transcendent to and other than his own rational perspective—since such a reality, i.e., the reality he himself finds himself in, of which the cause is unknown, is already there, outside his own perspective.

Moreover, the modern materialist position has no vantage point on reality outside of its own rationalistic one. Enclosed within its finitude and its philosophical predisposition, it lacks a critical viewpoint from which to critique itself, or from which to make a rational assertion about a transcendent sphere. Hence it is not rational for the nihilist to claim from within this finitude that no other reality exists than that which he himself posits. Such an assertion falls into the same self-contradiction as the metaphysical arguments for the existence of God that Kant critiques. The assertion is not being made on the basis of reason.

It being the case, furthermore, that there is a non-man-made reality there for all to see, it is rational for the Christian to argue that beyond this non-man-made reality which preceded his own existence, there may be another non-man-made reality that *made the one that preceded his own*; and it is irrational for the materialist to write off this possibility simply because it is not empirically knowable.

I have argued in this essay that modern men and women are trapped in the technological supermarket. Our stance toward the world is no longer to look upon it with wonder and to care for it with gratitude, as was the case before the rise of modern science changed the whole way human beings related to their environment. Our age is sullen, like an overcast sky in winter. Having eliminated the notion of "creation" from our rational discourse, and having absorbed, theoretically, the notion of "nature" into that of "history", we now find that nature itself—its actual reality—is being defaced, polluted, and damaged irrevocably by our technological invasion. Our abuse of our nurturing *mother*—this planet which is God's gift—is making of us *de facto* orphans. We are just beginning to realize what we are losing. We no longer trust anyone or anything. Underneath the effervescence and ceaseless distraction of technologically driven modern life, sadness is settling like a fog on our race. We are joyless. Fear stalks us. We are self-important and self-hating. Everywhere is cacophony. Inner emptiness has replaced interiority.

The underlying, inner drive in the human race—to push the Creator toward the margins of our life and finally out of it altogether—has been there from history's beginning, as we have seen, but before the seventeenth century we lacked the power to implement this drive effectively. That has changed. We live henceforth in a closed circle *of our own making* from which there is no exit *of our own making*. Only in God's grace can we find hope, and we are not naturally inclined to welcome grace. Enframing technology is totalitarian. If the nihilist is right, and there is no transcendent sphere, no spiritual reality beyond our empirical realm, then our fate must be a losing battle between our race and the reality we're trapped in, because our own self-aggrandizing disposition is the problem underlying all the other problems, and there is no way, *pace* the technocrats, that we ourselves can possibly change our own disposition *while remaining human*.

As David Hart observes in his moving book, *Atheist Delusions*, modernity's highest ideal of personal autonomy "requires us to place our trust in an original absence underlying all of reality, a fertile void in which all things are possible, from which arises no impediment to our wills, and before which we may consequently choose to make of ourselves what we choose."[16] The modern project is built on the *will* that there be nothing beyond ourselves—no Truth, no God, no Good. Nothing. This is the requisite condition for mankind to be able to believe and do whatever we *will* to believe and do. It is, as I have contended, an *irrational* project—a product of the will, not the reason. The notion that everything is possible is a recipe for anarchy. It cannot but lead in the long run to irrational behavior, to the

---

16. Hart, *Atheist Delusions*, 21.

dangerous couple of anarchy/despotism, and finally to the unraveling of the social and the ecological fabric of the world, and to chaos.

This is because it does not correspond to truth, that is, to the *reality* of the way things are. The positivist-secularist vision of life is at bottom not only reductionist, it is essentially *mad*. In the strict sense, it is *folly*. According to Scripture, he who says in his heart that there is no God, is a *fool* (Ps 14:1). This foolishness is at the heart of the paradox of technology in the modern age and of the human project it is carrying forward. By it we conquer, by it we are conquered. It is no longer a question of our civilization developing technology; it is rather technology that is dictating the course of our civilization. Our reason brings tool-making into being, but our will-to-be-gods turns that reason into unreason and the tool-making into a force that, in its negative dimension, threatens our race with perversion or annihilation. And so we are enslaved, even as we demand autonomy and what we call our freedom, and think we are achieving it.

I.II.6

Only the perspective of faith can provide a critique of technology; the cultural construction of the ideology of "constructivism"; coherence of the biblical/historical witness to divine revelation; incarnation/resurrection as the hinge between the transcendent and the material spheres; the limits on technology's alleged "limitlessness"; Christ and true freedom; the Church's call to proclaim the power of God for salvation

It is only possible for me to speak so boldly because I am a Christian writing from within the perspective of faith, that is, a perspective based on revelation that looks at our world from a point of view outside it. It is in the incarnation of the Son of God that men can find salvation, nowhere else. Our race is confined in a pit, and we cannot get out of it by ourselves. In a radically different way from the historicalizing approach to reality that I described above, which absorbs nature into history and so dissolves the idea of divine creation, Christians claim that the Son of God, the Word by whom the world was created, by coming down into human history and becoming man, redeemed not only fallen man/woman-in-history but the whole natural world over which the human race exercises control.[17]

That the historical figure Jesus Christ was the Son of God is, of course, a matter of faith and cannot be proved. So, obviously, is his physical resurrection from the dead. These are not scientifically demonstrable affirmations. Yet they are made about a historical figure and are recorded in texts that would have been considered at the time to be of the genre called "historiography" or "biography"[18] and that in turn have shaped the historical institution called the Church, comprising billions of people who, over the centuries and in every type of human society, have received the biblical testimony by faith and experienced in their lives its redemptive power. History—not just nature, which, as a revelator of transcendence, is opaque—is displayed here as being the setting of a divine revelation from a transcendent sphere, from a sphere altogether *outside* history, be it human history or cosmic history.

This claim is unique and compelling. Modern indifference to or denial of the existence of God, which is a movement of thought that positions itself aggressively within the historical/empirical realm, reveals its irrational and ideological nature by its refusal to take seriously the historical claims and affirmations connected with the person of Jesus of Nazareth, who is presented in the New Testament Scriptures as the fulfillment of promises and Messianic prophecies given over a period of hundreds of years. In view of the *historical* weight behind the claim that Jesus was resurrected from the dead, consisting in the texts, the institution of the Church, and the

---

17. In the context of the problematic we are discussing, it is instructive to consider biblical texts like Rom 8:18–24; Col 1:19–20; Isa 11:1–9, which show the cosmic and eschatological scope of the divine project of salvation.

18. Richard Bauckham, "Reading Scripture," refines Richard Burridge's argument, set out in his *What are the Gospels? A Comparison with Graeco-Roman Biography*, in favor of the Gospels as falling within the classical genre of biography. Bauckham contends that all the Gospels, but in particular the Gospel of John, are as close to the classical genre of historiography as to that of biography. In his special focus on John, he compares the Gospel with what was considered in the first century to be the characteristics of good historiographical method, especially the view that history-writing should be as accurate as possible in its chronological and topographical details and that history "could really only be written within the period in which the author could, if not himself an eyewitness, at least interview still living eyewitnesses" (19). The modern indifference to the New Testament accounts of the life, death, and resurrection of Jesus of Nazareth is based—contrary to what contemporary people might think—not on any solid *rational* argument but on an ideological position that simply rules out *a priori* any trace of miracle or the "supernatural" within the framework of history.

testimony of billions, modernity's dismissal of these claims as being merely human constructions of one sort or another without any objective basis, is clearly a reflection of the rebellious ideology I have been highlighting in this essay, according to which everything in human history is nothing more than cultural construction. This position cannot be taken as a rational, disinterested, scientific evaluation of the historical evidence.

There is no more conclusive, empirically-based proof of this bald assertion about the culturally constructed nature of all human reality, including the claims of the Christian Gospel, than there is of the biblical affirmations we are discussing. Indeed, it is easier to maintain that the constructivist position *itself* is a cultural/ideological construction, than to contend that the foundations of human reality as presented in Genesis texts, and the ground of faith in a redemptive intervention in human history by God as presented in the New Testament, are merely cultural inventions. Humankind *can* act, at least for a time, on the assumption that the biblical claim to be the written witness and bearer of God's self-revelation is false and outdated, nothing more than a cultural concoction from the religious stage of human development; but this assertion, grounded in our technological power but unfounded in reason, will be in fundamental tension with the ontological structure of human being as created by God, and will lead, as we are seeing in our day, to inner stresses in the race similar to those produced by tectonic plates inside the earth.

While it is not my present brief to elaborate this argument more fully, the point is immediately relevant to the other main concern of this essay. The startling eruption into public and global prominence in the last thirty years of the *question of homosexuality* finds here its most comprehensive context. The liberal position regarding homosexual practice that I shall be discussing in Part II of the essay is properly located within the *constructivist view of reality* that has been taking shape since the Enlightenment and has emerged in the West full-blown in the last two generations. This view of reality constitutes the core of the technological matrix that I have analyzed; it is the setting of that liberal position, in radical contrast to the vision of reality based on revelation coming into history from a transcendent realm—a revelation to which the Old and New Testament writings bear inspired witness. We have here the underlying explanation for the careless dismissal by liberal Christians of the biblical injunctions concerning homosexual practice, and for their thoughtless acceptance of the reigning cultural approval of this practice. It remains to be seen whether TEC and the other mainline Protestant Churches will allow themselves to be permeated by the underlying worldview of modernity to the point of losing altogether the vital content of Christian faith and becoming salt that has lost its savor and is fit only to be thrown out and trampled under foot (Matt 5:13).

God's self-revelation to humankind, made with a view to our salvation, is the hinge connecting the transcendent realm with earth. Here God's mercy and power are made available to our rebellious race. The incarnation of Christ, as the fulfillment of Old Testament prophecy and the fulcrum of history, provides the only perspective on this history from outside it. It alone provides history with ultimate meaning. The Eternal Son of God entered human history, but did not arise out of it. In his divine nature, he is not its product. After accomplishing his redemptive work, he returned to his heavenly Father. In Christ, a transcendent perspective and critique are brought to bear on humankind and human history. This includes, therefore, a critique of the technological frame that now encloses the world. There is no other critique imaginable, since this frame has become the very identity of Modern Man.

It is within this frame that humanity henceforth will live and die, until the Lord Jesus returns to judge the world and set it right. This "setting it right" will be the consummate manifestation of God's justice and righteousness, his faithfulness to his covenanted promise not to destroy or condemn humankind but to redeem it and offer salvation to those whose hearts seek God and desire Life. By reducing all reality to the measurable world around us, modernist ideology has imprisoned us. Death has always been humanity's limit, but to this has now been added the self-inflicted and suffocating limit imposed by this materialist vision. And yet this same vision (or lack of vision), which presumes to imagine a victory even over mortality, is fueled by its *refusal of limits*. There is a fundamental contradiction here. This most constricting philosophical stance, with its flag planted squarely in the soil of science/technology, actually flaunts its ambition to overcome all traditional constraints on the freedom of the human race. Inside our prison cell, we hear the message blared out: "There are no limits to your freedom!" Here, flagrantly, the City of Man is divided against itself. It is trapped in a paradox. But a kingdom divided against itself, Jesus says, cannot stand (Luke 11:17). So what, we must ask, is really going on in this era we call *modernity*? Where are we headed? What are we actually doing to our race? It is our responsibility as Christians to grasp more clearly and teach more boldly the inner meaning of what is happening to the world in our time.

To both the limit of death and that of materialism, Christian faith responds by pointing to the resurrection of the Son of God, the incarnate Second Person of the Trinity, Jesus Christ. If this Person, out of love for humanity and with a view to our salvation, has indeed been incarnated and come to live with us, has died, and has been resurrected in the flesh, with a body both like and unlike his earthly body and with the promise that those who love him are incorporated into a cosmic new creation and will be resurrected with spiritual bodies at the Final Judgment when he himself returns in glory to this earth, we are obviously dealing here with the decisive event of world history. God has manifested himself; the transcendent has penetrated with sovereign power our material sphere; all our natural limitations and frames, *including that of technology*, have been overcome. Herein lies the ultimate meaning of Jesus' pronouncement: "*If you hold to my teaching, you are really my disciples. Then you will know the truth, and the truth will set you free. . . .So if the Son sets you free, you will be free indeed.*" (John 8: 31b, 32, 36).

The Christian gospel "*is the power of God for the salvation of everyone who believes: first for the Jew, then for the Gentile.*" (Rom 1:16). The power of the human mind, using the tools of science and technique, has altered the face of the earth and the human condition for the better and for the worse, and undoubtedly will continue to do so. But technology cannot and will not *save* us. It cannot free us to live beyond ourselves, *toward* a metaphysical reality in which alone we can find hope, both for this life and for a life beyond the bourn of death. Technology has become humanity's supreme idol, separating us from our Creator.

Only the Church can tell God's story and so provide mankind with a coherent narrative of its own history. Only the Church, speaking on the basis of a transcendent reality outside of the technological frame, can declare the Truth that is Love and help people to receive this revelation by faith and live into the inner freedom it provides. No other worldview, philosophy, or ethic has purchase any longer on the modern world—all are contained, or are destined to be contained, within the technological matrix. They have no objective basis on which to critique that matrix. Only the resurrected Christ and the universal Gospel the Church proclaims have the power to overcome the universal ideology that is modern technology.

If the Church yields to the moral relativism and constructivism that characterize the *essence* of technology as I have analyzed it, it will lose its peculiar voice and become simply one more singer in the medley of modernity, exalting humanity under the cover of "God-talk". Wherever it neglects the power of the Gospel and opts instead for the fashions of the world, it will become a mere pantomime of truth and will decline into irrelevance. There are, happily, many signs of resistance by authentic Christian communities and by other concerned citizens across the world as well, to the widespread abdication of ethical responsibility so common today. This resistance necessarily involves the question of human sexuality and, ultimately, of human identity. What is the nature of Man? Either we—man/woman—are made in the image of God and enabled by God's grace in Christ to experience new life and flourish . . . or, in modernity's perspective, we have no fixed human nature and invent our own identity, including our sexuality, even our gender. Each individual concocts his or her own "sexual orientation". *We* decide what it is to be human. Anything goes, anything is possible—it is *we* who make the rules, it is *we* who determine what is "good" or "evil". Ultimately, from such *hubris*, only social dissolution can result.

Christians in our time are faced with this choice as to what we affirm about *human being*. The choice is fundamental. Let us pray that the Church may hold to the truth revealed to it through the Law, the Prophets, and the Messiah. If it does, its unique voice will continue to ring out, *despite inevitable persecution*. Many will hear about God's grace and power revealed in the crucified and resurrected Jesus Christ, and will be gathered into the communion of love that is his Body. There will be rejoicing on earth and in heaven, and God will be glorified. Then one day, at an unexpected hour, the Lord Jesus will come again and be united joyfully with those who love him.

Part II

The Question of Homosexuality in the Context of Modernity

"You turn things upside down, as if the potter were thought to be like the clay! Shall what is formed say to him who formed it, 'He did not make me'? Can the pot say of the potter, 'He knows nothing'?"

(Isa 29:16)

Section III

The impulse of theological liberalism is to adapt the Gospel to the standards of the modern world. Three recent practices in the Episcopal Church related to the question of homosexuality exemplify this impulse and demonstrate doctrinal and pastoral irresponsibility

II.III.1

Three practices in the Episcopal Church that break with Church tradition

IN RECENT YEARS THE Episcopal Church and the worldwide Anglican Communion have been severely shaken by actions related to the issue of homosexuality. It is no secret that for years many gay persons in mainline churches in the USA, especially in The Episcopal Church (TEC), have been ordained to the priesthood, and that the blessing of same-sex unions has been frequently practiced, even though official rites for this purpose have yet to be formally adopted. Notwithstanding, a shock-wave went through the Anglican Communion in 2003 when Gene Robinson, a divorced man living with his gay partner, was ordained bishop of New Hampshire prior to the triennial General Convention of that year. This was rightly seen to be an historic event.

At the General Convention of 2006, under pressure from Lambeth Palace, a resolution of "restraint" was passed that urged the church to refrain from electing more gay bishops, with a view to maintaining at least the appearance of unity within the wider, and generally more conservative, Anglican Communion. Three years later, at the General Convention of 2009, a resolution was passed, known as DO25, in which TEC claimed loyalty to the Anglican Communion even while insisting that God "has called and may call such individuals [gay and lesbian Christians] to any ordained ministry" in the church. The inner intent of this disingenuous resolution was clarified five months later when the Reverend Mary Glasspool, a lesbian in a relationship with another woman for twenty years, was put forward for ordination as suffragan bishop of the Diocese of Los Angeles. She was ordained Bishop on May 15, 2010, less than a year after the General Convention.[1]

It was agreed by another vote that the use of blessing rites for same-sex couples should continue to be at the discretion of bishops, more or less in line with what State laws prescribe in a given case with respect to this issue. This, it was thought, was a "generous pastoral response" to meet the needs of church members, in particular gays.

Another development of recent vintage that has gained currency in many parts of TEC and gone virtually unnoticed or uncontested is the practice of "open" or "inclusive" communion at the Eucharist, whereby the priest, at the moment of reception, makes everyone in the congregation welcome to come forward to receive communion. No mention is made of repentance, faith, baptism, or of being a member of the church in good standing, nor is any hint given that those living in a manner inconsistent with traditional Christian norms of behavior ought to think twice before coming forward. Clergy show no concern to make it clear that biblical norms of behavior must be followed by the would-be communicant if he/she is to avoid the undesirable consequence of "unworthy participation". There is, in effect, a total disregard of St. Paul's admonition to the Christians in Corinth in connection with the Eucharist, recorded in 1 Cor 11:27–29. After citing Jesus' words of consecration of the bread and wine at the Last Supper, Paul writes: *"Therefore, whoever eats the bread or drinks the cup of the Lord in an unworthy manner will be guilty of sinning against the body and blood of the Lord. A man ought to examine himself before he eats of the bread and drinks of the cup. For anyone who eats and drinks without recognizing the body of the Lord eats and drinks judgment on himself."* It is the clergy's responsibility to make this admonition known and to call their congregations to take it seriously.

In the event, the Apostle was dealing with issues of social discrimination and selfishness in the church, leading to division amongst those who

---

1. I must point out here that the final manuscript for this book was submitted for publication before the General Convention of 2012, making it impossible for me to refer to resolutions taken at that meeting with respect to these issues.

made up the local body of Christ. The Lord's Supper at this early stage in the Church's history was a full meal, to which participants brought their own food. The particular focus of Paul's ire was undoubtedly the tendency of the richer members of the congregation to show contempt for the poorer members by not sharing their abundance with them (1 Cor 11:20–22). Before God, all members of the Church of God were equal; by God's grace they had been called, and social status was no longer to determine the way they related to each other; each had responsibility for his/her fellow Christians. By their behavior, the rich showed that they were not discerning the Lord's body. By humiliating their brothers and sisters in Christ, they were perpetuating the social divisions Christ had overcome. Paul saw this as a travesty, a defilement of the Lord's Supper.

All the people whom Paul was addressing would have been baptized, of course, which makes the scandal he was confronting very different from the question of "open communion" that I am discussing. But the Apostle's admonition can surely be applied to other kinds of matters than those with which he was immediately concerned. It does not seem inappropriate to invoke it in connection with the practice of "open communion" as described above. The clergy authorizing this procedure seem to have no concern whatever with spiritual matters such as repentance and baptism or with ethical matters of conduct, as these might bear on the conditions for the proper reception of Christ's sacramental body and blood. *Anyone* can come forward and receive the bread and the wine—no instruction given, no requirements made. "Communicants" need not even be believers. This makes of the Eucharist nothing less than a nonsense.

How far we are here from the traditional practice of the universal Church, or indeed from Anglicanism's own founding convictions and documents, such as Article 28 of the Articles of Religion, and the exhortation to repentance in the Confession of Sin in the Eucharistic Liturgy![2] Under a benign appearance, "open communion" is an affront to the

---

2. The first paragraph of Article 28 reads: "The Supper of the Lord is not only a sign of the love that Christians ought to have among themselves one to another; but rather it is a Sacrament of our Redemption by Christ's death: insomuch that to such as rightly, worthily, and with faith, receive the same, the Bread which we break is a partaking of the body of Christ; and likewise the Cup of Blessing is a partaking of the Blood of Christ." And in Rite I of the Holy Eucharist—BCP (330)—we read: "Ye who do truly and earnestly repent you of your sins, and are in love and charity with your neighbors, and intend to lead a new life, following the commandments of God, and walking from henceforth in his holy ways: Draw near with faith, and make your humble confession to Almighty God, devoutly kneeling."

Lord Jesus Christ and shows an almost blasphemous indifference to the meaning of Christ's sacrifice and to the grandeur and horror of his suffering on the Cross. TEC—a Church that prides itself on its "catholicity"—is, moreover, thumbing its nose at both the Church of Christ down through the ages and the rest of the Church across the world today, in particular those parts of it that seek to be faithful to biblical and liturgical tradition. Any sense of collegiality with the worldwide Body of Christ is absent here.[3] The "natural man" is "baptized" in the name of some sort of notion of "equality" or "justice", and this within a wider, overruling American cultural imperative of "freedom". Indeed, there is a cultural imperialism operative in this spreading practice that presumes to be "prophetic", out in front of the rest of the world, providing the example that everyone else should, or ultimately will, follow. Unbeknownst, perhaps, to many of the priests who endorse "open communion", Jesus is being recruited here for a cause other than the Gospel. "Open communion", when practiced in this way, is a travesty, no less than, though different from, the travesty denounced by St. Paul.[4]

3. This point is made with devastating force by Philip Turner and Ephraim Radner in chapters 1 and 2 of their co-authored book, published in 2006, *The Fate of Communion: The Agony of Anglicanism and the Future of a Global Church*. Referring to the undisciplined way that TEC has gone about making a succession of innovative ecclesial decisions in the last forty years, and noting in particular the Robinson election in 2003, Turner and Radner argue that the American liberal social economy, which is based not on publicly agreed notions of the *good* but on personal *preferences*, is subverting Christian belief and practice by the logic of autonomous individualism. The Episcopal Church—not to mention the other Protestant churches and even the American Roman Catholic Church to some extent—is acting more and more like a denominational "niche" church, rather than like a member of a worldwide communion of churches. This clearly calls into question its vaunted self-identity as a "catholic" church in space and time bound by a practice of "mutual submission" to churches elsewhere, in favor of a parochial denominationalism with an agenda largely determined by local cultural influences.

4. Bishop Thomas Breidenthal presents an interesting reflection on open communion in a recent article in the Sewanee Theological Review. Using as a framework for his analysis a (somewhat confusing) dialectic of "insiders" and "outsiders," Breidenthal considers the issue of whether one must be baptized in order to partake of Holy Communion. In the last part of his article he reflects on the admirable street-church movement gaining momentum in the Episcopal Church, noting in particular a community in Columbus, Ohio that holds street services for homeless people. The homeless eagerly partake of Holy Communion, without reference to the matter of whether they were ever baptized. Breidenthal approves of this openness, although he does not, barring exceptional cases, support a similar policy for ordinary parish communities. I agree here with Breidenthal, but I would wish to underline more strongly than he does that the basic

It cannot be objected that this increasingly common practice in TEC is no different from the practice of "open table" in the United Methodist Church. This "Methodist exception", as Mark Stamm calls it, has the genuinely prophetic function of reminding people that Jesus welcomed sinners and showed hospitality to everyone.[5] The notion of Holy Communion as a "converting ordinance", dear to the Wesleyan tradition, can be correlated with the traditional normative order for Christian initiation that regards baptism as a precondition of Eucharistic participation, provided one sees a movement of repentance as the prior and primary response to God's grace in both cases (see Rom 2:4. With respect to infant baptism, this "prior response" is represented on behalf of the infant by the gathered church and the godparents, and is meant to be enabled by the completion of the baptismal sacrament at Confirmation). "Its positive witness of generosity notwithstanding," cautions Stamm, "the open table must not contradict the biblical expectation that those who eat and drink with Jesus will repent, opening their hearts to new life."[6] Something like catechumenal pre-baptismal formation and discipline, he goes on to insist, must be provided for in the church, and an open invitation to the table must be accompanied by appropriate warning and an open invitation to a disciplined life. Stamm writes cogently: "Eucharist is banquet and feast—the joyful marriage supper of the Lamb—yet it is not that alone. If emphasized to the exclusion of other themes, focus on banquet and feast can become a new form of docetism, a denial of the Paschal

---

issue is not baptism but repentance and faith. The ritualization of baptism has tended, ever since the early centuries when infant baptism became the norm, to cover over the prior change of heart and faith in Christ of which baptism is the sacramental expression and seal. If the priest in Columbus is preaching the gospel and calling his hearers to repentance and faith, as Peter did at Pentecost (Acts 2:38, 41; 3:19), and these men and women are flocking to receive the sacrament, it may be surmised that a measure of faith and a hunger for forgiveness and a new life have arisen in their hearts, making them eligible, in due time, for baptism and "formal" inclusion in the Church, of which their repentance and welcome of Christ have already made them members (Acts 2:41). What is objectionable about "open communion" as increasingly practiced in the liberal parts of TEC is that it has no evident link with a call to authentic faith and a change of life, a call that is addressed to all of us equally, whatever our social status and condition. Our equality here is a matter of our being sinners in need of God's forgiveness—it has nothing to do with inherent "rights" or "merit", or even with our inherent "human dignity" or our "belovedness" in the eyes of a loving God.

5. See Stamm's comprehensive article in *Quarterly Review* on the practice of open communion in the United Methodist Church, especially 266–69.

6. Ibid., 269.

character of the Christian life. The eucharistic mystery is far deeper than the conviviality shared at a church coffee hour. Again, those who eat with Jesus enter into the dynamics of his death."[7]

The three recent developments in The Episcopal Church that I am instancing—the ordination of gay bishops, the blessing of same-sex unions (which surely will lead in time to the blessing of what will be called same-sex "marriages"), and "open communion" as I have described it—have emerged in the space of one generation and turned the Church into something very different from what it was forty years ago . . . or nineteen hundred years ago—and there lies the problem. The three developments are closely connected, even if more attention is usually given to the first two. Those who espouse these positions, even though they provide what they sincerely take to be a Christian rationale for the moves—namely, God's unconditional love of all his creatures—appear unconscious of the fact, or are simply indifferent to it, that they are taking their cue essentially from secular society and simply conforming the Gospel to current social norms. While declaring that their actions are in prophetic continuity with the essence of the Gospel, they fail to see that what they are proposing subverts the Gospel both theologically and anthropologically. These actions represent, in fact, a radical *dis*continuity with the Gospel, to the point of being a heresy, in the triple sense of *treating the "natural man" (man/woman)* as if he were already holy and worthy *in himself* of approaching God; *of flattening God* into a sentimental figure of human construction; and, with respect to Jesus, *of eviscerating the Cross* of its inner meaning. By inviting people to follow a manmade cardboard divinity, a "designer" God, these new trumpet calls of the progressive elite are the very opposite of prophetic.

The word "heresy" is strong, and my first task will be to unpack what I have just said and explain in what way I consider these actions to be heretical. My second task, to be accomplished in Section IV, will be to reflect on reasons why, according to the Scriptures, God is opposed to homosexual practice.

II.III.2

Theological liberalism's impulse to "domesticate" God

7. Ibid.

The position I find myself in is a complex one, because I certainly commend the concern of TEC and other churches similarly motivated to right the wrongs done for centuries by the Church and by society in general to people of homosexual orientation. What might be called the *uprising* of the gay community in our day is undoubtedly, at one level, a spring-back from centuries of rejection. In this sense it is an entirely legitimate demand for recognition and civil rights. If I reprove the "in your face" stridency of the radicals who make up the constituency called the "Gay Lobby"; and if I stress the wider technological and social context of the sexual revolution and insist on distinguishing what is appropriate sexual behavior within and without the church, this is not because I discount the rightful concerns of gay persons, in particular of the majority who simply want to be left alone to get on with their lives, or have any wish to see rejection of gays continued. I distance myself absolutely from those who might rightly be accused of homophobia. The desire of TEC and of many other churches to express to people of homosexual orientation God's love for them is altogether praiseworthy and long overdue. And yet at the same time, the manner in which this is being done, while rehabilitating gay persons in one way, in another way does them a severe injustice, as I shall make clear below, by papering over or falsifying aspects of the homosexual condition and by ignoring both the truth and the power of the Gospel. There is a real contradiction here that can only be resolved by theological analysis, with input—unbiased—from the social sciences.

The churches moving in this direction believe strongly in virtues such as justice and equality, and affirm with conviction the Judeo-Christian vision of the dignity of every person, as created in the image of God. This is admirable, and I must insist from the outset that my accusation of heresy with respect to TEC's position on this issue does not impugn either the integrity of the persons involved or the motives for their actions. But I believe there is enormous confusion here, and culpable ignorance of what is at stake; theological vacuity, deceit, and cowardice go hand in hand, paradoxically, with what appears to be the earnest and laudatory motive of seeing justice done and extending God's love to all.

The majority of Christians have little idea of the import of these novel policies; indeed, part of the scandal in all this is that the TEC bishops and seminary professors have made so little effort to inform and educate their people as to the real nature and significance of these developments. The hullabaloo surrounding the homosexual issue in the last decade and especially since 2003 has centered on procedural and canonical issues far more than on the underlying theological ones. The whole matter has been "managed" juridically rather than debated in a genuinely open and theological manner. Many of us are astonished to realize that it is only after these new policies have more or less taken hold in the praxis of most of the TEC dioceses that the hierarchy is at last agreeing to undertake something like a serious, and supposedly dispassionate, theological analysis of the issues concerning homosexuality and its place in the church. As for the issue of open communion, it has received practically no comment or analysis at all, despite its far-reaching theological significance. These facts in themselves reveal the theological indifference that characterizes TEC in our day, and why it is so open to fundamental doctrinal and ethical deviations, to the point that the word "heresy" is not out of place in this connection.

It needs to be pointed out here that this theological indifference is the fruit of a regrettable indifference to practical moral reason that has characterized liberal Christianity for a hundred and fifty years. Theological liberalism arises from a deep impulse to "domesticate" God, to "integrate" him into the world; it resists the Gospel's basic message that the world is fallen and that humankind is irredeemably corrupted in both its thinking and its action on account of its idolatrous focus on the creature—itself—rather than the Creator. This project of human self-justification, rooted in pride, has the effect of enhancing humanity's status and diminishing, even de-legitimating, God's; it orients liberalism's approach to dogma and ethics in a constant effort to discount the antithesis of world/church in favor of a progressive narrative of human history that owes at least as much to Hegelian idealism as to Kantian rationalism. The doctrines of original sin and divine judgment on a rebellious world are fudged or simply denied, and a kind of moral intuitionism prevails, rooted in the conviction that men and women can and should devise their own moral rules as they go along and needn't take account of or make reference to what the Church used to call "revelation".[8]

Emancipation from the authority of a tradition based on the New Testament's construal of truth about our fallen human condition and our redemption through Christ, is liberalism's driving force. "Reason" is co-opted to serve that purpose. Far from being the guiding torch of liberal thought, as liberals often contend, "reason" as the means and instrument

---

8. I am indebted to Oliver O'Donovan for clarifying this perspective on the liberal tradition. See his *Church in Crisis*, especially ch. 1. See also Radner and Turner, op. cit., ch. 1.

of serious debate on doctrinal and ethical issues has been gagged by a sentimental humanity-affirming ideological stance that resists rational inquiry. Oliver O'Donovan sums up the matter thusly:

> In the interests of finding the modern world God-enchanted, it [theological liberalism] closed down on the serious deliberation with which Christians ought to weigh their stance of witness in the world. Potentially world-critical questions were suppressed. Liberal moral commitments, though sometimes urged with a passion verging on outright moralism, were not steered from the helm of discursive inquiry but set adrift on the moral currents of the day.[9]

This has been notably evident in TEC's handling of the issues connected with homosexuality, from which "discursive inquiry" has been strikingly absent.

II.III.3

Egalitarianism and inclusivism; discrimination; "rights"; justice

The word "heresy" has the meaning of choice, a choosing, and is associated with the idea of a faction, a sect, that has chosen a path divergent from a consensual body of thought or practice. The word has often been used in the Christian Church to designate an opinion or a current of thought that has been at variance with what has been taken broadly to be traditional and authoritative catholic/orthodox belief. There is the idea of plucking an idea up from its context, of selecting it out from its wider biblical/theological setting, and then making it stand on its own as a new or deeper truth. Most heresies in the history of the Church have arisen in connection with fundamental theological, Christological, pneumatological, or anthropological dogma, such as the Trinitarian structure of the Godhead, the status of the Person of Christ or of the Holy Spirit, or the essential nature of humankind.

By using the word "heresy" in relation to the recent actions of TEC, I am suggesting that these actions involve a choice to interpret the inclusiveness of God's love for humanity as manifested in Christ's incarnation in a way that lifts this inclusiveness from its dogmatic setting and in doing so subverts its meaning. Those carrying out these actions certainly do

9. O'Donovan, op. cit, 11.

not mean to do this; they see themselves as prophetic, not heretical; but the choice to make this interpretation reveals the source of these actions to be not the Gospel as conveyed in Scripture and tradition, but a twist exerted on the Gospel by the prevailing cultural climate. The actions do not represent, as their practitioners imagine, a legitimate *development* in our understanding of God's love, but rather a *distortion* of it on the basis of the modern notion of egalitarianism coupled with the application to the Church of a political/secular construal of justice. The historical origin of this heretical distortion lies in the movement of thought alluded to above, which sought—and seeks—to "liberate" the human race from what was seen as its tutelage to God and to a Gospel that proclaimed the fallenness of men and women and their need of redemption by divine intervention.

The practice of open communion provides the key to understanding the nature of the heresy involved. Insight gained from an analysis of this practice will illuminate TEC's attitude toward the ordination of homosexuals and same sex unions. The guiding word is "inclusive", which, when applied by TEC to its ecclesial practices, means that all persons concerned are welcome to participate in the practice in question, without distinction. To make distinctions, for instance, as to who might be welcome at the Lord's Table, would be to discriminate, and discrimination goes against the Christian Gospel of love. Christ died for everybody; thus, to "discriminate" as to who is eligible to receive Holy Communion and who is not is to contradict Christ's universal saving purpose and relapse into the world's ways of exclusion and prejudice. Likewise with the questions of the access of gay persons to priestly or episcopal ordination, and to unions or, ultimately, marriages with partners of the same sex. Before God, and therefore in his Church, everyone is on the same level, in perfect equality. Because God loves everyone equally and is no respecter of persons, distinctions between persons allowed to come to the Lord's Table and those who are not, or between those who may join together in (marital) union, or be ordained, and those who may not, are unjust and must be abolished.

It is, of course, quite true that God loves everyone and, in Christ, calls everyone to himself. He is indeed no respecter of persons. *"For God so loved the world that he gave his one and only Son, that whoever believes in him shall not perish but have eternal life. For God did not send his Son into the world to condemn the world, but to save the world through him. Whoever believes in him is not condemned, but whoever does not believe stands condemned already because he has not believed in the name of God's one and only Son*" (John 3:16–18). And the Apostle Paul in his Epistle to the Romans writes similarly: *"But God demonstrates his own love for us in this: While we were still sinners, Christ died for us"* (Rom 5:8).

The problem lies on man's side, not God's. God welcomes all sinners—that is to say, he welcomes all human beings—but not all sinners welcome him. Receiving God's grace in Christ is not on the same level as changing jobs or nationalities or even genders. It is a matter of dying to self and being reborn. This is the condition attached to our entrance into the new life God offers us: it is called repentance and involves, in principle, renunciation of any number of habitual beliefs and practices, followed by costly commitment to follow Christ, often in defiance of accepted social norms. *"You were taught,"* writes Paul to the Ephesians, *"with regard to your former way of life, to put off your old self, which is being corrupted by its deceitful desires; to be made new in the attitude of your minds; and to put on the new self, created to be like God in true righteousness and holiness"* (Eph 4:22–24). Paul could hardly write this way to the average liberal mainline church today. The people are *not* normally taught to "put off the old self and put on the new", that is, to let the presence of Christ by the Spirit irradiate the "inner man", transforming attitudes and motivations and disposing the heart to reject its deceitful ways and embrace and cultivate the virtues of holy living, what the Apostle calls the "fruit of the Spirit" (Gal 5:22–23).

God in Christ is turned toward us, yes; but we as sinners living in a fallen world are by nature turned in upon ourselves and away from him, and we cannot authentically go toward him unless we first turn around, or change course, which is what repentance means. In Matthew's Gospel, the first words Jesus speaks as he undertakes his ministry are: *"Repent, for the kingdom of heaven is near."* And in Mark's Gospel, he declares: *"The time has come. The kingdom of God is near. Repent and believe the good news!"* (Matt 4:17; Mark 1:15). And in the Book of Acts, chapter 2, after Peter's speech to the *"men of Israel"* (v. 22) on the day of Pentecost, when they were convicted of sin and cried out to the apostles, *"Brothers, what shall we do?"* (v. 37b), Peter replied, *"Repent and be baptized every one of you, in the name of Jesus Christ for the forgiveness of your sins. And you will receive the gift of the Holy Spirit. The promise is for you and your children and for all who are far off—for all whom the Lord our God will call"* (Acts 2:38–39).

In order to receive the gift of forgiveness of sins, the promised gift of the Holy Spirit, and the gift of eternal life won for us by the atoning passion of Jesus Christ, we must repent and believe, and this will involve going in the opposite direction from the self-focused one we were travel-ing in before. The Bible calls this *"metanoia"*. It is a matter of conversion. Jesus becomes our Lord and Master, instead of our own ego. The way we experience this "turning" away from self and towards God will vary greatly from person to person, but it must happen if we are to be incor-porated genuinely into the "new creation" that the authentic Church, as a corporate society, *is*, and that each believer, as a member by faith of this corporate society, *is* (Gal 6:15; 2 Cor 5:17; Eph 4:24). In our "natural" selves, we are impure, full of self-serving attitudes and behavior, heedless of divine glory and truth, deceitful, condemning others and justifying ourselves, altogether unfit to stand before a Holy God. All of us, even those raised in loving homes where kindness and service to others were the norms, carry the self-centeredness of original sin and are marked by wounds inflicted by others and by circumstances to which any number of self-defensive mechanisms and unloving attitudes such as fear, bitter-ness, jealousy, and a desire for vengeance and power, will have been our response. As the prophet in the last part of the Book of Isaiah put it: *"All of us have become like one who is unclean, and all our righteous acts are like filthy rags"* (Isa 64:6a). For our wounds, we need healing; for our sins, forgiveness and cleansing. We need to be sanctified, and only a holy God can accomplish such a miracle.

And this, of course, is precisely what we don't want to hear, especially in our day when so much of the Judeo-Christian anthropological view of man/woman's inherent dignity and value has been absorbed into the hu-man bloodstream, albeit in a completely secularized and self-glorifying idiom and without due recognition of its biblical origins. TEC admirably gives expression to this view of human value, as it welcomes in principle all comers into its churches and defends the civil rights of minorities, in particular the civil rights of homosexuals whom the Church and society in general have grievously mistreated over the centuries. And for this, as I said above, TEC and the other churches that have moved in the same direction, are to be commended. They have learned from the movement of contemporary society in favor of inclusive civil rights, and this is very much to their credit.

But this does not change for a moment the reverse side of the coin, namely, the truth of what the Bible says about our righteousness being as filthy rags and our need to repent if we are to enter the Kingdom of God. We are here in another realm from the human value that is claimed as the basis for civil rights. It is the Church's privilege to recognize this truth about human nature, teach it, and preach God's grace in response to it. But this is not a popular stance today in many parts of the Church, where a secular political agenda is often substituted for the proclamation of the Gospel. Rebellion against the Creator, which makes us unrighteous in his sight, is the default position of fallen humanity—the biblical word for this disobedience is "sin"—and no tacit or overt appeal to our inherent dignity as made in God's image can obviate the need for a change of heart and conduct. It is utterly presumptuous to imagine that we can come into God's presence on the basis of some supposed "rights" or natural "goodness". The call of Jesus and the apostles is addressed to human beings made in God's image, equal before their Creator, loved by their Redeemer, yes; but the *first word* of that call, in whatever age or place, is "Repent!", because none of us is naturally in any state to stand before a holy God.

In the Gospel of John, Jesus expresses this same truth in a different idiom: *"I tell you the truth, no one can see the kingdom of God unless he is born again"* (John 3:3). By our self-sufficiency we are *alienated* from our divine Source and fundamentally ungrateful to him for our life and being. We are not by nature "nice"—far from it, alas. If we think we are basically "nice", we would do well to take a hard, honest look at ourselves in the mirror, considering our thoughts, emotions, words, and acts in our daily relationships with others. Nice? Always loving toward others? Without resentment or jealousy? Generous? Humble? Honest? Forgiving? Not greedy? Not nourishing lustful thoughts? Faithful in thought and deed to one's spouse? Never harboring grudges or hateful emotions? Going the second mile? Never arrogant? Never manipulative? Never seeking revenge where we have been wronged? We deceive ourselves if we think we are "basically good". We are masters at self-justification.[10]

Not for a moment am I saying that we have no good in us and are inherently evil. We are created in God's image, so obviously we are not inherently evil. The creation is good; men and women *as God's creations* are good; dominion over nature, properly understood, and human culture as the expression of this dominion, are good (Gen 1:4, 10, 12, 18, 21, 25, 31). A sense of right and wrong is built into us, as a law of nature. But we have turned away from God, which means we are sinners. That is not the same thing as being inherently evil, but it does mean that, as a

---

10. The clearest, kindest, and most trenchant analysis of right and wrong in our daily behavior, and of our constant inclination to justify even what we perceive to be our faults, is made by C. S. Lewis in *Mere Christianity*, chapters 1–5.

consequence of our rebellious self-will, we *do* evil, as well as good. Our hearts are *impure*. We're all about *ourselves*. The cultures we create are inherently ambiguous, morally speaking. The communion with God that we are created to have, we do not naturally have; to the contrary, we stand over against God and are idolaters and self-worshippers. Therefore, even in our righteous works, double-mindedness will be present. Self-focus, which is what sin is all about, breeds fear, jealousy, and violence toward others, with the result that much of human history is cruel and blood-stained. Without the sacrifice and mediation of the Messiah, the Son of God, on humanity's behalf, there is no way any of us could stand before our Creator without being condemned.

This is what the Good News of the Gospel is all about, but in today's secular climate, it is Bad News that inspires only indifference or contempt among the theologically illiterate intellectual classes and the untutored general population. Sadly, that general population includes large numbers of church-goers and their clergy, people who would presumably call themselves "Christian" but who seem to have very little idea of what this means. The actions of TEC that I am criticizing suggest, for instance, that TEC believes that we are "fine"—OK—just as we are and can stand before God and come to his altar with no real change of heart or behavior. In view of the "open communion" policy now generally accepted among the liberal sectors of TEC, this would appear to be TEC's conviction not only for all baptized persons (whether or not they have ever really confessed anything or repented of anything), but for *anybody*, baptized or not. There is a spiritual and moral carelessness here that, on the part of a body calling itself Christian, is culpable. It is not Pelagianism exactly, because the issue is not one of works-righteousness, as it was in the fourth century and at the time of the Reformation. The issue is rather one of what might be called *rights*-righteousness: the pretension, as I have reiterated, that, on the basis of our inherent human dignity and of God's equal love for all of us, we have "rights" before God, as we have come to have rights in the political and social spheres, and so have no need to change our ways at all in order to come into God's presence. We have usurped God's gift to us of dignity and turned it into a kind of entitlement, on the basis of which we justify ourselves before God. This is a remarkable example of the deceitfulness—indeed, the *cunning*—of the human heart (Jer 17:9).

This is the heresy behind open communion—what I have called the "baptism of the natural man"—and, as I shall try to show, behind TEC's actions affirming the "rights" of sexually active homosexuals to ordination and liturgically blessed "unions". It is an example of what is called "cheap grace". The notion that it would be *discriminatory* to reserve reception of the bread and the wine to baptized persons and refuse it to anyone else, is absurd, a shameful bow in the direction of political correctness and in contradiction with over nineteen hundred years of Christian tradition. The sacrament of baptism is rendered meaningless by this new Eucharistic practice, as is the sacrament of the Eucharist itself. An egalitarian ideology is operative here, forcing different realities, different spheres, into a single mold. The spiritual sphere, in this case, is being conformed to and absorbed into the political. The kingdom of Man is usurping the Kingdom of God.

Moreover, as I observed above, no teaching of any sort normally accompanies this global invitation to all in the congregation on any given Sunday to come forward at reception. No effort is made to justify the open invitation theologically, and the sad fact is that most churchgoers do not even seem to notice the novelty. If, as is more and more the case, the average baptized person in a mainline church pew in the West today has only the dimmest understanding of his or her faith and of the significance of Christ's atonement, it goes without saying that all those on a given Sunday who are not baptized and who happen to be in church for one reason or another, will have virtually no notion *at all* of what Holy Communion is about.

It is a travesty of Christ's sacrifice that persons lacking instruction about the Person and work of the Son of God, and having no idea of personal commitment to Jesus or of what is involved in partaking of his body and blood, should be "welcomed" at the communion rail. The lame pretext that this "welcome" is a user-friendly form of "evangelism" and will incline people to want to become "members of the parish" is disingenuous and theologically jejune. There is no authentic evangelism without a call to "repent and believe", and becoming a member of a parish provides no evidence in itself that one is a disciple of Christ, part of a *new* creation, intent on leading a *new* life.

Doctrine, spiritual discipline, and the cultivation of Christian virtue need to be taught and carefully explained, more so today than ever before, but in the liberal churches such teaching is a rarity. The "cure of souls", as it used to be called—what is today called "inner healing", the penetration, through anointed pastoral prayer, of Christ's forgiveness into the deep heart and the repressed regions of the soul—needs to be developed and practiced regularly in our parishes. This is a necessary feature in building authentic Christian community, of the sort that will be attractive to non-believers because they will see people renewed and revitalized through the power of the Holy Spirit (see Jas 5:13–16, for example, along with the paranetic portions of the Pauline Epistles). God is not in the business of patting his children on the back and telling us that our, say, angry or resentful or fearful or lustful temperament is "just the way it is" and that nothing can or needs to be done about it. He has incorporated the Christian believer into a cosmic "new creation" (2 Cor 5:17) and given him/her the gift of the Holy Spirit, and the believer is then summoned by Christ to live into that new reality that he/she *is*, as an adopted son or daughter of God (Rom 8:14–17)—the believer is certainly *not* called to act as if this new identity were nothing more than a new way of talking about what he/she was before having faith and being baptized, with the fact of God's love thrown in. We are called to be *conformed* to Christ, renewed in mind and spirit, not to carry on just as we were, warts and all. The true person each of us was made to be, with the particular personality that God foresaw (Eph 1:4; Ps 139:13–18), will emerge as we allow Christ to live his life in us (Gal 2:20) and are progressively transformed into his likeness (Rom 8:29; 2 Cor 3:18; cf. Rom 6:1–14; 8:1–17; 12:1–4; Eph 4:20–24; 5:1–14; Col 3:1–17).

"God loves you" is pretty much the sum of what one hears from many liberal pulpits today, with only the scantiest explanation of what this affirmation means and implies. "Sin" is a word seldom spoken or defined, "repentance" virtually never, "judgment" never. Authentic faith and participation in Christ's cross and resurrection are themes rarely broached in any systematic way. That becoming a "new creation"—the reality recognized sacramentally at baptism—is expected, on the basis of Scripture and tradition, to give rise to a radically new self-understanding and progressively changed way of life, is a declaration practically unknown to the average Episcopalian congregation. The new buzz-word, ironically, is "transformation", but it is transformation without content. I shall have more to say about transformation later, but in the context under discussion, the word has little meaning.

The Episcopal Church is under the sway of an ideology called "inclusivism". By requiring little more of parishioners beyond a measure of financial support for the parish and frequent attendance at Sunday worship, the contemporary liberal establishment in the church has turned Christian faith into a free pass to an utterly superficial "acceptance", a churchy version of the secular mantra, "I'm OK, you're OK". In the pulpits of the Western liberal church, first doctrine, then ethics, are disappearing like the Cheshire Cat in Alice in Wonderland, and congregations are left with the vanished cat's bland smile: "God loves you!" All are welcome, all are "OK". Nothing is required, no questions are asked. *We're modern!* The name on our product is "Jesus Christ", but apart from that, we, The Episcopal Church, are just like everybody else, with the noteworthy exception that we accompany our presentation with a polished liturgy and sophisticated music. *We're proud of our tradition!* In any case, nothing substantial needs to change in the way we live, for to suggest that God could require such a thing as changing direction and dying to certain attitudes and behavior, would make his love conditional . . . and would be *discriminatory*! God loves us all just as we are, full stop. The most grievous thing about this kind of discourse is that there is scarcely any mention of our being summoned to *love God*, which is, after all, the First Commandment. "Loving God" and "following Jesus", with the radical obedience and re-orientation that this will entail, are not hot topics in the liberal churches—and yet that is precisely what being a Christian is essentially all about.

"Discrimination" is perceived to be the great contemporary sin. In its proper sense, of course, it *is* a sin, an arrogant and prejudicial judgment and devaluation of one person or group by another. Homosexuals, for instance, certainly have been and sometimes still are discriminated against, as are many other groups. This is altogether unacceptable, morally speaking, and the greater awareness in our day of human rights must be credited with making all of us more conscious of our hidden prejudices against one group or another. But in the age of political correctness, this is not the way the word "discrimination" is used. In current parlance, it means the making of moral distinctions of any kind regarding persons or things, suggesting that some beliefs or patterns of behavior are better than others. This is ethically unacceptable in the West today except when it comes to what are loosely called issues of "justice". To suppose that some behavior or belief is morally superior to other behavior or belief is seen to be condemning of another person and an insult to his or her integrity. It may even be an attack on his/her rights as a person considered to be of equal value and dignity to the person making the judgment. To do such a thing is to presuppose some sort of objective moral standard of the sort that used to be taken for granted in all cultures but can no longer be imagined in today's relativistic climate. What is rarely perceived in such tendentious thinking is the perfect platform it presents—contrary to its egalitarian pretensions—for manipulation by interest groups using "rights" ideology as a weapon to dominate others and assert the superiority of their own views.

Justice is the one area where even a priest (!) or a pastor (!) can suggest that a certain kind of behavior needs to be changed. If a priest perceives that a person is acting unjustly toward another—that is, is discriminating against another—he or she is seen as having an obligation to take action to call the offending person to order. Inclusivist ideology here finds its limit. What this means in the context of the present discussion of inclusivism as it may pertain to the issue of homosexuality is, however, ironic. A person attending a church and engaged in a homosexual lifestyle must not be asked, even from the pulpit in a general way, to consider whether such a lifestyle is in line with God's perfect will, because to ask this would be an aggressive infringement of the gay person's rights. A person—let's say a priest—who suggests that such a change of lifestyle might be God's will must be made to understand that such a suggestion is discriminatory and presumptuous, an attack on the gay person's integrity. The ideology of inclusivism, inspired by a concern with justice and equality, reveals itself to be, in fact, discriminatory against those who oppose the ideology of inclusivism. Critics of homosexual practice and the gay lifestyle, even when they are welcoming of gays and eager to help those who wish to change their lifestyle, are labeled "homophobic" and are subject to the severest condemnation by those who see themselves as morally enlightened. On account of the politicization of this issue through pressure from the powerful Gay Lobby and its political supporters, it will soon become a criminal offense to offer such criticism, and Christian organizations such as churches or Christian schools that cleave to traditional, biblically based ethical doctrine and practice will come under attack in the courts and even find their leaders being dragged off to jail.

II.III.4

Inspiration and interpretation of Scripture; issues around the statement that "God loves us just as we are"; justice and the question of equal rights of gay persons in the wider society and also in the Church

The liberal majority in TEC clearly has come to approve of homosexuality and of same-sex unions, and will probably officially approve same-sex marriage when the time is ripe. Given its track record, once gay marriage has become commonplace in civil society in America, it is likely that the TEC majority will find a way to adapt its rulings on same-sex unions to same-sex marriages. Although such a revisionist stance fundamentally alters the understanding of Christian marriage, a traditional image of marriage—already used in experimental liturgies for same-sex unions—is preserved by stressing the importance of commitment and monogamous fidelity and opposing the promiscuity commonly associated with the gay lifestyle; inevitably, however, this nod to tradition, while praiseworthy in itself, coexists with a basic tolerance, even approval, of homosexuality in general, which the liberal church is neither able nor willing to critique. It functions, in the end, as a whitewash. The incidence of successful and enduring monogamous same-sex unions and "marriages" in the wider society has not been high in the past, though it does appear to be growing. Since the reality of such unions is here to stay, we can only hope this trend towards a measure of stability will continue.[11] Unquestionably this is better for the common good than the promiscuous conduct that often characterizes the gay lifestyle. In no way, however, does it justify calling into question the traditional understanding of marriage; and it certainly should not alter the teaching and practice of marriage in the Church.

TEC's inclusivist stance being in line, it is believed, with Christ's will and God's perfect love for all his human creatures, the startling departure in the course of one generation from the settled teaching of the historic Church and from its long-standing tradition going back to apostolic times, must be seen as a decisive prophetic move taken under the inspiration of the Holy Spirit, which the rest of the Church will eventually come to recognize and approve. We live in a pluralistic, relativistic, multicultural, postmodern age, it is argued, when people in free democracies determine their own moral standards and do as they want, "provided there is mutual consent and nobody gets hurt", and therefore, says the liberal majority in TEC, any Scripture or tradition that questions this new reality must be considered to be outmoded and should be jettisoned. Our context being different from that in which the Scriptural prohibitions were enunciated means, we are told—often flippantly—that those prohibitions are irrelevant and we may ignore them.

Many books have been written in the last twenty years (albeit very few by Episcopalians) to show conclusively that the Old and New

---

11. See Gagnon, op. cit., 465–66.

Testament Scriptures are against the practice of homosexuality in any form. The special pleading of *exegetes* favorable to homosexual behavior has not carried wide conviction, and the argument on *hermeneutical* grounds for equal rights for gays in the church has proved to be extremely problematical.[12] Grounds other than hermeneutical must be found to support this position. I shall examine some of this material in the next section when I ask the question—assuming the Scriptures, and therefore their condemnation of homosexual practice, to be expressing God's will—why this should be so and why God should be opposed to homosexual conduct. This is a proper question, to which those committed to the historic position of the Church based on apostolic teaching, and to the authority of the Scriptures as expressing the mind of God in matters of morality and worship, must provide thoughtful answers.

Christians have indeed traditionally believed the Scriptures to be divinely inspired and authoritative, subject to interpretation, of course, and not without distortions and errors, but dependable in matters to do with salvation, and wise in matters of ethics. This is certainly the position long held by the Anglican churches around the world and enshrined in the Articles of Religion, Article VI. It is beyond the scope of my essay to develop this point, but I feel obliged to underline it.[13] I have already shown, but need to reiterate, that the current stance of the liberal majority of TEC clearly rejects this traditional position, not only when it comes to sexual ethics but also sometimes in dogmatic matters as well. With respect to the homosexual issue, they advance the notion that the texts concerning

---

12. See, for example, Robert A. J. Gagnon's comprehensive and decisive analysis, *The Bible and Homosexual Practice*, and Richard Hays, *Moral Vision*; also, Ronald Springett's essays on the Old and New Testaments in Yamamoto, *Crisis of Homosexuality*, in which he criticizes the forced exegesis of Scriptural texts concerning homosexuality as this appears in the works of D. S. Bailey, *Homosexuality and the Western Christian Tradition*, 1975, John Boswell, *Christianity, Social Tolerance and Homosexuality, Gay People in Western Europe from the Beginning of the Christian Era to the Fourteenth Century*, 1981, and Robin Scroggs, *New Testament and Homosexuality*. Springett points out that most biblical commentators do not agree with this tendentious exegesis (137, 142). See also, for example, the critique by Richard Hays in "Relations Natural and Unnatural, 184–215. Gagnon, in an article critiquing Jack Roger's book *Explode the Myths, Heal the Church*, cites three well-known authors sympathetic to homosexual unions—Louis Compton, Walter Wink, and Dan O. Via—who admit that the Bible from beginning to end is categorically hostile to same-sex behavior and that no responsible hermeneutic can make it say otherwise.

13. Two books that treat this subject with clarity and theological depth are Schneiders, *Revelatory Text*, and Davis and Hays, *Art of Reading Scripture*.

homosexuality are limited in application to their historical context and part of an outdated worldview, and in any event clash with our contemporary democratic understanding of human rights and equal justice for all. Obviously, it is argued, to condemn homosexuality is discriminatory and unjust and could not possibly be in accord with God's capacious, inclusive, loving heart. The Church, to be sure, should urge fidelity in relationships, but basically from now on we must see homosexual and heterosexual relationships as on a par and press for equal consideration and opportunity for persons of both sexual "orientations" at every level and in every corner of society, including within the Church. This necessarily applies to all matters of civil rights, of course, notably the right to marry and adopt children, but it also is seen to apply to matters of Church polity and to encompass the additional right of equal access to ordination.

TEC and other likeminded churches base their position on two theses that I examined earlier. The *first*, theological, is that God loves all of us just as we are, so that there are really no requirements to enter his Kingdom, one simply hears from the Church about God's love, takes this assertion on board, and does one's best, with very little guidance provided, to discern what it is to be loving in the daily circumstances of life and to act that way. Such is the content of faith, recalled at each liturgical celebration. That God's love is proclaimed is laudable, but without systematic explanation of the doctrinal basis for this assertion and the ethical consequences of it, the proclamation in the end is hollow and without transforming power. What it might mean to say that it is *only* by the Holy Spirit, and with the guidance of Scripture, Tradition, and Reason rightly understood[14], that the Church is empowered actually to *live* according to God's love in day-to-day experience, is a subject rarely broached in concrete terms. The pastoral issue of how *practically* to go about living this Christian life, is hardly ever addressed.

14. "Reason" in classical Anglican thought is rooted in divine law and cannot be divorced from divine authority, as expressed quintessentially in Holy Scripture. Within the sphere of the Church, and with the assistance of grace, man can, with his reason, perceive the Good and, with his free will, choose it. Faith and reason go together, in response to grace. This is a very different understanding of reason from the rationalistic construal that has predominated since the Enlightenment, where reason is man-centered and basically cut off from any reference to divine law, authority, or even reality. This is a reversal of the traditional Christian position, as the title of Kant's famous treatise—*Religion within the Limits of Reason Alone*—makes clear. The Enlightenment's understanding has yielded some remarkable political and social fruit, but its moral and spiritual reductionism has had disastrous consequences.

Of *course* God loves us "just as we are"—he died for us *while we were still sinners*" (Rom 5:8). This is the heart of the Gospel, as John 3:16 reminds us explicitly. But as responsible human beings, we are called to *respond* to that love, and this, as I pointed out above, involves repentance and transformation of the "just as we are" persons that we are when God meets us. The liberal "gospel" refuses this call. Such a call is seen as demeaning, indeed "judgmental". Human beings are good and should not be treated so roughly. In requiring repentance, God shows us humans a lack of respect. He is not being amiable. This is unacceptable. In our human omnipotence, we judge God's judgment to be unjust, so we must revise it.

This kind of sentimental, flabby moralism takes us back once again to the liberal movement of thought that "domesticates" God by evacuating all "hard" content from the Scriptural revelation and turning the Father of the Lord Jesus Christ into a "Nice Guy" who approves without question whatever we consider to be, on the strength of little more than our subjective feelings and "intuitions", our own "loving" actions. The death that Jesus suffered on the Cross is evacuated of all meaning, to the point that it is not an exaggeration to say that in this regard the liberal Church is crucifying Christ again.

The *second* thesis, politically driven but also theological at its root, is that, since God has created all persons with equal value and dignity, it follows that justice, as defined by secular law, requires that all persons have equal rights before the law *and in the Church*. This must include, logically, equal access to social and ecclesial positions and roles. Therefore, according to this understanding, there is no reasonable ground within the Church on which to impugn the right of persons of the same sex to marry if they wish, or the right of practicing gay persons to be ordained priest or bishop in the Church if they are qualified and have completed the necessary studies and received liturgical training.

I have already indicated a fundamental flaw in the first thesis, which I have named a heresy and an example of what Dietrich Bonhoeffer called "cheap grace". According to the Judeo-Christian vision of reality, God made the human creature good, but we have turned away from our Creator and rebelled against his ordinances, aspiring to be like God ourselves. (I explored this issue in Part I of this essay). We have fallen from our first estate and are sinners, which means, in practice, that our race strives to deny its creature-hood and to live without reference to the true God. As a consequence, history is marked by strife and violence rather than harmony. There can be no unity or peace if a lie underpins civilization; if finite man/woman rather than the transcendent Creator God is the measure of truth. Only contention—tribal, ethnic, religious, national, gender—can result. We cannot change this state of things by any thought or action of our own, try as we might; being ourselves the problem, we cannot by ourselves find the solution.

In Christ, the Church proclaims, God has shown us grace and redeemed us from our fallen, broken state, opening the way to new life. The Creator God has come into our fragmented humanity to make possible a new community rooted in him, beyond our divisions. He is our peace— our peace with God and our peace with each other—and in him our mutual distrust and hatred are overcome eschatologically—with respect to the life to come—and can effectively be overcome already in this life, as Christians have demonstrated time and again in the last two thousand years. *"You are all sons of God through faith in Christ Jesus, for all of you who were baptised into Christ have clothed yourselves with Christ. There is neither Jew nor Greek, slave nor free, male nor female, for you are all one in Christ Jesus. If you belong to Christ, then you are Abraham's seed, and heirs according to the promise."* (Gal 3:26–29). That the Church, along with its remarkable successes in transforming society down through the centuries (e.g., hospitals, schools, humane attitude toward the poor and the weak, affirmation of the equal dignity of all men and women), has often failed—sometimes grievously—to realize substantially this peaceful community and indeed has not infrequently acted contrary to what the Gospel requires and enables, does not give the lie to this extraordinary new vision and the hope it mediates.

It cannot be doubted that the Church, for much of its history, has often sought worldly power and acted out of its own natural strength and according to political rather than spiritual criteria, rather than by the Holy Spirit; and undeniably this sad truth has resulted in much profoundly un- or sub-Christian behavior and has severely distorted the general understanding of what the Gospel is all about. But the Holy Spirit, making available, in and through the Church, God's mercy and transforming power in Christ, is not for one moment less present in Christ's Body here on earth for all that, ready to be received through faith and then to work at changing individuals and societies. The Life in Christ is not itself diminished or destroyed by our disobedience or unbelief; it is rather *eclipsed*, like an eclipse of the life-giving sun by the barren moon— and is ready to spring forth wherever true faith is found.

But to enter into this new life, we must, as I have argued, turn from the lordship of self to the Lordship of Christ. This is the first step of faith, as the Scriptures make clear. Humankind, as a corporate entity and as so many individuals, must cease to be the measure of all things. We men and women must recognize and accept our creature-hood. This means concretely putting off attitudes and behavior condemned by the Word that God has spoken into history, as the Holy Spirit has elucidated it within the Church through the centuries, and taking on the yoke of Christ, allowing him to be our master. The Holy Spirit then begins to work within us to conform us to Christ. This is the only way of experiencing true peace and freedom, because only Christ, who mediates our peace with God, can set us free from the impulse to distrust, fear, and dominate the other, and from the egocentric desire to do what we please with our bodies, our finances, and our time. It is only the veneer of civilization that makes us think otherwise.

As far as the notion of our race's *fundamental* moral progress is concerned—a notion dear to the Enlightenment and that did indeed inspire and generate real progress in many areas of social life, yet that also engendered the reductionist aberrations to which I have already alluded—it has become evident to any thoughtful person that the cataclysms of the twentieth century must put an end to any such pretension. What moral advances have been made—and they are many, undeniably—have been made at the *conceptual* and *legal* levels, not the ontological, and these have been achieved largely by virtue of the yeast of the Christian Gospel in Western society, wherever the Church has been faithful to its mandate and inspiration, and notwithstanding its frequent disobedience and lapses into authoritarianism, legalism, cupidity, or cowardice.[15]

The attitudes and behavior condemned by the Word of God encompass all manner of things, lengthily detailed in many parts of Scripture, both Old and New Testaments. Included are varieties of sexual indulgence, including homosexual practice, that are judged to be impure and unworthy of human creatures made in the image of God. The postmodern liberal church, TEC in particular, jumps from the affirmation of God's love as this finds expression in the redemptive grace in Christ, to the affirmation that a person living a gay lifestyle need not put off that

15. The highest social ideals of the Enlightenment were an example of this yeast, under a secular form. The Enlightenment, followed by the French Revolution, emerged in part as a reaction to Roman Catholic authoritarianism and the Church's association with oppressive State power.

lifestyle but can simply carry on as before "because God loves him/her as he/she is". This is a deceptive twist of the truth, a false "half-truth" that is an affront to God's holiness and contrary to the Gospel. It is a *false doctrine* that perfectly illustrates man's manipulation of God's Word and usurpation of the Creator's prerogatives. The churches that choose this path are not taking Christ's yoke upon them but throwing it off altogether, often without having any idea of what they are really doing. As a result, far from extending the peace and freedom that are in Christ, they are provoking new divisions and hostilities and new forms of bondage, which are contributing to the breakdown of coherent family structures and strengthening the forces of disorder in society.[16]

Of course, the liberal churches don't see it that way. Quite the contrary. The second thesis just mentioned, which favors blessings on same-sex unions *in the church*, as well as the ordination of practicing homosexuals, maintains that issues of justice and equality, now front and center in our Western democracies, *overrule* biblical injunctions in the area of sexuality. As far as the wider secular society is concerned, justice may be seen to require that homosexuals should benefit equally with all other citizens from the civil rights approved by federal and state law, including same-sex unions, but the criteria that may be construed to require this in the secular context must not be imposed in the different context of the Church, which is under God's rule before it is under the State's; and the Church should certainly not simply apply to itself the criteria taken to be valid in the secular sphere. The Church should argue its

---

16. My references in this essay to the breakdown of "family" and "family structures" must not be taken to mean that I see marriage between a man and a woman, and the family that normally follows, as always successful. Far from it. It has often been oppressive and abusive, especially where misogyny has been present. Sin affects all our human structures. The breakdown of countless heterosexual marriages in the West today (and across the world) demonstrates the fragility of this institution. Indeed, I would argue that one of the chief causes, along with others that I mention in this essay, of the homosexual "movement" in the last generation is the widespread crisis besetting the institution of marriage. But this is all the more reason to seek to strengthen this institution, instead of using its vulnerability as a stick with which to beat it. The fact that it is in crisis today is no reason to dismiss it as outdated. The social unit of the family, based on the institution of marriage between a man and a woman, has always been, and remains, the basic, universal structure of stable human societies that perpetuate themselves through time, and from this empirical fact alone we may deduce that it is willed by God. Scripture, natural law, and historical experience bear this out. The polygamous practice of the Old Testament patriarchs and kings was not normative law, but a contingent historical phenomenon manifesting the domination of women by men, and which was opposed by the prophets, Jesus, and the New Testament writers.

case cogently in the public square against gay "marriage", presenting reasons for its opposition, as it has every right to do in a democratic society and as it has done on the issues of abortion-on-demand and euthanasia; but obviously it cannot enforce its position. What the long-range effect will be on Western society of the general trend to accept gay "marriage" as normal, is a moot point at this stage. Undoubtedly this development will exacerbate gender confusion and personal identity issues, and, when children come into the picture, make immensely complicated the questions of filiation, resulting in increased tension and deeper psychological anxiety in the population at large. The gay community is a small minority, but its influence in recent years has become immense. As I discuss in this essay, the whole understanding of human sexuality is undergoing a sea-change in modern society. The tremendous disturbances this is causing will surely continue to destabilize our nations and add to the rising general disorder in our institutions and societal relationships. As far as the Church is concerned, in any case, it is unquestionable that general acceptance of gay "marriage" among the liberal denominations would fundamentally alter the nature of the Gospel that these churches would be proclaiming.

II.III.5

Two unscientific assumptions about homosexuality; pastoral irresponsibility and the injustice done to gay persons by denying the possibility or desirability of change

A chief problem with the liberal argument that justice and equality issues overrule biblical injunctions in the area of sexuality is that it is based on two assumptions that are scientifically false, and on a pastoral position that is ideologically biased and unjust.

The first unscientific assumption is that *homosexuality is genetically based* and therefore "natural". "God made me this way," is a statement often heard in gay Christian circles. This is simply false.[17] It is true—and

17. See Gagnon, op. cit., 395–408, for a thorough discussion of this issue. See, also, the article by Stanton L. Jones in *First Things*, "Same-Sex Science," 27–34. Jones, a professor of psychology, cites numerous studies in the last decade, carried out in several countries, that address the question of whether there is solid scientific evidence to show that homosexuality is biologically determined. His findings are negative, even though he makes it clear that biological factors can definitely influence

I shall discuss this later—that many gay people have experienced same-sex attraction from a very early age, for which they are not themselves responsible, but this does not mean that these people are congenitally homosexual and that there is nothing they can do about it. Influence coming down through previous generations can also obviously have an effect, as with other behavioral dispositions in a family. Pre-natal hormonal imbalances may play a role. Instances of a testosterone deficiency in the uterus of a mother carrying a second male child may, on occasion, present yet another influencing factor. Genetic anomalies may occur. But such biological influences are a different matter from normal genetic inheritance. Furthermore, it should be evident from an evolutionary standpoint that any population with a homosexual gene that it allowed to condition its behavior would have become extinct long ago.[18] God most assuredly did not create a portion of the human race so that it could become extinct.

The second unscientific assumption is that *the homosexual orientation cannot be changed.* Like the first assumption, this is simply false. Both these false assumptions, to be considered more lengthily later in this essay, are based on the ideologically driven propaganda of the activist homosexual lobby. They are mere assertions. There is no unbiased scientifically demonstrated evidence to prove them. To the contrary, ample evidence demonstrates, on the one hand, the great variety of biological, psychological, social, and relational causes of the homosexual orientation, and on the other hand, the considerable success, in both secular and religious contexts, in the reorientation of the homosexual to the heterosexual lifestyle for gay persons *who want to change.* This evidence is out there, available, easily accessible.[19] Numerous organizations exist, both secular and religious, that

---

sexual orientation, along with psychological and environmental variables. He points out moreover that "sample representativeness," obviously influenced by the bias of the researchers, is a major problem in all such studies, especially in a numerically small community such as the gay community. With respect to the question of whether or not sexual orientation can be changed, Jones concludes, on the basis of a study that he himself carried out with a colleague, that it *can* be, provided the motivation for doing so is strong and a network of support is available. He observes that overall, up till now, value judgments, not science, lie behind the "determinations" of most studies. We know much more now about homosexuality than we did thirty or even ten years ago, but scientifically speaking, our knowledge remains elementary at best. "The contributions of science to this area," Jones writes, ". . . .remain sketchy, limited, and puzzling. It is remarkable how little scientific humility is in evidence given the primitive nature of our knowledge" (33).

18. See the discussion of this subject in Goldberg, *Light in the Closet,* 59–61.

19. See, e.g., Satinover, *Homosexuality*; Goldberg, *Light in the Closet*; Nicolosi,

help homosexuals who wish to leave their lifestyle behind, such as Desert Stream, Exodus International, Courage, Homosexuals Anonymous, Redeemed Life Ministries, Pastoral Care Ministries, and Jonah.

This being said, it is undeniable that there have been scandals and fraudulent cases in some of these organizations, and reports of changed life-styles have sometimes been trumped up. Some of those men or women who came through programs successfully have later fallen back into their old habits. This is indisputable. Given the range and varying intensity of those old habits among members of the gay community, and given the enormous temperamental variety among gay persons (as among heterosexuals), it is not surprising. One "cure" does not fit all, certainly, and some "cures" are ill-adapted or simply don't work. But this does not give the lie to the testimony of the many gay people who have navigated the course from a gay to a straight lifestyle and gone on to live well-adjusted heterosexual lives, either as married or as celibate persons.[20] Of course, as with ex-alcoholics, they must be vigilant for the rest of their days, and their renewal, to whatever degree it has occurred, must never be taken for granted. It may be a long slog. They remain vulnerable, especially in their emotions, and they may have falls. But the change is real, and many gay persons have experienced it. It is inexcusable on the part of gay advocates, outside and inside the Church, to go on playing this down or denying it outright, even mocking the organizations that devote themselves to caring for and guiding gay persons who want to change. Ideology, not love for their fellow gays, is what would seem to motivate such hostile behavior. The liberal clergy of TEC, as a case in point, have so far taken no account of such programs to exit the gay lifestyle, and have bought

Reparative Therapy; Anatrella, *Règne de Narcisse*; MacNutt, *Can Homosexuality be Healed?*; Scott, *At Variance*; Comiskey, *Pursuing Sexual Wholeness*; Payne, *Broken Image*; *Crisis in Masculinity*; *Healing of the Homosexual*; Bergner, *Setting Love in Order*; Moberly, *Homosexuality: A New Christian Ethic*; Gagnon, *Bible and Homosexual Practice*.

20. The example of Jesus himself, whom the Church looks upon as the very model of perfect humanity, demonstrates that neither heterosexual nor homosexual "intimacy" is needed for the fulfillment of human nature. Anthony Thiselton writes in Bradshaw, *Way Forward?*, 149: ". . . the narratives of the New Testament contain no suggestion that Jesus could not fully affirm and live out what it is to be human without experiencing sexual intimacy. It is nowhere suggested that celibacy hinders truly human development in the case of Jesus." The New Testament doesn't for one moment suggest that the state of celibacy is *superior* to marriage, but the Christian conviction, contrary to what current modernity insists on saying, is that human plenitude consists not in sexual expression, but in our being *in Christ*, the perfect Man.

into both the false assumptions I have been discussing. They have made no effort to discredit these assumptions or to point Christian gay persons who might wish to change their sexual orientation in the direction of persons or organizations—secular, Christian, or Jewish—capable of helping them. They have swallowed whole the propaganda of the activist Gay Lobby—the radicals who push the homosexual agenda—without any attempt to critique it theologically or even factually.

This betrays a level of pastoral irresponsibility that is nothing short of scandalous. It is a betrayal of the truth and hence, ultimately, of Jesus, who speaks of himself as the Way, the Truth, and the Life (John 14:6). Critical reason and open discussion tend to be ruled out, along with any need to defend and argue the revisionist position taken. In many congregations, as I mentioned earlier, the whole subject is off bounds, and parishioners are profoundly confused and destabilized but dare not ask questions, fearing that they will be condemned, ridiculed, or called "homophobe". From the pulpit of liberal churches no clear voice is heard on this subject; indeed, no voice is heard at all—the gay agenda is simply adopted or swallowed without argument or discussion, and any contrary position is sidelined or ignored. Congregations are left disoriented and without any guidance whatsoever. Most of the liberal clergy themselves are content to flow passively with the current and have not seriously examined the issues. Even conservative clergy rarely address the question squarely, using rational theological arguments from Scripture and natural law to support their case, as well as material from the social sciences. They are often content to let it be known that they are against homosexual practice, without making the effort needed to show why; and in the past, shamefully, they have often failed to offer to gay persons the respect and welcome such persons deserve.

All this undermines any claim that TEC is acting justly toward either its gay or its heterosexual constituents. By withholding or distorting factual information concerning the homosexual condition, and by accepting hook, line, and sinker the Gay Lobby's party line, the liberal majority is abusing gay people, and others too, simply by suppressing the truth, and abusing in particular all those gay persons who are stuck in the gay lifestyle but want nothing more than to leave it behind them. By not informing them of the possibility of change through the power of the Holy Spirit, and by in fact confirming them in their homosexual orientation and simply telling them that "God made them that way", TEC is depriving these persons of the transformation their *deepest* heart, as made in God's image, would desire.

TEC may speak of God's love, but in this regard it is not demonstrating either the meaning or the power of that love.

The majority of gay persons are not Gay Lobby activists with a political agenda; like most people, they see themselves in a certain way and simply want to get on with their lives. Their intention, obviously, is not to worship false gods or indulge in idolatrous practices. No more than the average heterosexual person do they think of themselves as pagans indulging in pagan behavior. But, as with heterosexuals, the way gay persons see themselves is not the last word on the subject. TEC and gay activists may wish it were, but they are mistaken. There is more to say, which can open other horizons to those gay persons (or to heterosexuals) not satisfied with their lives, who may be troubled or anxious, or who feel somehow that things are not the way they should be. This "more" is the love of Christ and the power of his Cross. It is the Church that should be revealing this "more" to them, not with condemnation—God forbid!—but with a combination of gracious pastoral concern, biblical teaching, and cogent argument. But the "progressive" wing of TEC and of other mainline Protestant churches is not doing this, and even the conservative wing is often failing in its responsibility.

God, it is suggested, is the one who has changed, since his biblical injunctions no longer apply; and the ethical standards of the Church have also changed, evidently, according to the liberal hierarchy's pronouncements of the last generation. But gay persons themselves, TEC is declaring, *cannot* change, nor should they even consider such a thing, since the modern world has made the momentous discovery after all these centuries that God created them that way in the first place and, as I observed above, rather oddly put into them a gene that would guarantee their early extinction as a minority group if such a gene were commonly the cause of their condition.

Homosexual activity, we are told, is altogether different today from what it was in Greek or Roman culture. Robin Scroggs goes so far as to argue that the Apostle Paul's target when he attacks homosexuality in his Epistles was specifically the various forms of pederasty to be found in the prevailing Greco-Roman culture, in which inequality of the partners, domination, and impermanency of the relationships were the norm, and that it is impossible to know what he would think about the phenomenon of homosexual love and monogamous relationship as we find these in today's culture.[21] This new cultural reality, Scroggs asserts, totally changes the way we are to view homosexual practice and makes obsolete the Scriptural condemnation of homosexuality as we find it in the Old Testament and in the Pauline Epistles.[22]

Monogamous same-sex unions and "marriages" are a growing but still very much of a minority phenomenon in the gay community, as I mentioned earlier. They clearly respond to a deep need in today's atomistic culture, where traditional forms of community are disappearing rapidly in the West, and loneliness is endemic. The *qualities* of mutuality and commitment that the partners in these unions wish to institutionalize in the wider society are, *as such*, to be commended, of course; but the assumption underlying them that homosexual practice, at least under these circumstances, is *good*, should be resisted. Wholehearted approval of same-sex unions by TEC and other liberal factions in the mainline churches inevitably has the effect—whether this is intended or not—of appearing to accommodate, even *encourage*, homosexual practice in general, whatever its form. Within the Church itself, particular instances of the affective mutuality of some gay couples must not be allowed to determine the shape and course of the principled debate about the theological significance of homosexual practice and, ultimately, of marriage itself.

One wonders if the liberal leaders in TEC, in their capacity as pastors, have given any thought to the distress and confusion caused to heterosexual parents—the large majority of the population—facing the disruptions in society caused by the Gay Lobby's intimidating propaganda—now invading the media and the school systems in the West—and its resulting effects on their children. Clear and honest teaching on these issues by TEC and other churches, both liberal and conservative—the kind of work I'm arguing for in this essay—could alleviate some of this

---

21. Scroggs, op. cit., see especially chapter 3 and 117, 128. Scroggs' argument has been strongly criticized by a number of authors, as Thiselton shows in his essay in Bradford, op. cit. Thiselton points out that there is evidence of other, more positive, sorts of homosexual relationship in the Greco-Roman world, with which Paul, sophisticated and well-traveled, would certainly have been familiar. The Apostle's condemnation of homosexual practice, while showing obvious affinities with Hellenistic-Jewish and Stoic ethical stances, had its roots deep in the Hebraic vision of a disjointed world in rebellion against its Creator, as Romans, chapters 1and 2, make clear. Paul sees homosexuality, whatever its form, as one among many distorted expressions of human nature and behavior, neither worse nor better than others but peculiarly symbolic of the human will to flout God's creation order and lawful ordinances.

22. Ibid., 127.

confusion, while also helping the ultra-right churches, which often do veer toward homophobia, to repent of their fear and condemnation and adopt a more Christian approach to the question of homosexuality.

The fact that justice and equality are being touted as the reasons for TEC's actions, while at the same time alternate viewpoints—and ones with solid evidence to support them—are being deliberately derided or suppressed, can only give rise to a charge of hypocrisy. There is nothing holy or just or prophetic about such actions—TEC is simply aping the ideology and behavior of the gay radicals. This is certainly not an expression of love. It is cowardly and sentimental. Everyone will be happier, it is blithely affirmed, if we just let people do what they feel like doing—and God, of course, wants people to be happy! This is naïve, theologically jejune, and irresponsible. One must ask: what justice and equality are being shown to members of the gay community who want only to get out of it; who sense that their attraction to persons of their own sex is not a destiny, that they are not *fated* to act in the way they are acting, but who don't know how to overcome their compulsions; who fear for their physical and mental health but are told there is no way they can change and that the answer to their anxieties is simply to accept their condition; who find the conflict between their conduct and what they read in Scripture and in Christian tradition to be intolerable, but who are told that the texts in the Bible that worry them are obsolete and not to be taken seriously? What is TEC offering these people? Not only is its liberal wing proposing a Gospel without responsibility, a simulacrum of grace calling itself "inclusiveness," but it adopts the patent lies of the secular Gay Lobby as it militates for "gay rights."

The heresy underlying these ignoble and unfaithful actions is this: TEC and the churches going down the same road have simply ceased to understand themselves as a separate society, a holy and eschatological community set apart from the "world" (*spiritually speaking*, in the biblical sense I have described, as in 1 Pet 2:9–12; John 15:19; 17:16) and called to think and act in ways often at variance with the world's ways: *"But you are a chosen people, a royal priesthood, a holy nation, a people belonging to God, that you may declare the praises of him who called you out of darkness into his wonderful light."* (1 Pet 2:9). The "new birth" and its revolutionary theological significance, sacramentally expressed in baptism, have ceased to have any effectual meaning for large sectors of TEC and the other liberalizing Protestant churches. Far from acting like a *new creation*, eschatologically oriented to the Kingdom of God, these churches seem hardly different from secular institutions that do socially approved things, except that they do "religious" things as well like talking about God's love, celebrating rites called "sacraments", and observing "feast days" that commemorate events in the life of Jesus Christ.

These are all excellent, vitally important things to do, undoubtedly expressing the sincere Christian faith of many, but in light of the New Testament one must ask: where is the emphasis, so characteristic of the New Testament writings, on the life of the Kingdom of God? On the "new heart" and the "new spirit" of which the prophet Ezekiel speaks (Ezek 36:26–27)? On an altogether new way of living, a whole new morality and behavior, grounded in the ontological/theological transformation that is involved in death to the egocentric, grasping self and in new birth through identification with Christ on the Cross and in his Resurrection? (Rom 6:1–14). Where do we find any notion of conformity to Christ (Rom 12:1–2; 8:29) and of the progressive transfiguration, through the healing and sanctifying work of the Holy Spirit, into Christ's image of those who follow him? (2 Cor 3:18; Col 3:10f.). In a word, where is Good Friday, beyond its liturgical celebration? And where is Easter? For without the death of the self-focused sinful nature—the "old man", the "*palaios hemon anthropos*", in St. Paul's language (Rom 6:6)—there can be no risen life in the Spirit in any way approximating what the Apostle means in his classical discussion of this subject in Rom 8: 1–17. And where, moreover, is the Ascension and our session with Christ at the right hand of the Father, whereby, as heirs of the Kingdom, we share even now in God's life and are able to exercise Christ's authority? And finally, where is Pentecost, when the Holy Spirit, the promise of the Father, is poured out on the disciples by God the Father and by the risen Lord, and the Church is born? Without the Spirit, there would be no Church, and Christ's work in history—singular though it was—would have remained just that: a series of (remarkable) events that happened two thousand years ago. Christ's passion and resurrection would have no effectual bearing on the present. We wouldn't even have the inspired New Testament writings. Without the gift of the Holy Spirit there is no eschatology and no new creation. *Practically* speaking, one fears that something like this is not far from being the case in the liberal mainline churches of the West: the daily round simply goes on as before and as it does anywhere else, and eschatological living, with respect both to life here and now and to future matters like divine judgment, the return of Christ, and the transfiguration of creation, gets little attention, if any at all.

II.III.6

Commitment to social action, but a neglect of teaching on personal ethics; justice and love; the adaptation of the Gospel to the standards of the modern world; decline of collegiality and indifference to catholicity

This is the nub of the matter. The focal question of this essay is homosexuality in the context of modernity, but the more fundamental issue is our *crucifixion with Christ*, the crucifixion of our "old nature", of "lord Self", and our *resurrection in Christ* into new life. In what ways are the members of these churches, heterosexual or gay, being called by their bishops and priests to live in a manner palpably different from the world's way, in attitude and behavior? It is not just the sphere of sexuality that is at issue here. I have already observed that issues to do with ethics (other than "justice" questions), and with sin, personal holiness, and conformity to Christ, are rarely preached about from liberal pulpits. Yet such issues tend to take up about half of Paul's Epistles, not to mention the place they occupy in other New Testament Epistles and in the Gospels! They have been replaced by commitment to social works and social justice (admirable in itself, of course, but not to be taken as a substitute for personal holiness—in an authentic Christian life, the two necessarily go together), or by something called "spirituality". In contemporary parlance, outside of the Church but sometimes even inside it, this last often consists in syncretistic, even New Age or occult mixtures, in Jungianism,[23] or in benign

23. See Satinover, *Empty Self*, for a lucid analysis of Jung's development of gnostic spirituality, in accordance with his studies of alchemy and his psychologizing re-symbolization, via his theory of archetypes, of the Judeo-Christian heritage. "In polytheism, ancient or modern," writes Satinover, "each [social] group [type] has its own god [or goddess]. In Jung's view, these are the *spiritual faces of the instincts*, which he named 'archetypes'. . . . Each archetype is the image of an underlying instinct. In other words, the 'gods' of polytheism are merely the images of our own instinctive drives. The pagan psycho-theology that lurks behind Jungianism, and that has spread so widely within the church, is simply *the psychologized worship of instinct*" (55). The notion to be found in Jung of a union of opposites, of the incorporation of darkness into light to form a "higher" more psychologically realistic image of God and of mankind, has its root, according to Satinover, in alchemy and processes of chemical transformation (39, 30), and represents another modern variant on the theme of our race's quest to get "beyond good and evil" in some sort of "superior" synthesis—beyond the reach, that is, of Judeo-Christian morality and of the God who is wholly good and who demands holiness and obedience. In the Gnostic "spirituality" that profoundly influenced Jung, the

feelings of a vaguely "spiritual" nature (whatever that means), turning on concepts such as "love", "tolerance", "peace", and "inclusion"—God is Love, God is within me (which, in this context, means basically: "I am God"), so I'm fine, we're all fine. This is little more than a religious equivalent of the feel-good sentimentality associated with the self-actualization movement. In some persons, of course, it may translate a genuine hunger for truth, but often it is simply self-indulgence.

Christians in the liberal churches are known for their strong commitment to "social action" and humanitarian aid—TEC dioceses, for example, fund or run scores of hospitals and schools in poor countries such as Haiti[24]—and this laudable work is genuinely motivated by God's love as mediated by the Gospel. I want it to be clear that I strongly support all such work and have been personally engaged in it for years as an ordained priest and theologian. I see in it manifest evidence of Christ's presence and the Holy Spirit's action. But teaching about the substance of the Gospel that inspires this sort of labor in the first place is being neglected, and the good works done are in fact hardly distinctive in our day from what humanitarian organizations with no open Christian affiliation do abundantly and well.[25] It is of great importance for their future that

---

fundamental Judeo-Christian doctrine of atonement is set aside as unnecessary (46). Distinctions and boundaries are blurred, opposites are amalgamated in favor of an "inclusive" vision of lifestyles, where good and evil are reconciled and made obsolete as categories. Such a psycho-theology, essentially pagan, which in effect can be used to justify virtually any variety of sexual behavior, fits perfectly with the thrust of modern technology to overcome all limits. In Jungianism, psychology replaces theology, the psyche replaces God as the source of wisdom, and our instinctive drives, labeled with the scientific-sounding title "archetypes," become idols.

24. TEC has long been associated with philanthropic actions, and, in this, commendably illustrates Christian motivation and generosity. To give just one example, it has been doing energetic work in Haiti since the earthquake of 2010 through its Episcopal Relief and Development Fund, in cooperation with a number of American dioceses and its populous parishes on the island, most of which support schools and local clinics. TEC is also a strong supporter of the Millenium Development goals and of causes such as immigrants' rights. Its concern and labor in these areas is to be applauded. Social work of this sort is, and has always been, an absolutely basic part of Christian mission.

25. This fact, it should be noted, is owing ultimately to the Christian worldview and respect for human dignity that underlies modern humanitarian operations, even those among them that are patently secular. Concern for the weak and suffering, in a universal sense, including the acknowledgement that their value is equal to that of the strong, is not "natural" to post-lapsarian humankind, though scholastic natural law theory, operating within a theological framework based on the doctrine of creation, held that the equality of human beings is a foundational *given* in God's good creation. The widespread recognition in the modern world of the dignity and equal value of all human beings is

these churches not lose the basis for the revolutionary dynamism that lies behind the love and hope to which these charitable works bear witness.

The New Testament does not talk about human rights or even justice in the conventional sense of that term, that is, the giving to others their due, neither more nor less. The New Testament's standards are those of love and are far more rigorous than the standards of justice, which are more strictly characteristic of Old Testament ethics. The Sermon on the Mount does certainly stress *dikaiosynē*, translated as "righteousness/justice" (Matt 5:20, as the basis for the antitheses in vv. 21–48), but Jesus' injunctions go beyond the understanding of righteousness/justice in the Old Testament. Broadly speaking, one might say that in the Old Testament, love for neighbor is to be understood in terms of justice—rendering to him his due—whereas in the New Testament justice is to be understood in terms of love. To go the second mile, or to turn the other cheek, or to forgive (and to keep on forgiving) those who have wronged us, or to show love to one's enemies instead of rendering to them what we may consider their due, are expressions not of justice in the strict sense, but of love—*authentic* love, not mere sentimentality. Nor is there any question in the Bible of "human rights" as such. Human dignity, as we have seen, is strongly affirmed on the basis of our being creatures made in God's image, but in no way does this serve as ground for making claims on God or for asserting what we human creatures have a "right" to do or demand of him, especially if such claims contradict God's Word as set out in both Old and New Testaments.

Justice is indeed the foremost operative virtue in the social and political spheres. But the standards by which the new creation that is the Church is called by its Head to govern itself are not in the first instance those of even the most just and equitable societies. They are rather the standards of the Kingdom of God, for which, according to the King himself, the Scriptures provide the criteria. The requirement of justice is subsumed under the requirement of love. Love, entailing respect and openness, is to be shown by the Church equally to all persons—and obviously this includes homosexuals—in ways appropriate to their situation,

---

the fruit of the Christian Gospel and is inconceivable outside its sphere of influence. Specifically, the modern affirmation of human dignity and equality is rooted ultimately in the anthropological affirmation in Genesis 1:27 that man/woman is created *imago Dei*, and in the Christian affirmation that Jesus Christ is the very *Imago Dei*, who made manifest human being as it is meant to be (2 Cor 4:4; Col 1:15; cf. Heb 1:3). By fulfilling thus in himself our human vocation, he was able likewise, as our perfect representative, to bear our sin and guilt and make redemption for us.

but this does not mean that secular standards of equality, as defined by secular interest groups or law, are to be applied across the board to Christians or incorporated wholesale into the Church's canonical law. The Church is a proper entity responsible to God first, not to the State or society. As it is unacceptable for the State to impose standards on the Church not in keeping with the Church's own standards—and when this is done, the Church must resist—it is inappropriate for the Church to adopt for itself without further ado the standards of civil society. In both cases boundaries are being unduly and inappropriately crossed.

There are, of course, many matters not addressed by Scripture that the Church must make decisions about, but the responsible practice of hermeneutics does not warrant departures from Scripture that contradict or undermine clear biblical teaching and praxis. If the modern concepts of human rights and equality before the law are rooted ultimately in Judeo-Christian anthropology—and they are—this does not mean that all distinctions between human beings are to be effaced, or that different standards and criteria of judgment and action are not to be applied in different contexts.

The Church cannot hold secular society to the same ethical standards as those to which it holds itself, or, at least, as those to which God holds it, even though it is certainly called to proclaim these standards and to argue, on both rational and spiritual grounds, for their universal value. The holiness that is supposed to be the mark of God's people cannot be an applicable objective or ideal for people who do not believe in the biblical God. In principle the reverse is also the case, and the Church ought not to be required to approve or abide by the moral standards governing a given society in which it finds itself, where these may be construed as being in opposition to or tension with biblical standards.

According to the Church's Scriptures and its own traditional standards, for example, persons of the same sex are not to be united *within the context of the Church* in "same-sex unions" or in "marriage", regardless of what the surrounding society may think about the matter; and persons exercising authority in the Church are not to be practicing homosexuals, since Scripture and Christian tradition—not to mention natural law theory, as it may be applied to homosexuality—uniformly and explicitly oppose homosexual practice and therefore cannot legitimately be made to endorse such practice on the part of its members and in particular on the part of those who govern God's people and represent the Church to the world. The issue has nothing to do with "equality" and "justice", but with the Church's time-honored morality and its traditional, biblically-based norms as these apply to its ethics and canonical practice. To its credit, TEC has insisted that gay persons be treated in all circumstances justly and with no less consideration than heterosexual persons, being altogether equal with them before God and as made in the divine image; but not for a moment does this warrant the conclusion that distinctions in the order of creation are no longer pertinent and that Scriptural markers are henceforth irrelevant.

In the light of the Church's traditional, nearly two thousand-year old self-understanding and the teaching in the Hebrew Scriptures from before the Christian era, this is simple logic. With respect to the three recent actions of TEC that are here under discussion, however, this logic has been peremptorily set aside in favor of a logic imposed by the contemporary cultural climate. According to this logic, if modern democracies are ruled by an ideology of autonomous freedom interweaving human rights, equality, individualism, and moral relativism, the Church, in order to remain "relevant" and keep up with the times, must adopt that ideology for itself and make its ecclesial decisions accordingly. The proclamation of Christ and what St. Paul calls the *"law of the Spirit of life in Christ Jesus"* (Rom 8:2a) has been co-opted by the proclamation of homosexuality and the "law of equality". This indictment may approach being a caricature, but in the liberal sectors of TEC it is not far from the truth. The ultimate reference and source of meaning and practice here is clearly human society, not God's Word. Lip service is paid to that Word, of course, but the toolbox of hermeneutics is then brought in and used to twist the Word into bright new shapes that fit current secular belief and practice. "Love", meaning in this context approval of sexual behavior that has been considered sinful in the past, is the operative principle here, "inclusiveness" the operative concept.[26]

The fact that the results of that interpretive exercise have not, as mentioned earlier, proved convincing to many of the leading exegetes of

26. See Gagnon, op. cit., ch. 5, for an exhaustive critique of the numerous hermeneutical devices used by liberal writers to deny or twist the plain meaning of the biblical references to homosexuality, deploying a variety of sociological, psychological, behavioral, and "scientific" criteria to justify the acceptance of homosexual practice in the Church today. And, as mentioned earlier in relation to Robin Scroggs, Anthony Thiselton, in op. cit., ch. 12, also develops a cogent critique of exegetical and hermeneutical arguments that are intended to show that what Paul is talking about in relevant New Testament texts does not correspond to the "loving" aspects of homosexual behavior today.

our day apparently gives no cause for alarm to the "progressive" population in TEC, because, at bottom, the Word itself, whatever results exegesis
may give, is not taken seriously by this population as being an objective,
perennial authority. It is *not* divine revelation given through inspired
men, but merely a human construct relating religious experience in those
ancient, primitive societies. Therefore it can be legitimately de- and re-
constructed in new ways to fit changed cultural modes and perspectives.
What carries final authority is the prevailing climate of opinion, which,
as adopted by TEC, is called "prophetic". Theological rationale for this
extraordinary move is neither needed nor provided, judging by TEC's
way of proceeding. Nor does the wider Church need to be consulted; the
sense of collegiality is absent. The "new revelation", it would appear, has
been received and enunciated in one part—the "progressive" part—of the
universal Body of Christ, and as it is prophetic, eventually all the other
parts will come around, or ought to.

This is nothing less than a sell-out, a betrayal of the Gospel. It is a
form of idolatry, masquerading as a "Spirit-led" development. It shows
contempt for the universal Church of Christ and gives the lie to its confession, made each week when reciting the Creed, that the Church is "one,
holy, catholic and apostolic". Here I must repeat something I alluded to
earlier. By proceeding in this way, TEC is acting like a Congregationalist
"local church", in contradiction with its own ecclesiology. It is acting in
isolation from the rest of the universal Body of Christ. The idolatrous focus on this single issue—this "cause célèbre"—reveals—or perhaps results
from—the absence of any authentic sense of the Body of Christ in time
and space. Arrogance has caused TEC to lose its ecclesiological moor-
ings. This should be—but appears not to be—a cause for consternation in
a Church that prides itself on its "enlightened" and catholic ecclesiology.

The heart of the biblical message consists in a call to the human race
on the part of a merciful and holy God to turn from its rebellion against
its Creator and line up again with his graciously revealed will and ways, of
which the aim is our redemption and transformation. Of course, this must
cause offense to those who refuse to do it. At bottom, the persecution of
Jews and Christians through the ages always has had to do primarily with
this call that they have received to "leave Ur" (Abram), "be saved out of
Egypt" (the Israelites), "repudiate idolatry" (Israel), "repent, die to sin,
and be reborn to new life" (the Church). This call presupposes that the
"natural" state of affairs—what is called *paganism*—is, from God's point

of view, "unnatural" and not in conformity with his will. This is totally unacceptable to the pagan mind, of course.[27]

27. The persecution over the centuries of Jews by the Church is a different matter altogether. It arose from a neglect of the mature Pauline theology in Romans, chapters 9–11, regarding the relation of the Jews to the Church. Under the pressure of the persecution—mentioned frequently in the New Testament—that the young Church, made up largely of Jews, experienced at the hands of other Jews (like Paul himself, before his conversion), we find a "replacement" theology emerging in Matthew and the Letter to the Hebrews, and, in John, an anti-Jewish stance even more extreme. This perspective, which later hardened into a rigid supersessionist doctrine, eclipsed Paul's reflections in Romans, where, in an effort to demonstrate God's faithfulness to his covenant with Israel, he wrestled theologically with the meaning of the refusal by the majority of Jews in his day to receive Christ as the long-awaited Messiah. He saw this refusal as spiritual blindness and disobedience on the part of his own people, and struggled to see how God could both judge them and yet remain faithful to his covenant with them. This is not the place to expound his argument, but Paul's reasoning provided theological meaning to what was for him the most vexing question he faced in the course of his ministry, to which clear and altogether satisfying answers were simply not forthcoming. Along with the indifference by the wider Church to Paul's arguments, one must point out the understandable but regrettable failure of the early Church to respond with love to the Jews who rejected its claims that Jesus was the Messiah and who opposed its preaching of the Gospel—sometimes violently, as we see in the Book of Acts and in allusions elsewhere in the New Testament: e.g., 1 Thess 2:14–16; Heb 10:32–34.

In this the primitive Church was disregarding Jesus' own words about loving one's enemies that, ironically, Matthew himself records in his Gospel (Matt 5:43–48). The anti-Jewish prejudice that turned into anti-Semitism as the centuries advanced and as the Gentile Church became politically powerful and dominating—and, where this happened, distinctly *un-christian*—was the greatest, and most shameful, tragedy to befall the Church in its long history. It is a sign of the Holy Spirit's work to confirm Christ's promise that the gates of Hell shall not prevail against his Church, that this same Church, disobedient as it has often been—just like Israel in the Old Testament—has recognized its sin with respect to the Jews and begun to repent, opening the way for significant moves of *rapprochement* between Christians and Jews. It is this, in part, that is prodding many Jews to face squarely the question of the Messianic identity of Jesus of Nazareth and the theological meaning of the suffering of their people in the light of their refusal to take seriously their own prophetic Scriptures and to recognize Jesus as their Messiah. In any case, the pagan mind, supremely represented in our day by despots like Hitler and Stalin, would wish at all times to eradicate *both* the Jews and the Christians, because *both* recall to it the transcendent God they wish to deny and eliminate—the God who is their *rival* and judge and whose Word declares resoundingly that the world as it stands—the pagan world—is under divine judgment and altogether unable to save itself. The pagan mind cannot tolerate the ethical standard of holiness set forth in the Old and New Testaments, or the invisible One God who establishes this standard; it is so much more "natural", so much easier, to worship multiple idols in the form of man-made things of this world. With respect in particular to Christians, the genocidal attempt by the Ottoman Sultan Abdul-Hamid and later by

The modern liberal Church has turned this call upside down. What is important is *not* to cause offense to non-Christians by doing or claiming anything fundamentally different from what they claim or do. The Church is *not* called to "leave Ur" or be "born from above" (John 3:3), but to integrate "Ur" into itself. To do otherwise would be discriminatory, judgmental, and presumptuous. Not holiness, but political correctness, is the criterion here for action. The will and ways of God, as set forth in Scripture, are thus relativized and reinterpreted in conformity with this option. The Gospel is "adapted" to modern society. What remains of the liberal Episcopal Church in the long run, if these actions are representative of its definitive orientation and continue decisively to influence its future, will, along with its commendable and energetic humanitarian initiatives, be its dignified liturgy, fine hymnody, and a somewhat parochial and smug self-satisfaction. Its handsome rituals will provide a beautiful *reflection* of the tradition and the Christian faith. Not for one moment do I wish to say that these are small or bad things. Far from it. The tradition of the Episcopal Church, as part of the wider Anglican tradition, is commendable. The earnestness of TEC's emphasis on liturgy is laudable, especially since the importance in today's secular society of powerful liturgical celebration, as a presentation of the story of God's acts to create and redeem the world, cannot be exaggerated. But except in pockets here and there, the *foundation* and *spiritual substance* of that glorious tradition and liturgical expression will grow pale indeed if the current trend continues. The Cheshire cat will have gone; only the smile will remain.

---

the Young Turk government during and after the First World War, to annihilate the several Christian populations of the Empire, most notably the Armenians, is a salient example—arising this time from within the Islamic world—of the inclination of the "natural man" to eradicate those who proclaim the Gospel of Christ. Such persecution of Christians within the Islamic world by exponents of radical Islamism is increasing in our day. Undoubtedly the mistaken *identification* in the Muslim mind of Christian faith with Western culture is a contributing factor in this persecution; but the religious factor, based on Qoranic texts from the latter half of Muhammad's life in Medina, is at least as important and should not be overlooked or underestimated.

Section IV

The biblical opposition to homosexual practice is rooted in the Creation order, founded on the complementarity of man and woman and on the Creator's high view of the body, sexuality, and marriage. A deficient or defective love and a lack of personal affirmation underlie most cases of homosexual orientation. In Christ are to be found both wholeness and holiness

II.IV.1

Idolatry, sexual license, and the Holiness Code of Leviticus 18–20

IN THIS SECTION I want to explore the question of why, according to the Scriptures, God is opposed to the practice of homosexuality. I emphasize the word "practice", because it is absolutely vital to distinguish the sexual practice, which is condemned, from the person engaging in it, whom God has created, loves, and wishes to redeem. In the Book of Leviticus, what has traditionally been called the Holiness Code runs from chapters 17–26. Chapters 18–20 contain ethical ordinances applicable to the whole people of Israel. The injunctions concerning male homosexual practice are severe: *"Do not lie with a man as one lies with a woman; that is detestable [an abomination]."* (Lev 18:22). *"If a man lies with a man as with a woman, both of them have done what is detestable [an abomination]; they must be put to death; their blood will be on their own heads."* (Lev 20:13).

For the contemporary mentality, such a severe reprobation for the homosexual act is totally unacceptable, and we must try to understand the reasons behind it. In the New Testament, though the reprobation takes a different form, it is no less severe, even if the death penalty for this transgression is no longer applicable. I shall consider first the Holiness Code, then Rom 1:16–32, in an effort to draw out theological and anthropological principles that may help modern people to understand better why the biblical texts condemn homosexual practice. After considering other aspects of homosexuality that help to explain the reasons for the traditional Judeo-Christian position, I will conclude Section IV with a brief look at 1 Cor 6:9–11. An extensive literature has been devoted to these texts, of course, and I have no pretensions to do exhaustive exegesis; but in the context of my overall discussion, certain points do need to be drawn out.

The word translated "abomination" is *to'ebah* in the Hebrew. Arthur Goldberg, in his detailed book on homosexuality, *Light in the Closet*, points out that Bar Kappara, one of the eminent Second Century Sages of the Talmud, proposes a popular etymology for the Hebrew term that suggests "that those who engage in homosexual behavior are 'straying' or have been 'led astray.'"[1] This reading broadens the term's connotation and opens the way for a lengthy discussion of *teshuvah*, or repentance, e.g., the possibility held out by God to sinners—to all (all of us) who "go astray" and leave the path of divine Law—to turn and recover themselves and receive forgiveness. Divine grace is held out, for this as for all sins. It remains the case, however, that it is this strong word *to'ebah* that is used here as a characterization of the male homosexual act, which, as Goldberg observes, "is the only prohibited activity to which the Torah applies the label *to'ebah* twice—that is, in two separate places."[2] And it remains the case that this act, along with other acts, principally sexual, that are under God's curse according to the Old Testament Holiness Code, incurs the death penalty. Why is this?

Chapters 18 and 20 of Leviticus deal primarily with sexual sins (bestiality, incest, male homosexuality), sorcery and the practice by mediums of consulting the dead, and the sacrifice by Israelites of offspring to the Canaanite god of the dead, Molech. All these practices are considered to be detestable and worthy of death because they are forms of idolatry that defile the people of God and lead to death and disorder. They involve the crossing of natural limits and the annulment of fundamental distinctions, such as those between male and female, father and daughter, human and animal. It is precisely this kind of crossing of natural limits that is leading to moral confusion and rampant social disorder in our own day, as I argued in Part I. Chapter 19 of Leviticus, sandwiched between chapters 18 and 20, sets out commandments bearing chiefly on ordinances and social

1. Goldberg, op. cit., 192.

2. Ibid., 300–301.

relations that promote order and justice in the community. It is significant that chapter 19 opens with an injunction to be holy: *"The Lord said to Moses, 'Speak to the entire assembly of Israel and say to them: Be holy because I, the Lord your God, am holy. Each of you must respect his mother and father, and you must observe my Sabbaths. I am the Lord your God. Do not turn to idols or make gods of cast metal for yourselves. I am the Lord your God."* (Lev 19:1–4). This call to holiness is set over against the defiling practices listed in the previous chapter, common to the inhabitants of Canaan whom God is punishing for their iniquity by driving them out of the land; and the same call concludes chapter 20, after a reiteration of the same defiling practices: *"You are to be holy to me because I, the Lord, am holy, and I have set you apart from the nations to be my own."* (Lev 20:26).

The Holiness Code is directed specifically to the people of Israel and involves precise ordinances and commandments. Holiness involves being separated out from the nations and consecrated to Yahweh, the Holy God who has revealed himself to this Semitic tribe, the descendants of Abraham. At the heart of the Holiness Code is the presence of Yahweh himself, the true and only God. He is not like other "gods", he is not an idol; worship offered him cannot be like worship offered to the idols/gods of the surrounding pagan tribes. The statutes and ordinances Yahweh prescribes to this Semitic people, chosen to be the vehicle of God's self-revelation to the world, are the juridical equivalent and confirmation in the context of Canaan of the separation from the pagan world signified by the exodus from Egypt. *"The Lord said to Moses, 'Speak to the Israelites and say to them: I am the Lord your God. You must not do as they do in Egypt, where you used to live, and you must not do as they do in the land of Canaan, where I am bringing you. Do not follow their practices."* (Lev 18:1–3). The call to be holy as God is holy; the call to belong to this holy God, to live in his presence and obey his commandments, is thus to be understood as a call to freedom from idolatry and the injustice, oppression, and uncleanness that accompany it, as expressed in the defiling practices of the nations.

These practices lead to disordered social relations where exploitation and injustice prevail and sexual anarchy is rampant. It is not by chance that the Second Commandment of which Jesus speaks in Matt 22:39, Mark 12:31 and Luke10:27, appears in the middle of the Holiness Code: *"You shall not pervert justice; do not show partiality to the poor or favoritism to the great, but judge your neighbor fairly. . . . Do not hate your brother in your heart. . . . Do not seek revenge or bear a grudge against one of your people, but love your neighbor as yourself: I am the Lord."* (Lev 19:15,17a,18).

As suggested in the text at the beginning of Leviticus 19, quoted above, revering father and mother and keeping God's Sabbaths are central to holiness, as is the rejection of idolatry. These commandments, in context, refer first to social relations, as ordered basically by the family; then to the relationship with God, whose being as Creator and Redeemer is recalled by the weekly practice of the Sabbath (see Exod 20:8–11 and Deut 5:12–15); and finally to the idolatrous relation with false gods that turn men and women from proper sexual relationships within the bond of marriage, ordered to mutual satisfaction and procreation, to perverted, sterile relationships that defile those who practice them, give rise to physical illnesses and psychological disorder and instability, and destroy familial and social harmony.

Both in the beginning of chapter 18 and in the end of chapter 20, the practices of the pagan nations are condemned. The words in Lev 20:22–23 echo those in Lev 18:1–3, cited above: *"Keep all my decrees and laws and follow them, so that the land where I am bringing you to live may not vomit you out. You must not live according to the customs of the nations I am going to drive out before you. Because they did all these things, I abhorred them."* The bulk of practices condemned in the Leviticus texts have to do with sexual sins, some of them associated with public rituals. These involved the exaltation of lust and self-serving passion. Such practices break down family structures and so undermine social stability and the integrity of the nation. The individual ego and its gratification are at their core, rather than the family, the wider community, and God. Attention—indeed, *worship*, in the case of the public rituals—is deflected from the Creator to an aspect of his creation—to that aspect, in fact, which involves fertility, i.e. creation/procreation, the very work of the Creator himself. This is why, ultimately, these sexual practices constituted idolatry and were abhorrent to Yahweh.

The fact that many of the pagan religious practices in Canaan and elsewhere are devoted to gods and goddesses of fertility and involve "sacred" prostitution and orgies, is proof of their idolatrous nature. Sexuality as such and its perverted—unholy—expression is one of the chief vehicles of the proliferation of "gods", as over against the One God, Holy and Unique, before whom the Israelites are commanded to have no other (Deut 5:6–8). This goes far toward explaining why, according to this and other Scriptural texts, God condemns unbridled sexuality and commands his people to separate themselves from the surrounding nations that indulge in it. Exclusive allegiance to a Holy God is the unifying theme that underlies the entire Holiness Code.

The sexual impulse is, of course, one of the most powerful forces in nature. If uncontrolled, it leads to personal and social breakdown. Indeed, uncontrolled sexuality in a given society is a sign that the society is already beginning to disintegrate. Pathologies and violence of various kinds accompany this breakdown. In Near Eastern ancient pagan societies, the obvious association of sexuality with the fertility necessary to the perpetuation of the society tended to lead to religious practices of an orgiastic nature, in which the appeasing and imploring of gods and goddesses like Baal and Ishtar served as pretexts for unbridled sexuality. Again, idolatry and sexual license are seen to go together.

It is against this background that the words to do with man and woman in the beginning of Genesis take on their full meaning: "*So God created man in his own image, in the image of God he created him; male and female he created them. God blessed them and said to them, 'Be fruitful and increase in number, fill the earth and subdue it.'*" (Gen. 1:27–28); and "*For this reason a man will leave his father and mother and be united to his wife, and they will become one flesh.*" (Gen 2:24). At the heart of the mandate given by the Creator to mankind—to his created image in his creation—is the command to be fertile; but this fertility is to be ordered within and disciplined by the institution of marriage. Woman belongs to man and man to woman; it is together that they make up a whole—human being—which represents God in his creation. Both fertility and marriage are gifts from God, for man's benefit and the Creator's glory. Sexuality and fertility together are posited as being at the absolute center of the Creation order and God's purpose for his world. It is because of this truth that they occupy such a central place in biblical ethics, and that their misuse and perversion are so severely reprimanded.

II.IV.2

Moral decadence; the breakdown of the social order; identity confusion

None of this has changed. By that I mean: the *moral* prescriptions of the Holiness Code, the *sexual practices* the Code prohibits, the *breakdown of the social order* when these practices are indulged in—none of this has changed. God has not changed. God has not modified the call to holiness and the basic ethical requirements that he makes of his people. Of course, many of the ordinances in the Torah have been rendered obsolete, even for Jews, by changed social conditions and, for Christians, by the fulfillment of the just requirements of the Law by Jesus Christ (see Rom 8:1–4); but the prohibitions connected with sexuality, which have their theological *raison d'être* in the Creation order itself and are clearly linked with idolatry and the maintenance of social order and proper boundaries, have not been annulled. To declare that they have been because the modern context is "different", is an arbitrary assertion. The fact that Western society, including parts of the Western Church, wants to make this assertion, and that the liberal sectors of the mainline Protestant churches loudly proclaim the provisions of the Holiness Code to be obsolete because a supposedly new form of homosexual expression has emerged in our time—i.e. monogamous union—changes nothing whatsoever about God, the truth of his commandments, and the responsibility of human beings—in particular those who call themselves God's people and have in principle received his revelation—to obey them.

The disorder, impurity, and violence that God's prohibitions are meant to prevent are as evident in our contemporary secularized Western societies as they were in Canaanitic society three thousand years ago. The existence today of monogamous homosexual unions, where these may be found, does not alter this, even though such unions are undoubtedly superior to random promiscuity and pederasty. I want to insist, again, that God is against *practices*, not persons. Indeed, his opposition to the *practices* of homosexuality, incest, and bestiality, as well as the other behavior condemned in the Holiness Code, is for the *good* of persons, individually and corporately. It is because of the modern ideology of individualism/consumerism, which provides no criterion for ethical action other than pleasure, and no social vision beyond the demand for individual "rights", that Western people today are more and more blinded to the rising social chaos and confusion due to the overthrow of the Judeo-Christian spiritual and ethical heritage. The moral decadence in Western society today, the compromised leadership, the corrupt politics, the rapacious corporate practices, the acceptance of casual abortion, the sexual profligacy, the aimlessness, dispiritedness, and fear to be seen in the lives of so many young (and not so young) people—all result in large measure from the collapse of the moral consensus. The *baby* of our Christian heritage is being thrown out with the *bathwater* of the Church's not infrequent failures at many levels to live up to its calling. And it must be added, as I wrote in Part I, that the strident, warped religiosity of many people in America today who call themselves "Christian" can only contribute to this rejection.

Self-righteous neo-pagans, with their furious judgment of God and the Christian Church and their willful refusal to recognize the fruits of the Gospel in human society, seem to have no notion that their unrestrained "rave party" is nudging their society to the edge of a precipice. Or perhaps they *do* have a notion of this danger and, in their inner despair, are simply intent on committing suicide. The rave-party and the technological accoutrements that make it possible confine the party-goers to an inebriated immediacy and set out no hope for any desirable future. It is not incidental that procreation is by no means the highest priority in Western populations today. If in the ancient world the association of sexuality with fertility rites provided at the public level a pretext for orgiastic license, in our own day it is the *dissociation* of sexuality and fertility, made possible by the techniques of contraception, that provides such license.[3] Consumerist behavior, orchestrated by the big corporations

---

3. In a recent issue of *Touchstone* Douglas Farrow, alluding to an article by Elizabeth Anscombe published in 1975 entitled "Contraception and Chastity," points out that contraceptive intercourse, by eliminating the bond between the unitive and the reproductive aspects of marriage, eliminates with it "any solid reason for confining sexual intimacy to the marital act" (Farrow, "Why Fight Same-Sex Marriage?"; online: *Touchstone Archives*, 9).This technological intrusion into the natural processes of reproduction opens the door to utilitarian sex and to every form of manipulation that can be imagined and performed according to the modern idol/ideology of pleasure and convenience. The sexual act is abstracted from the natural order that entails the possibility of pregnancy and fecundity, an order that is pre-political and objective, in that it does not depend either on a prior humanly devised political entity or on the feelings or will of the persons involved. Less noticed perhaps is that, with this deliberate removal of the reproductive possibility, the *unitive* power of the sexual act is *also* diminished, since personal pleasure gains precedence over mutual commitment and its consequences, there being no longer the constraint of a potential pregnancy and child that normally engages the shared moral responsibility of the parents towards that child. Modern persons living by the norms of pleasure and convenience may think their individuality and self-fulfillment are enhanced by their liberation, through contraceptive devices, from the "fear of pregnancy" or the "burden of a child", but there is grave self-deception operating here. It is not recognized that both they and the child/children they avoid having are being "depersonalized", precisely to the extent that the sexual relations are *self-* rather than *other*-focused. The dignity of all concerned is being diminished as ephemeral satisfactions displace long-term bonding in a mutual love and commitment that willingly makes room for the struggles, ups and downs, and self-sacrifices required to build deep relationships that are of permanent public

and the media and exacerbated by the pornography and the "encounter culture" promulgated over the internet, finds in hedonism and sexual profligacy its consummate expression. Baal and Ishtar are no less present with us today than they were in the ancient Near East.

To the Israelites, to the Church, and to the wider world, God is saying through the Holiness Code that such behavior, which is contrary to the Creation order and an affront to the Creator, can lead only to societal disintegration. This is what is happening to Western civilization in our time. The decline of the traditional family, the devaluation of marriage understood as a lifelong covenant between a man and a woman, the frequency of abortion, the banalization of adultery and divorce, the spread of the practice of euthanasia, all these trends lead to the psychological instability and identity confusion of millions of fathers, mothers, and children. Inevitably, as a consequence, we are seeing homosexual expression gaining general acceptance in Western societies, along with a growing approval among people who consider themselves "progressive", of gender confusion, trans-sexuality, pornography, and promiscuous sex in general. All this is accompanied by a rising rate of international sex-trafficking, child abuse, drug abuse, delinquency, crime, and the spread of a penal culture. Sexually transmitted diseases like HIV/AIDS are affecting tens of millions of people across the world. In America, distrust and hostility between the sexes and between the generations is more common than it used to be, as is domestic violence and violence between young people themselves. Taken together, these are symptoms of societal crisis. We do not have statistics from the past with which to compare current behavior patterns in every one of these areas, but judging by the ever-increasing exposure these issues receive, it does not seem unreasonable to infer that their incidence, on the whole, is also steadily increasing.

The flouting of God's ordinances is leading not to greater freedom but to the breakdown of law and order in general and, in reaction, to increased surveillance and repression by the "guardians of order". Modern men and women, while experiencing unprecedented mobility, at the same time, ironically, feel squeezed from all sides, unable to breathe, their lives terminally constricted. We are always on the run—running away from something or running to get somewhere. A common form of our

---

interest because they structure the kind of solid marriages and families needed to sustain a healthy society. Abortion as a common recourse to avoid embarrassment or unwanted responsibilities flows naturally from the contraceptive disposition, as does, eventually, the notion of same-sex "marriage".

running is our refusal to take moral responsibility for our actions. The typical modern individual has no time for moral reflection. He may experience guilt at wrongdoing, but tends to justify his actions and avoid taking blame. Bombarded by information, solicited ceaselessly by noise and images that flit across her mind like specks across her retina, she is perpetually *distracted* and knows neither stillness nor silence. Contemporary forms of what is called "meditation"—a widespread practice intended to offset the centrifugal forces of modern life—normally lack an ethical component and are focused narcissistically on the "self" and the self's "actualization" (whatever that means). As I suggested above, these are properly to be understood simply as *techniques*, characteristic of the technological nature of everything we do, rather than as genuine quests for spiritual and moral enlargement.

Fear and anxiety track contemporary men and women. In reaction to our sense of impotence and self-hatred, we fall into desolation or resort, as I have said, to "technical" solutions or diversions, which in turn lead not infrequently to forms of dependency and addictions, or to the greed, dishonesty, and abuse that we find today at every level of society. I pointed out earlier that the suicide rate in the West, and particularly among the young, increases from year to year, signaling the exhaustion and inner hopelessness of our contemporary culture.

Identity confusion is everywhere. With regard to the family, fathers in particular have lost the sense of their position and responsibility, with the result that families lack proper authority, discipline, and direction.[4]

4. There are many reasons for this, such as the terrible decimation of men in the wars of the twentieth century; the nature of work in a free market capitalist economy, where the imperatives of mobility and flexibility imposed by deregulated labor markets put enormous stress on families; the often prolonged absences from home of men in particular, due to the demands of their jobs and the frequent requirement to travel; financial pressures that often make it necessary for both spouses to hold jobs and to work away from the home; the expansion of women's rights and the changing place of women in society, with the challenge this poses to men and their natural drive to be dominant; the rise in divorce and in one-parent families; the decline of the sense of family cohesion, with the parents and children going about their separate business with their separate schedules, and all of them spending much of their time staring mutely and uncommunicatively at screens or manipulating handheld electronic gadgets to the exclusion of everyone and of everything around them; the elimination, by technological advances, of a great deal of the heavy physical labor that validated men and gave them a clear identity that women could not emulate or equal; the feminist movement *as an ideology*, in particular on its negative side, with its rejection of the man and the father; and gender theory, with its flattening out of gender distinctions. The apparent increase of overt homosexual practice is undoubtedly caused in part by

The feminist movement, in its aggressive "anti-men" dimension, is partly a result of this and partly a cause. Often the fathers simply cop out and run off, to find another woman (or man!) or to make more money. The children flounder, and the number of single mothers increases from year to year. This is a cause of great suffering and resentment. The problem of delinquent fathers, single mothers, and effectively un-parented children (despite the mothers' best efforts), is at the heart of many problems in contemporary society, not the least of which is what certainly appears to be an increase in homosexual behavior, or at least in the degree of publicity attached to homosexuality. The father-figure is rejected, and with it the figure of God-the-Father, the Father of Jesus Christ, from whom, as St. Paul puts it, *"his whole family in heaven and on earth derives its name"* (Eph 3:15). We judge God by the standard of our earthly fathers, whereas in truth, authentic fatherhood, without which no society can have stability and peace, is rooted ultimately in God the Father, of whom God the Son—Jesus—is the perfect reflection (John 14:7–10).

People are *dis-oriented*, in the strong sense of that word. Bitterness and acrimony are corroding the social fabric. Respect and courtesy are disappearing from the spheres of education and politics. Contempt for authority of any kind, and gratuitous denigration of those one disagrees with, is now commonplace. The old fear the young, the young despise the old. Despite major moral advances today in areas like the demand for equal rights for women, the concern for the rights of handicapped persons and for minorities (including homosexuals), the battle against sexual slavery, the development of international tribunals to prosecute crimes against humanity, and the expanding "green" consciousness that the planet and other living species must be treated with respect, our society is oriented *spiritually* downwards towards death and is growing increasingly chaotic. In Part I of this essay, I outlined the basis for this judgment.

Moral license, resulting itself from the rejection of transcendence and the divine order and expressing itself most visibly in the areas of sexuality, corruption, and rampant greed, is at the root of this disorder. It is "politically incorrect" to say this, a fact that is itself a symptom of the underlying condition. Moral relativism and laxism have so undermined our ethical sense that few people in our culture today can even tolerate the notion of moral wrong-doing, much less condemn it as the

---

the "flight of the father" in contemporary society, and this in turn contributes to the uncertainty and confusion many men feel today about their male identity and what it means to be a man.

basic cause of the irresponsible narcissism, self-indulgence, and deceit prevalent in our society. The flaunting of homosexuality as a way of life equal to, even superior to, heterosexuality, constitutes the most obvious outward sign of this disorder and the ultimate emblem of humanity's rebellion against God the Creator. It is not that homosexuality is essentially worse than other transgressions prohibited by the Torah, but its nature is so flagrantly at odds with the principles of male/female *complementarity* and *fertility* enshrined in the created order, and with the fundamental distinctions and limits which that order establishes, that it serves as a patent symbol of human rebellion against the Creator and is a clear indication of the breakdown in healthy relationships between men and women.

God gave to the Hebrew people centuries ago a code of behavior intended for their good and ultimately, as disseminated worldwide by the Church's proclamation of the Gospel, for the good of all humankind. To the extent that, under the influence of the Christian Gospel, there has been an aspiration in Western civilization over the centuries to adhere, at least somewhat, to the ordinances of that code, in particular to the statutes concerning justice and sexual behavior, conditions for human flourishing have been created that have progressively brought great benefits for the nations of the world, even if the failures and sins of the West have wrought havoc alongside those benefits. The modern refusal to abide by the moral terms of that code is a key factor leading to the moral subversion and decline of Western civilization.

II.IV.3

Repentance by much of the Christian Church for rejection of homosexuals in the past; Gay Lobby propaganda, adopted by the liberal Churches; in Christian community, we are first of all sons and daughters of God: divisions between social groups are transcended and become sources of diversity

I have already pointed out that in the past the Church has gravely erred in condemning homosexuals rather than focusing on the *practice* of homosexuality and helping persons with same-sex leanings to enter into the new life promised through the Gospel. As a result, people of homosexual orientation, who have not infrequently suffered abuse or been brought up in dysfunctional families, have been marginalized and made to feel like a noxious sub-group, when what they have needed and need—like all of us—is compassion and kindness. Many Christian confessions have repented of this sinful and completely un-Christian attitude, and thousands of gay persons are being welcomed by the Church and helped to find the fullness of their gender identity.

It is vital for the Church at large to understand that this help, to be effective, must take the form of *authentic community*. Such community has to be at the core of Christian life and mission in our day, as it has always been at the core of any successful implantation of the Gospel in the past. Church culture, especially in the West, has put so much emphasis on the good of *marriage* that single persons, voluntarily or involuntarily celibate, have often felt left out. This has discouraged them from participation in the Church, and surely it laid the ground for the move of many singles toward the gay community once the wider social conditions were ripe, in a quest for the warmth and comradeship the Church was failing to provide. As was evident when the HIV/AIDS crisis broke out in America in the 80s, the gay community displayed genuine solidarity and care for its own, of the kind that Christian churches are always called upon to show but sometimes *fail* to show.

Our churches should welcome gay persons, whether or not at the outset they have any intention of modifying their behavior. The Gospel, the summons to holiness, and the power of God to change us, must be declared clearly from the pulpit; but it must also be declared clearly from the pulpit that we are called to honor others for and in themselves, quite aside from, and prior to, any conversion they may experience. That is the way God loved us in Christ (I John 4:10,19; Rom 5:8). For persons seeking to leave the gay community and a gay lifestyle, individual pastoral counseling, even the most compassionate and perspicuous, cannot alone bring them into the liberation they may be seeking. The gay identity is shadowed by an inner loneliness. The narcissism of the homosexual community, while providing an *ersatz* shelter and "home" for its gay members, as was evidenced in the AIDS crisis mentioned above, cannot satisfy the human being's need for the "other". Gender tribalism is out of line ontologically with the way men and women are made. We need *each other* in order to be fulfilled. It is obvious that coming out of the gay lifestyle and entering upon a *baptismal* lifestyle in its place is a messy and prolonged operation and requires the sustained love and support of others, both men and women. Authentic Christian communities can provide this. Regrettably, their number is not great, and church parishes are often far from being such communities; but where they exist, and where the Holy Spirit is powerfully active, the means are present to assist gay persons to enter gradually into the freedom of Christ, through the identification with Jesus' death and resurrection to which the Apostle Paul alludes in Rom 6:10–12: *"The death he [Jesus] died, he died to sin, once for all; but the life he lives, he lives to God. In the same way, count yourselves dead to sin but alive to God in Christ Jesus. Therefore do not let sin reign in your mortal body so that you obey its evil desires."*

But two phenomena are pulling in a different and dangerous direction from the picture I am presenting here: first, the radical Gay Lobby, and second, the positive acceptance by the liberal Protestant churches, notably TEC, of the Gay Lobby's propaganda and political/social agenda. Both of these movements are hostile to rational discussion with those who oppose their views. It is not just acceptance they are after, but power and wide influence. The epithet "homophobe" is flung viciously at anyone and everyone who doesn't assent to the Gay Lobby's line, without the slightest nuance or respect of persons. Traditional positions on sexuality are scorned. A hunger for vindication, even revenge, for the contempt shown towards homosexuals in the past, manifestly drives the Lobby, to the point that to speak of the idolatrous absolutization of their goal is not an exaggeration. One can understand this, as I have said several times in this essay; but such an agenda must be strongly contested. As to the liberal churches, a species of fixation on this issue drives its own agenda, with the aim of appropriating and refashioning the ethical vision of Scripture and the Christian tradition under the deceptive banner of "justice and human rights". This too must be strongly contested.

The issue of idolatry is as important here as it was in biblical times. All across the spectrum of the liberal churches, one finds the presence of "gay and lesbian groups" that, as such, meet together to discuss their particular situation. Homosexuality and its acceptance by the Church at large, not the Gospel or the possible transformation of their lives, appear to be their chief preoccupation, and their guiding assumption, apparently unquestioned, is that God created them gay and that this is their fundamental identity (I examined this point in II.III.5). The whole reality of a life transfigured through the *"power of God for . . . salvation"* (Rom 1:16) hardly gets a look-in, since the clergy of these churches believe firmly in "the cause" and do not countenance the traditional biblical perspective. Operative here is what the chairman of the St. Andrew's Day Group calls "affective fundamentalism": *This is the way we feel, so this is what we are.*

Christ is made captive to sexual *feelings* and "orientation". "Here lies the path to the secret domestication of God, far from the historical Jesus and his theological context."[5]

I do not question the sincerity of these "special interest" groups, for they find themselves in churches that pose no challenge to their assumptions about their gay identity and offer no assistance to those who wish to move from this identity, through the strength of Christ's love, into a heterosexual lifestyle, either as celibate or as married. Nor, surely, are their intentions idolatrous, as I observed earlier, though the intensity of their preoccupation with themselves and their own "sexual identity"—a pervasive self-referentiality—can have an obsessive, idolatrous feel to it, as if their sexuality were the fundamental source of their identity, rather than Christ and the *new being* that they are in him. However this may be, in the conservative churches they may still—most regrettably—feel a lack of real communal welcome, and in the liberal churches they are left with their inner confusion and the vain labor of poring over Scripture to find some way of reinterpreting its texts to justify their position. Clearly they still find their primary identity in their gay orientation, not in their being sons and daughters of the Father. Christianity ought to have no place for *categories* of Christians, such as "pygmy" Christians, or "Japanese" Christians, or "white" Christians, or "Tutsi" Christians, or "female" Christians, or "gay" Christians. Believers in Christ who are baptized and seek to follow him are Christians, *tout court*. To *categorize* Christians is to fall back into the world's way and place a perceived natural identity before, or above, the son or daughter of God that the person becomes who dies and rises in identification with the crucified and risen Christ (John 1:12; Rom 6:4).

Regrettably, in the present climate of self-pity coupled with vindictiveness that characterizes the culture in general, gay people tend to see themselves as victims. For Christians, this self-understanding, even when there is some truth in it, is to be left behind upon commitment to Christ. Jesus became voluntarily a Victim for us, precisely so that any sense we may have—for whatever reason—of ourselves as being in some fundamental way "victims", might be overcome and replaced by our self-understanding that we are persons in whom Christ lives his risen life ("*On that day you will realize that I am in my Father, and you are in me, and I am in you.*" John 14:20; Gal 2:20). In Christ we are "conquerors"

---

5. Bradshaw, op. cit., 221.

(*"No, in all these things* [sufferings] *we are more than conquerors through him who loved us."* Rom 8:37). Gay Christians are, at the very least, in a state of confusion and need the truthful love of the Good News mediated through the Church. They do not need to be confirmed, even "blessed", in their "orientation", and told that all is well, *when it isn't*.

The primary social categories that differentiate and, in the disorder of the fallen world, *divide* human beings from each other, are transcended in Christ, as persons are lifted from the confining conditions of their natural birth into the new reality of the Kingdom of God. This is what the new birth and baptism are all about, and what makes possible the love that characterizes *authentic* Christian community and the ethics that give that love practical expression. The primary identity of a Christian, whatever his or her natural state or sexual proclivity, is to be an adopted son or daughter of God the Father in and through the Eternal Son, Jesus Christ, and a brother or sister of all other believers, incorporated into the family of God. It is on this basis—this new identity—that a person can go on to grow in virtue and spiritual maturity and be progressively transformed into Christ's image:

> *Before this faith came, we were held prisoners by the Law, locked up until faith should be revealed. So the Law was put in charge to lead us to Christ that we might be justified by faith. Now that faith has come, we are no longer under the supervision of the law. You are all sons of God through faith in Christ Jesus, for all of you who were baptized into Christ have clothed yourselves with Christ. There is neither Jew nor Greek, slave nor free, male nor female, for you are all one in Christ Jesus. If you belong to Christ, then you are Abraham's seed, and heirs according to the promise.* (Gal 3:23–29)

For Christians, the fundamental distinguishing categories of human life, whether natural or conventional, are not annulled, obviously, but are henceforth placed on a secondary plane relative to the unifying identity as children of God in Jesus Christ. Gender, race, and ethnicity cease to have the *absolute* value as identify tags that turns them so easily into objects of idolatry and hence of fear, hatred, and violence.[6] The "other" moves from

6. Proponents of the gay agenda often cite Gal 3:28 as evidence that gender is no longer final as a category for the Christian, and that therefore the argument against homosexual practice based on gender complementarity loses its force and is rendered basically obsolete. This is tendentious exegesis. The context for Paul's assertion is a discussion of Law and faith. The Jewish Law, given by God, radically separated Jew from Gentile, that is, God's chosen people from pagans who had no direct revelation from God; but both Jew and Gentile were imprisoned under the power of sin, and the Law

being an object of fear and suspicion to being an object of wonder and delight, as is so simply and paradigmatically portrayed in Gen 2:21–23, before the Fall, when Eve is presented to Adam: *"So the Lord God caused the man to fall into a deep sleep; and while he was sleeping, he took one of the man's ribs and closed up the place with flesh. Then the Lord God made a woman from the rib he had taken out of the man, and he brought her to the man. The man said, 'This is now bone of my bones and flesh of my flesh; she shall be called 'woman', for she was taken out of man.'"*

It is this text, underwriting the fundamental diversity in creation, which is followed by the text cited earlier concerning marriage: *"For this reason a man shall leave his father and mother and be united to his wife, and they will become one flesh"* (Gen 2:24). The union of the two distinct yet homogeneous persons retains the distinction between them even while incorporating them into a fertile unity that embodies and expresses love. This diversity in unity is both an image of the Trinity—the Father, Son, and Holy Spirit who, being of one divine essence, constitute the One God—and emblematic of the whole of the created order, in which the infinite diversity of creatures is coordinated in a vast ecological unity. Of this harmonious unity, it was the Creator's intention that humankind— man and woman—be the keeper and cultivator, preserving, observing, and serving his created handiwork.[7] The relevance to this divine plan of the phenomenon of homosexuality will be explored shortly.

---

itself was unable to make the Jew righteous. Jesus the Messiah, through his obedient faithfulness to God, fulfilled the Law and so overcame sin and the curse of separation and division between human beings that it created, of which the Jew/Gentile hostility was a patent social example. The oppositional categories listed in the Galatians passage remain intact as realities in the natural sphere, but Christ's redemptive achievement opens the way for those who are in Christ by grace through faith (Christ's faith and their own God-given faith in him) to live in peace and harmony with each other in the *Spirit*, where before, in the *flesh* (used here in the Pauline sense of the unredeemed "natural man"), there was antagonism. The fact that henceforth, for the new creation in Christ that is the Church, the natural divisions are overcome *in principle* and natural categories become *secondary* identity tags rather than primary, does not mean that these categories are relativized and lose their significance in the order of creation (gender) or in the reality of culture. Where the authentic Gospel has spread and taken root and not been co-opted by political or racist interests, it has in fact slowly undermined some of these oppositions at the social level, such as "slave and free", and made inroads into ethnic and racial hatreds, and it has tended to improve relations between men and women; but this positive social effect has no relevance as such to the issue of ontological male/female identity and complementarity.

7. Davis, op. cit., 30–31, in the context of a discussion of the centrality of the land in the Genesis 2 creation narrative.

In chapter 3 of Genesis, this unity falls apart because of human-kind's pride and willful disobedience to the commandment of its Creator. Distrust between man and woman, and alienation of human beings from each other and from other creatures, immediately follow, with the tragic consequences that all cultures throughout history demonstrate.

It is on account of this broken reality that God called out Terah and his son Abraham from Ur of the Chaldeans, and then sent Abraham on toward the land of Canaan (Gen 11:31—12:3), as the first step in bringing communion and order back into an unruly and violent world. Abraham and his descendants, the Hebrews, later called the Jews, were "set apart" unto God as the bearers of the new covenant between God and human-kind that would be fulfilled ultimately by the Jewish Messiah, Yeshua (Je-sus). With Moses came the Law that codified the distinctiveness of this people through a fuller revelation of their God and an ethics that brought the holiness he demanded into their social structures.

The "specialness" of the Jews and their separation from Gentiles came to be seen over the centuries by both parties as fundamental and everlasting. In order to realize God's redemptive plan for humanity, which involved unity in diversity, both the Holy Law that set the Jews apart from the Gentiles and the unholy, idolatrous practices that characterized the pagan Gentiles, would have to be transcended, though no reconciliation of these two groups by merely human means was desired—or even imag-inable—by either party. It is this miracle that Christians believe occurred in the life and death of Jesus, the Son of God, who fulfilled the Law of love of God and neighbor required by the Mosaic revelation and thus brought within reach of all men and women the promise of blessing first made to Abraham so long before: *"I will make you into a great nation, and I will bless you; I will make your name great, and you will be a blessing. . . . and all peoples on earth will be blessed through you."* (Gen 12:2,3b). In Christ the fundamental barriers between human beings, represented paradigmati-cally by the "wall of hostility" between Jews and Gentiles, were broken down (Eph 2:11–22). The text quoted above from Paul's Epistle to the Ga-latians sums up this universal blessing rooted in the promise to Abraham and shows it to be precisely the restoration, through Christ's faith and our responding faith in him, of the unity in diversity and diversity in unity that characterized the original creation as represented by Adam and Eve, and that finds completion in God's Kingdom.

This reconciliation, achieved by the Jewish Messiah and made ac-cessible to men and women through his bloody but willingly accepted death on Calvary, has been met over the centuries more often than not with incomprehension and resistance by both Jews and Gentiles. Not for a moment, however, has this sad reality altered the truth of the reconciliation wrought by Christ, which stands available forever to those who will seize it by faith. At the heart of this resistance, of course, is the very sin that motivated God, in his mercy, to separate out for himself a people in the first place, in order to make his true Name and nature known to unruly men and women. At the core of that sin is the prideful rebellion against God the Creator and hence against God the *Re*-Creator in Christ. This rebellion has generated countless forms of idolatry in diverse cultures down through history, of which the most basic and visible is sexual depravity, the refusal to accept the norm of sexual fidelity within the frame of monogamous complementarity that was laid down in the Genesis creation texts and developed in the negative mode by the interdictions in the Holiness Code that we have looked at.

II.IV.4

Redemption in Christ; Romans 1 and divine judgment; the "natural" and "unnatural" with respect to homosexual activity

It is now time to look at the question of idolatry from a New Testament perspective and to go further by examining other reasons—all of them linked ultimately with idolatry—that will make it easier to understand the Scriptural hostility to homosexual practice. The New Testament text that refers most explicitly to homosexuality is Rom 1:16–32. To understand what is being said about homosexual practice, the references to it must be placed in their theological context. The Apostle Paul strongly disapproves of homoerotic activity, but his text is not about specific ordinances in the manner of the Holiness Code but about the rebellion that describes the general human condition and God's response to it: The text needs to be quoted at length:

> *I am not ashamed of the gospel, because it is the power of God for the salvation of everyone who believes: first for the Jew, then for the Gentile. For in the gospel a righteousness from God is revealed, a righteousness that is by faith from first to last, just as it is written: 'The righteous will live by faith'. The wrath of God is being revealed from heaven against all the godlessness and wickedness of*

men who suppress the truth by their wickedness, since what may be known about God is plain to them, because God has made it plain to them. For since the creation of the world God's invisible qualities—his eternal power and divine nature—have been clearly seen, being understood from what has been made, so that men are without excuse. For although they knew God, they neither glorified him as God nor gave thanks to him, but their thinking became futile and their foolish hearts were darkened. Although they claimed to be wise, they became fools and exchanged the glory of the immortal God for images made to look like mortal man and birds and animals and reptiles. Therefore God gave them over in the sinful desires of their hearts to sexual impurity for the degrading of their bodies with one another. They exchanged the truth of God for a lie, and worshipped and served created things rather than the Creator—who is forever praised. Amen. Because of this, God gave them over to shameful lusts. Even their women exchanged natural relations for unnatural ones. In the same way the men also abandoned natural relations with women and were inflamed with lust for one another. Men committed indecent acts with other men, and received in themselves the due penalty for their perversion. Furthermore, since they did not think it worth while to retain the knowledge of God, he gave them over to a depraved mind, to do what ought not to be done. They have become filled with every kind of wickedness, evil, greed, and depravity. They are full of envy, murder, strife, deceit and malice. They are gossips, slanderers, God-haters, insolent, arrogant and boastful; they invent ways of doing evil; they disobey their parents, they are senseless, faithless, heartless, ruthless. Although they know God's righteous decree that those who do such things deserve death, they do not only continue to do these very things but also approve of those who practice them.

That Paul calls the gospel "*the power of God for the salvation of everyone who believes*" (v.16), is the first point I want to stress. Richard Hays, in his finely crafted book, *The Moral Vision of the New Testament*, sums up the matter thus: "The gospel is not merely a moral or philosophical teaching that hearers may accept or reject as they choose; it is rather the eschatological instrument through which God is working his purpose out in the world."[8] The Gospel manifests God's righteousness in that it is the fulfillment of his promise first given to Abraham to bless humankind.

---

8. Hays, *Moral Vision*, 384. In the discussion that follows, I am indebted in particular to Hays for his careful analysis of the NT texts that refer to homosexuality.

It expresses his faithfulness to his own word, which is a word of mercy. In virtue of God's righteousness, the Father gave up his Son and the Son gave himself up in order to make salvation available to broken humanity.

This manifestation of divine righteousness has *power*—the tremendous power of *re*-creation, which is what the salvation proclaimed by the Church is all about. The same God who created and creates, also *re*-creates, and that *re*-creation is *redemption*. Through Christ, God grants forgiveness to the repentant sinner, puts to death the self-focused principle of rebellion in the person's heart, provides a new heart and spirit through the indwelling of his own Spirit, and raises up a new being, eager and able to live a life *unto God*. Entering into this new baptismal life, *"working out your salvation with fear and trembling"* (Phil 2:12b), is a slow and often painful process, as we shed one life and take on another. But the Spirit of God is working in us to make it happen: *". . . for it is God who works in you to will and to act according to his good purpose."* (Phil 2:13).

It is indifference to this re-creative power, and to the need for that power to be exercised on behalf of fallen human beings, including practicing homosexuals if they are to be made whole, that TEC is guilty of, as I have argued above. The power of the Gospel is the power to transform human lives from the inside out, to change the way we feel, think, and act. It is the same power that God deployed in his original act of creation. Its aim is not to dominate, as is so often the case when human power is in play, but to *redress, heal,* and *transfigure*. This truth, indeed, points us to the heart of the current problem, because it is precisely the nature of that original creation, as conveyed through the Scriptural revelation, that is called into question by the modern liberal churches. If one questions that revelation by reinterpreting it, one will question the *re*-creation in Christ—or the *need* for such a re-creation—that restores the original communion between a holy God and humankind. Churches that move in this revisionist direction make themselves liable to the indictment leveled by St. Paul in his Second Epistle to Timothy against some people in the *"last days"*, who are in the condition of *"having a form of godliness but denying its power"* (2 Tim 3:1, 5a).

The Torah, including the Holiness Code, had been given to Israel, and Israel had failed to abide by it. God's elect nation had frequently resorted to idolatry and pagan practices in the centuries preceding the destruction of Jerusalem and the deportation to Babylonia in the early sixth century BC, and later it had inclined to an exaggerated legalism on the one hand and then, under the Greek and Roman oppressors, to a heightened nationalism on the other, in which the sense of the nation as called ultimately to be a light to the Gentiles was lost sight of to a large extent in favor of an inward-turned, self-defensive posture of intrinsic superiority as God's specially elected and cherished people. At the time of Jesus, in certain sectors of the population, the Law itself and the election it objectified, had become practically an idol, drawing attention away from the Holy God himself to the instrument he had given—the Torah—the purpose of which was to train his people to know him and so to become like him, not just for themselves and because of some imagined spiritual superiority but for the sake of their own salvation and, through them, of that of the pagan Gentiles.[9]

It is the belief of the Church that Jesus Christ, as representative of Israel and hence of humanity as a whole, whose redemption was the ultimate aim of God's election of Israel, fulfilled the Law by showing unswerving love both to God and to man/woman and by making atonement in his own blood for the sins of his people and of all mankind. This love was the consummate manifestation of God's holiness and righteousness, of which the fruit in the context of human society, when human beings respond with gratitude and faith, is order and harmony between God and all his creatures. Love—or simple human devotion—without righteousness is quickly sapped and poisoned by selfishness, which is why the liberal Church's proclamation of divine love without a corresponding proclamation of God's holiness and the demands he makes upon us to be "born again" (John 3:3), to love him, our Lord, above all else, and to lead obedient, righteous lives, constitutes a radical distortion of the true picture of God and of the Gospel.

---

9. A number of passages in the New Testament point in this direction. See, for example, Jesus' diatribe against the Jewish scribes and Pharisees in Matthew 23, whom he accuses of hypocrisy because they adhere to the letter of the Law and neglect its ethical substance; and, in his Epistle to the Romans, Paul's reprimand of the Jews who boast of being a light to those who are in darkness but who do not act accordingly. Several texts in Deuteronomy make clear that God's election of Israel was because he *loved* them, not because they were superior or more righteous or more numerous than other peoples: chapters 4:35–38; 7:6–8; 9:4–6. God drove out the Canaanites because they were wicked, not because the Israelites were especially righteous. As to the vocation of the people of Israel to be the bearers to the whole world of the knowledge of the true God, it is implied in God's promise to Abraham in Gen 12:1–3 and then developed in the prophets, especially Isaiah. See Isa. 11:10; 42:5–10; 49:5–6; and Pss. 117:1–2 and 19:1–11, where the revelation of God given in creation is textually linked with that given in the Law.

Christ's fulfillment of the Law through his love and faithful obedience to the Father's will is the vehicle of salvation. In his own body, Jesus
took our sin and its penalty, death, down to death; then the Father raised
him into new life by the Holy Spirit. As our humanity was identified with
him in his death, it is identified with him in his resurrection. What God
accomplishes through Christ's redemptive act is the veritable *re-creation*
of humanity, the opening up for men and women of a new possibility
utterly beyond any power humanity has on its own. Human power has
many channels of expression and can accomplish many things, both
good and evil, but it is altogether powerless to re-establish communion
with a holy God. Humanity cannot save itself, try as it might; the history
of mankind has been marked by sustained tragedy to the extent that that
communion has been refused. I have investigated this theme in the Part I
of this essay.

In the Romans text cited above, the "*power of God for . . . salvation*",
which is the Gospel of Christ, is set alongside the "*wrath of God . . . being
revealed from heaven against all the ungodliness and wickedness of men who
suppress the truth by their wickedness . . .*" (v.18). In what follows, Paul ex-
poses the fundamental *sin* of humankind and then enumerates a variety of
sins that flow inevitably from it. The *sin*—what we may call "original sin"—
is rebellion against the Creator, that is, the prideful refusal to acknowledge
him as Creator and Master and to give him thanks for his work of creation.
Ingratitude is at the very core of what the Bible means by *sin* (see Rom
1:21). Men and women refuse to honor God and assert their autonomy, in
defiance of the obvious reality of the invisible God as seen notably in the
wonderful order and beauty of the visible universe he has made. Those who
rebel in this way are ungodly and become futile in their thinking, which
is a short way of saying that they think like fools and misuse God's gift
of reason. They become idolatrous, worshipping creatures rather than the
Creator. They "*. . . exchanged the glory of the immortal God for images made
to look like mortal man and birds and animals and reptiles.*" (v. 23). At the
heart of this idolatry is self-worship, the worship of Man. All the other idols
and ideologies that men and women erect and devote themselves to, which
take the place of the living Creator, come out from under the cloak, so to
speak, of this central idol, Man himself.

What is striking in the text that follows is that the "wrath of God"
is not said to be God's punishment visited like lightning—or like the
Flood—on deviant humankind; rather, it takes the form of God "giving
over", or "giving up" human beings to the consequences of their rebellion

and idolatry. The word in the Greek is *'paredoken'*, from the root *'para-didomi'*. Three times in short succession Paul uses it to describe God's action: vv.24, 26, 28. Interestingly, the same word also appears in Acts 7:42a, where Stephen, speaking before the Sanhedrin and recounting the history of the Israelites, recalls the idol of the golden calf in the desert and says: *"But God turned away and gave them over ('paredoken') to the worship of the heavenly bodies"*, that is, to demonic powers taking the form of idols and masquerading as divinities.

Divine judgment, we are being told, consists here in our being "given over" to the rotten fruits of our own idolatry, whose roots lie in our pride and covetousness. The Scriptures provide many instances of more direct divine judgment on evil, but in this passage judgment takes a more indirect form. The "fruits" of idolatry generate the havoc in human society and—we can add today—in our relations with nature and all other creatures. We cannot be under God's full blessing if we refuse to honor him by being grateful for his creation and obedient to his Word. The parallel with physical law is patent: if a person jumps off a high bridge, he/she will fall and die. Likewise, if he acts in an unholy way and goes against God's creation ordinances, he will be hardened spiritually and morally and will end up in a state of *confusion unto death*. This is the expression of God's wrath. We bring it upon ourselves. We act irrationally, misusing the moral freedom God has given us by thumbing our nose at the Giver of that freedom. God will not constrain us—he leaves us to our own devices. As the Scriptures make clear, he seeks ever to redeem us by his grace. Through our conscience and the Holy Spirit he calls us to repent; through the preaching of the Gospel he calls us to turn towards Christ: *"Or do you show contempt for the riches of his kindness, tolerance and patience, not realizing that God's kindness leads you towards repentance?"* (Rom 2:4). But God won't force us. If we pay no attention, he lets us go our way.

This is the human condition described by the Apostle in the Romans text. He is not detailing for God's people, in the manner of the Holiness Code, specific unlawful acts forbidden them, or saying that every human being does all these evil things; he is providing an empirical picture of the state of fallen humanity in which all of us are implicated. Homosexuality, again, is highlighted, not because it is a worse sin intrinsically than the other sins enumerated later in the text, but because it so manifestly demonstrates the rebellion against the Creator's design. "Paul's choice of homosexuality as an illustration of human depravity," comments Hays, "is not merely random: it serves his rhetorical purposes by providing a vivid image of humanity's primal rejection of the sovereignty of God the Creator."[10]

In parallel to the theme of God's "giving humanity over" to the degrading consequences of our own rebellion, Paul speaks three times in succession of our "exchanging" something divine or divinely approved for something depraved: vv. 22–23, 25, 26. This "exchanging" is idolatry. Truth about reality, evident from within the creation itself, is ignored and replaced by arbitrary human conceptions and immoral behavior. The right use of reason is perverted to serve the self-indulgent and self-glorifying aims of men and women. *"They exchanged the truth of God for a lie, and worshipped and served created things rather than the Creator—who is forever praised. Amen."* (v. 25). It is for this reason, declares the Apostle, that God "gives over humanity" to our degrading passions, and this statement is followed directly by the illustration of homosexuality, female and male (vv.26–27).

Paul calls homosexual practice "unnatural": (*para physin*) in v. 26. Although this was a commonplace way of describing homosexuality in Roman times, the growing number of defenders and proponents of homosexual practice in contemporary society would deny Paul's assertion and argue that such practice is in fact perfectly natural (*kata physin*). Of course it is natural in the sense that some human beings do it, but this obvious point cannot do hermeneutical justice to Paul's usage. Hays observes that Paul identifies "nature" with the *created order* and that his understanding "does not rest on empirical observation of what actually exists; instead, it appeals to a conception of what ought to be, of the world as designed by God and revealed through the stories and laws of Scripture."[11] Robert Gagnon, concluding his analysis of Paul's use of *physis*—"nature"—in his Epistles, writes: "In all these instances, 'nature' corresponds to the essential material, inherent, biological, or organic constitution of things as created and set in motion by God. Neither in Paul's thinking nor in our own do any of these uses pertain merely to personal preferences or prejudices, custom, a culturally conditioned sense of what is normal, or social convention. 'Nature' in these verses goes beyond what one feels and thinks to what simply 'is' by divine design."[12]

10. Hays, op. cit., 386.
11. Ibid. 387.
12. Gagnon, op. cit., 373.

In the fallen world that we live in, sin is "natural"; but, observes Gagnon, Paul himself never uses "nature" to refer to "conditions that are innate but due to sin operating in human flesh since the fall of Adam."[13] Coming at the issue from a different perspective, Jeffrey Satinover writes: "Sin is defined by God, not by nature. Sin is therefore not against nature but against God. . . .So natural is sin, and so unnatural are God's requirements, that almost the entirety of the Bible tells the story of man's inability to obey these requirements through his own natural effort."[14]

Modern skeptics, including homosexual activists, will scoff at the notion of a "created order" and call the concept of the world "designed by God" a myth. It is precisely this sort of mockery that the Apostle condemns as being the hallmark of human rebellion. Yes, God is invisible and the harmonious world he designed is not empirically observable; but both God's existence and that harmonious world can, Paul argues, be reasonably *inferred* from what is visible and demonstrable. The world as we have it points in numerous ways to the ideal order of nature that Paul evokes. O'Donovan makes the case, for example, that in the sphere of "values" we are perfectly aware of the difference between health and sickness and between life and death,[15] and while both sickness and death can be considered "natural" in one sense, in another sense the human yearning for health and peace and everlasting life reflects a hunger for an *ideal reality of which the source can only be in the creation itself*—intuited by the creature man, *imago Dei*—and not in some fantastical "elsewhere". This intuited ideal reality is sensed to be both prior to the "natural" world we know—the "fallen" world, theologically understood—and beyond it, awaiting eschatological fulfillment. Moreover, as I observed earlier, the incarnation of Christ reveals both divine and human nature as they truly are, and in the light of the Second Adam we can infer the godliness of the First Adam before the Fall.

At another level, modern science is providing stunning evidence for the amazing order of the universe and inter-connectedness of all reality, clearly pointing to God's *"eternal power and divine nature"* (Rom 1:20) for those whose minds are not blinded by the irrational thinking rooted in human pride.

13. Ibid.

14. Satinover, *Homosexuality*, 153. The author provides a thorough theological discussion of this point in ch. 10 of his book.

15. O'Donovan, op. cit., 94–96.

Returning to the question of homosexuality in connection with the "natural" and the "unnatural", we have abundant physical and sociological evidence in our day demonstrating the "unnaturalness" of homosexual practice. The health hazards—both physical and mental—of homoerotic activity are numerous and well-documented[16]. Anal intercourse and oral sex involving ejaculation in the mouth are unnatural in the sense that it is obvious to any disinterested observer that the organs involved are not naturally made for these purposes; but they are also unnatural in the sense that the lesions and diseases they frequently generate (e.g., rectal cancer, liver disease, bowel infections, streptococcal infections of the throat, mouth ulcers, high vulnerability to AIDS) are clearly harmful to health and life and the well-being of the individuals and the species. Not only are these sexual practices sterile and incapable of producing progeny, their uncleanness and inappropriateness militate against those who do them—against the *living*. Their evolutionary usefulness, to formulate the matter differently, is negative.

This is further confirmed by well-established data showing that the life expectancy of homosexuals is, on average, considerably lower than that of heterosexuals, and the suicide rate is higher. Older gay persons of both sexes are more likely than older heterosexuals to suffer from chronic physical and mental health problems, especially as the gay culture tends to be youth-oriented, with the result that acute loneliness or a lack of available care are common complaints among elders in the gay community. Facts like these patently demonstrate the "unnaturalness" of these "natural" practices that I have been discussing. That such practices are becoming common in Western society, even among heterosexual persons, in no way proves the contrary. What it *does* prove is the willful self-indulgence of fallen men and women and the *confusion unto death* that this entails, both for the individuals concerned and for the society at large. Any society welcoming such activity, even *promoting* it, as is the case in the West today, is fated to pay a huge cost, material, psychological, spiritual, and social. In light of this fact, the effectual endorsement by the mainline Protestant churches, with TEC in the lead, of homosexuality and the gay "identity", not only in society at

16. A thorough treatment of this subject is given in Jeffrey Satinover, *Homosexuality*. Francis MacNutt, *Can Homosexuality be Healed?* is also helpful, as is Goldberg, *Light in the Closet*. At the psychological level alone, in addition to the more commonly recognized physical problems arising from homosexual activity and listed above, gay persons frequently experience deep inner loneliness, depression, and sexual identity confusion, which cause great distress and suffering, often repressed by the sufferers themselves and unacknowledged by others.

large but also within the Church, is not only an affront to Christ, the author of life, but an astonishing example of shortsightedness and social irresponsibility. "*Although they know God's righteous decree*," writes the Apostle Paul disapprovingly, referring to a long list of vices including homosexual practice, "*. . . they not only continue to do these very things but also approve of those who practice them.*" (Rom 1:32).

II.IV.5

Complementarity of man and woman; solitude and homosexuality; decline of friendship; the quest for love

We come now to another reason for divine hostility to homosexual practice, rooted in the creation order. In Gen 1:27–29 the fundamental *equality* of man and woman is posited. Here we have the anthropological foundation for all human cultures. In chapter 2 man and woman are *differentiated*, within the framework of the established equality. The first description of woman that is found in the Creation account in Genesis 2 is that of "helper": "*So the man gave names to all the livestock, the birds of the air and all the beasts of the field. But for Adam no suitable helper was found.*" (Gen. 2:20) God then causes Adam (= *man*) to fall asleep and takes a rib from his side, with which he fashions Eve. Adam wakes, and God presents Eve to him. The man recognizes the woman as being *like* him—"*bone of my bones, flesh of my flesh*" (v.23a)—yet also *other* than he, *different*. He has found his partner. Ontologically, they are of one kind; yet they are two, *distinct*. Together—two persons with one essence—they are a reflection of the Creator—the Holy Trinity: Father, Son, and Holy Spirit—in whose image they are made, as Genesis chapter 1 reveals (v. 27). The verse that follows provides the natural consequence of this reality: "*For this reason a man will leave his father and mother and be united to his wife, and they will become one flesh.*" (v. 24). They are separate from each other, two human creatures, yet of one nature. They are complementary. Therefore they are attracted to each other irresistibly and cannot be fulfilled in separation. They are not self-sufficient. In their union is their fulfillment.

It cannot be so in the coming together of two gay persons. They join their solitudes, but cannot become a whole. At bottom they remain two solitudes. The yearning of Adam—man/male—for a mate/helper/partner *like him but different*—female—, as expressed in Gen 2:18, 20, is not satisfied. This is so even in a loving relationship where genuine affection and psychological satisfaction are experienced. Deep down there must remain an unfulfillment. This is because the two who meet in this relation are of the same sex. They are not counterparts. They do not complement each other, they *repeat* each other. In the other, each sees the *same*, not an *other*. It is not for nothing that sterility necessarily characterizes a "same-sex union". Life can only be engendered by the bonding of two creatures of the same species but having different sexual properties. At the highest level of physical creation—the human level—this aspect of biological life expresses *spiritual* life, that is, *love*, the mutual giving and receiving of two complementary, conscious, inspired beings, in a physical/spiritual union of which the fruit is new life. *Bearing*, as man and woman, the *image of God*, means that a man and a woman, coming together, can create (procreate)—they can *generate and bear children*. Procreation results from heterosexual union. The sign that even the most genuine and durable experience of love in a union of same-sex persons cannot bring deepest satisfaction and falls short of fulfillment, is its inability to engender biological life. The love it expresses falls short of the wholeness human beings long for.

Undeniably, heterosexual unions also invariably fall short of such wholeness—but *differently*. This is on account of sin, manifested in a different form. Indeed, the plenitude of our true humanity can only be discovered as we come to know the Creator who made us in his image and who redeems us in Christ so that we may be conformed to that image. But there is a "horizontal" corollary to this: our full humanity can only be discovered as we know and are known by the opposite sex. I am not talking here about sexual intercourse, but about the openness and availability of a person's deep heart to the other gender. Our sexuality and gender identity involve our whole person and are by no means limited to erotic contact. Celibacy therefore certainly does not rule out the possibility of fulfilled love and human flourishing, since celibate persons, in their deep heart, can be joined with persons of the opposite sex in friendship and work and prayer. Within the Church, of course, those Christians who receive an actual *vocation* to celibacy (see 1 Cor 7:7; Matt 19:12) are married to *Christ* in a special way—not a *better* way from that of married Christians, but a *different* way—being celibate members of his Bride, the Church.

Our humanity, as sexual beings, is fulfilled as we know the *other than ourselves*, that is, God and the other gender. Gay persons, at the deepest level of their bodies and souls, remain in some sense *solitary*, to the extent that their particular consciousness of who they are sets up, by definition, an inner barrier between themselves and the opposite sex. They may have warm relations with persons of the opposite sex, of course—perhaps even a yearning for real closeness—but to the degree that the inner barrier makes a deep *joining* with the other practically unthinkable, a profound loneliness—half-conscious, perhaps—will remain; and this will be the case *even if* they have found God—that is, have been found by him—or *even if* they have established a stable relationship with a same-sex partner and managed to stay clear of the promiscuity that so grievously manifests the innate hunger for love which generally characterizes the homosexual condition.

One of the saddest features of modern life is the decline of strong, non-erotic friendships between persons of the same sex, in particular between men. Such friendships between gay and non-gay persons exist, of course, as they do between gay persons living in a celibate way, but modern pressures make it difficult to develop these. Whether, statistically, there has been a big increase in homosexual practice in the last generation, cannot be proved, but there certainly has been a huge increase in the public focus on the phenomenon of homosexuality. This undoubtedly contributes to the decline of non-erotic friendships, though the phenomenon itself, to be understood, must be placed within the wider context of the breathtaking pace and complexity of modern life under the hegemony of technology.

Time and proximity are the matrix in which persons can put down roots in their relationships and achieve closeness and intimacy, but the technological advancements of our age, and the scientific mind-set that takes nothing for granted and that must put literally everything under the microscope, deprive modern people of both time and proximity. As I argued in Part I of this essay, we are "information addicts", slaves of the compulsion to pile up data and analyze and master everything in existence. We are constantly occupied, preoccupied, distracted, and driven forward deeper into the technological web. Every day there are new demands, new constraints, new possibilities, exhausting us with the need ceaselessly to make choices and decisions. At every moment there is something pressing that must be attended to, lest we "fall behind", lest we cease to be "on top" of our daily lives. But of course, we're not "on top" at all. Most of the time we're just struggling to "catch up". "Catch up with what?" is the question. Busy, restless, without peace, we're swept along relentlessly like flotsam in a flood. Most of us flail our arms desperately, trying to stay afloat. We have no time to live.

And *space* too, like time, is "unavailable", because we're constantly on the move. Time and space are no longer there for us, and we are not there for them. We are instrumentalizing them, as we construct an artificial world. They are becoming as abstract in our experience as they are in the mathematical equations we use to represent them. Since space and time are the matrix of our experience of reality, we find that *we too* are being instrumentalized by social forces beyond our control; that *we too* are becoming *abstract* in our sense of personal identity. We are losing contact with the ground—we are losing our *footing*.

We find it almost impossible to be still, both in time and in space. We have forgotten how to *contemplate*, how to stand in wonder before an object, an *other*, either God or a creature, organic or inorganic.[17] We strive to relax, because we sense something about this way of life is deeply wrong—but we fail, because, of course, striving to relax is a contradiction (the huge holiday/travel industry is a profit-making response to this problem, but as any contemporary traveler will confirm, practically the last thing we manage to do today when we go on a trip or a tour or "take a vacation", is *relax*). Cell phones penetrate our space, clutter our hours. Meaningless images, aimed to distract, seduce, and sell, saturate our brains, bringing profit only to the commercial interests behind them. From a younger and younger age, screens of one kind or another replace direct face-to-face contact and conversation. The internet phenomena of *Facebook* and *Twitter*, creating millions of ersatz "friendships", is a perfect example of this replacement, even deluding people into thinking that their virtual contacts are *really* friends. *Facebook* and *Twitter* links are not without innovative benefits, of course, and maintaining contact, especially with loved ones, is certainly better than having no contact at all; but in terms of personal *relationships*, the contacts that *Facebook* and *Twitter* sustain are like shadows—fleshless substitutes for something real and solid that is scarcely available any more. So-called "reality shows" on television reveal the pitiful loneliness in which many of us live today, to the point that men and women expose themselves shamelessly to an unknown public in the vain hope that somehow, by this exposure, they will actually *be known*, they will

---

17. It is pertinent to my overall argument to note that what is proposed in our society to compensate for this loss is a variety of *techniques* of meditation.

make contact with others. Dignity is lost, privacy betrayed.[18] Indeed, dignity and privacy are not cherished as they used to be, because a terror lurks in the heart of Modern Man—*underneath* the demand that his "rights" be recognized—that in fact he has no dignity to preserve, and "privacy", he fears, is just a sham that merely covers over his dereliction. "Let it all hang out!" is a suicidal cry of self-contempt.

Lastly, as the ultimate expression of all this, *silence* is banished or avoided, out of an unconscious dread that it might reveal a terrible emptiness at the core of our being. God speaks in silence; but, like Adam and Eve in Eden, we hide from God, we don't want to see him or hear his voice, so we run away and make noise, more and more noise. Earphones wired to electronic devices are, along with screens, the ubiquitous tags of contemporary existence.

Friendship with another person requires being together over time and simply enjoying each other, in a give and take of respect and appreciation. It is a form of love, without sexual overtones. In the New Testament, one is moved on reading of Jesus' "beloved disciple" John, pointing to a particular bond between these two men (John 13:23; 21:7, 20). In the Old Testament, male friendship is most beautifully represented by the love of David and Jonathan, as recorded in 1 Sam 18–20, and in David's heart-rending lamentation upon hearing of the death in battle of Jonathan and his father Saul, in 2 Sam 1:17–27. The faithful love between Naomi and her daughter-in-law Ruth provides a touching example of friendship between two women.

Gay advocates have asserted that these relationships were "homosexual", simply because deep love was shown between members of the same sex. This baseless assertion shows the difficulty many gay people have of even conceiving of intimate non-erotic same-sex relationships. The assertion is also self-serving, as an attempt to justify gay relationships by providing (bogus) biblical support for them. The normalization of homosexual practice in the West today is unquestionably a contributing cause—within the wider cultural context described above—of the decline of same-sex friendship in our culture. Any such friendship, as I observed earlier, is suspected automatically today of being homosexual. There is something close to tragic in this development. It impoverishes the range of human relationships, entailing an incalculable loss for our society.

---

18. An insightful discussion of certain technical issues connected with the growing problem of the *invasion* and *erosion* of privacy is to be found in Perera, "Friends or Fish?"

I mentioned that, fortunately, it is not uncommon for people with a same-sex orientation to have close friendships with non-gays, and this will be a source of strength for them; but between practicing gay persons, close non-erotic friendship will be much rarer. Speaking of men—and the same may be said of women—one of the key components in the life of any gay man who is disengaging from his homosexual orientation will be the development of non-erotic friendships with other males, both gay and "straight". It is precisely such relationships that he most needs to discover and affirm his masculine identity. A gay male's former eroticized relations with other males, which, unconsciously, he had hoped would provide on the one hand the affirming father-love he may never have had to the degree needed, and on the other hand the woman-love he was *created* to have, will only have confused and distorted his sense of his gender identity. It is through male-male friendships that his own maleness will be substantiated. Non-erotic friendships with men are indispensable to prepare "disengaging" gays either for a celibate life or for an eventual erotic relationship with a woman.

In talking about homosexuality, we are indeed talking about *love*, or rather the *lack* of it. We are talking about a lack of *affirmation*. Sadly, this lack is commonly not just a matter of individual circumstances, as the case may be; it is also the result of condemnation down through the centuries by society and by the Church. Such lack of affirmation will normally result in a measure of instability and identity confusion. Confusion about one's *sexual* identity is one expression of this.

Of course, notwithstanding the inner loneliness I referred to above, which I suspect is common, many gays are stable and well-adjusted in their identity, just as many heterosexual persons are unstable and maladjusted. Any general statements with regard to these matters must be tempered by the recognition that human affections and desires are multifaceted, that our feelings towards men and women will fluctuate, and that enduring stability will only come as we find our identity with reference to Christ, who redeems us from the vertiginous void that is the human self cut off from its transcendent source.

There are many possible causes of the homosexual orientation, and it is not the purpose of this essay to reiterate at great length the analyses of more competent authors than I in this domain. Much diagnostic uncertainty remains in this area, and even the biological and psychosocial factors that I will refer to, though supported by many, are strongly contested by other workers in the field. The mention of a number of the most common causes, however, will reveal the link of practically all of them with a lack of love/affirmation in some form. At what we may call the existential level as distinct from the ontological, this is a primary reason why God the Creator is opposed to homosexual practice: it is a *substitute*, a compensation for a lack, an attempt—in a quest to make up for love that *in some way*, in almost every instance, was missing or distorted in the early years of a person's life—to fill a void.

II.IV.6

Judgment of others condemned by Paul; common sources and causes of homosexual orientation and activity; we are all wounded, we all need love; the conflation of tendency and identity; the divorce in contemporary society of body from mind/heart

Before we consider these causes, it is appropriate at this point to return for a moment to the Epistle to the Romans. At the end of the text cited above, the Apostle Paul evidently realized that there would very likely be people hearing and reading his letter who would smugly congratulate themselves for not engaging in homosexual practices and for not committing the egregious sins listed in chapter 1:29–32. Some of these people would be Jews who believed in Messiah Jesus, who had tried earnestly to obey the Law, and who probably felt morally superior to pagan converts to the faith. Others would be Gentiles inclined to be judgmental towards the immoral pagan world from which they had come, or—perhaps especially—towards Jews for their scrupulosity. Paul, following the teaching of Jesus (Matt 7:1–5), roundly admonishes all who would self-righteously judge others, for whatever reason.

Discernment and rebuke of sin is one thing; a judgmental attitude that condemns the sinner is another. *All* have sinned, Paul insists, citing texts from the Hebrew Scriptures. *"You, therefore, have no excuse, you who pass judgment on someone else, for at whatever point you judge the other, you are condemning yourself, because you who pass judgment do the same things."* (Rom 2:1). Richard Hays calls this strategy a "homiletical sting operation". He adds: "The radical move that Paul makes is to proclaim that all people, Jews and Gentiles alike, stand equally condemned under the just judgment of a righteous God. Consequently, for Paul, self-righteous judgment of homosexuality is just as sinful as the homosexual behavior itself."[19] It is obvious that Paul's strong rebuke can be applied to those in the Church over the centuries who have categorically rejected people with homosexual tendencies or lifestyle, rather than extending to them God's welcoming hand and being respectful agents of his love and power to transform and heal. Ironically, the Church at large, for most of its history—and this is surely one of the main causes of the furious hatred of the radical Gay Lobby for traditional Christian sexual ethics—was guilty of the same irresponsibility towards persons of homosexual orientation that the liberal sector of the mainline Protestant churches, especially that of TEC, is guilty of today, though for the opposite reason and in an entirely different way: a refusal to propose and provide for such persons, if they desired or desire it, the affirming love of Christ *coupled with* the possibility of a change of orientation and the love and care needed to achieve this.

We are all wounded, we are all sinners, we all need love. Without this conviction, implanted deep in the heart as well as in the mind, it is difficult to keep one's head above water while negotiating the currents swirling around the homosexual issue. This is one reason why it is helpful to consider the issue from the *perspective of love.* God is love, John tells us in his First Epistle (1 John 4:8), and we, made in his image, are called to live in that love. But by turning away from him in rebellion, we have turned away from love as a way of life. We have all suffered from this and made others suffer. Gay persons have suffered more than many. It is vital to keep this in mind as we look briefly at a number of the recognized non-biological causes of the homosexual condition (I alluded earlier—II.III.5—to some of the possible *biological* causes).

I am aware that what follows is controversial and that some of the developmental causes of gay "orientation" that I shall adduce are contested or dismissed by many both in and outside of the gay community. But other respected voices, equally competent and professional, hold to positions similar to mine, and in a rational discussion such as I am attempting, these positions merit respect. There is a great deal of experiential evidence behind them, which it would be irresponsible to dismiss out of hand just because a new paradigm with respect to the phenomenon of homosexuality is now winning popular support. They fit, I believe, with my theological analysis and provide existential substance in support of it. It should be obvious that we all have more to learn about these vital questions. My overall

19. Hays, op. cit., 389.

aim in placing my analysis in the broader context of technology, is, as I have reiterated, to extend the discussion of the multiple aspects of these issues—including the psychological aspects I adduce, which cannot be separated out from the technological framework of modern life in which they take shape—beyond their current bounds. It is my sincerest hope that those who contest my position will produce substantive *arguments* of their own and not simply respond with polemics or indignant condemnation or biased studies disingenuously claiming to be scientific.

It is widely acknowledged by social workers and psychiatric professionals involved in treating gay persons who come for help, that a failure to bond with the same-sex parent is one of the commonest sources of the homosexual orientation. Francis MacNutt sums this up simply in the case of males: "Sometimes this lack of male bonding occurs because the father is harsh, abusive, demanding. In other cases the father, a decent man, is simply absent emotionally (or physically) and difficult to relate to. The son is left longing for his father's love; and when he becomes old enough for his sexuality to emerge, his longing may become sexualized."[20] What is technically called "defensive detachment" results from this mis-match. It may entail ambivalent or hostile feelings towards the father, coupled with a deep sense of unmet need. Experiences of detachment, whatever their cause, may have occurred in the earliest years of life and be buried deep in the unconscious mind.

Sometimes there may be jealousy between brothers, or envy of a favored sister. Difficulty in relating to same-sex peers may accompany the emotional detachment from the father. All this leads to an abnormal—and undesirable—emotional deficit in the boy's heart and a disruption in the normal process of his masculine identification. He will feel inadequate in his identity as a male, and experience a sense of gender inferiority (for different causes, the same will hold for a girl who lacks healthy same-sex bonding). Later, the young man will be drawn to other men for gender affirmation and in order to find the love missing originally in the relation with the father. This experience, common to a majority of homosexuals, is known in psychoanalytic literature as a "reparative drive", the "attempt to 'repair' a deficit in masculine identity".[21] If this attraction is eroticized, the young man in our example may end up thinking he is gay and living a gay life-style, when all the time the

20. MacNutt, *Can Homosexuality be Healed?*, 45; Nicolosi, *Reparative Therapy*, ch. 4.

21. Nicolosi, op cit., 70.

problem is basically not sexual but emotional, arising from a lack of masculine love and affirmation as he was growing up.

Another scenario may arise from a hetero-emotional wound and involve, in Arthur Goldberg's words, "a lack of separation, individuation, or differentiation from the opposite-sex parent, often owing to an abnormally close or, conversely, a particularly troubled or distant, relationship with that parent."[22] This departure from the normal bonding process between child and the opposite-sex parent can lead to all sorts of sexual deviance in later years, including homosexuality and lesbianism but also heterosexual promiscuity. A male may be drawn abnormally to feminine self-expression, represented by the mother, in an attempt to distance himself from the father's masculinity, experienced as cruel or remote; in a different kind of scenario, he may flee the mother and seek in relationships with other males the tenderness the mother, for some reason, was unable to give. A female lacking the father's affirmation may recoil from the masculine in general and bond abnormally with another female, seeking there the affirmation missing with the opposite-sex parent. Another common cause of a lesbian orientation is a desire to repair a poor relation with the mother by avoiding intimacy with men in the hope of establishing eventually a positive relation with the mother.

There are many possible sexual scenarios arising from disordered family relationships. The point to emphasize is that the erotic element in these scenarios is not basic but expresses prior unmet emotional needs. These will have been repressed for the most part, so that feelings of same-sex attraction of which the person begins to be aware around the time of puberty, or even earlier, will be taken to be "the way things are", whereas in fact the feelings involved are due to unbalanced or disordered relationships that can be healed through proper treatment. Normal sexual development has been diverted somehow from its proper course. Perhaps it has been arrested prematurely by a failure for some reason to get beyond the infantile incestuous stage when the child's sexuality is focused on his or her parents.[23] Such a failure may then have led to a mirror effect, with the child being fascinated by *itself* as "other", a fact that inhibits acceptance of the opposite sex. An identity confusion and a search for positive affirmation will have been the result. Persons with a same-sex orientation—*dis*-orientation—will obviously not be inclined to

22. Goldberg, op. cit., 129; Nicolosi, op. cit., ch. 8.
23. Anatrella, op. cit., 47–49.

seek such affirmation through a normal heterosexual relationship, since this is precisely where the initial problem—the *disorientation*—started; on the contrary, they will seek it through a narcissistic identification with persons of the same gender.

Homosexuality is a sexual *tendency* that is in conflict with the sexual *identity* of the subject.[24] Narcissistic pathology arises when the *tendency* is conflated with the *identity*. In today's narcissistic climate, subjective feelings and desires are considered to be determinative of what counts as real and ultimately important, and their expression is believed to be the source of personal fulfillment. Hence the conflation of tendency with identity is more and more common, resulting in the frequently heard affirmation by gay persons that they *are* homosexuals, that they always have been and always will be, and that their same-sex attraction and sexual expression reflect *who they are*. If they are Christians, they will say, "*God made me this way*".[25] Increasingly this sort of discourse is also heard from transvestites and transsexuals, even pederasts, such that the fact of gender is rendered more and more unclear and arbitrary. "Gender theory", which first became the object of academic attention in America in the 1970s, gives formal expression to this movement in contemporary society toward the idea that mankind can invent itself— re-create itself—and that the basic structures of the original creation are not determinant and definitive of human identity.[26] I have already considered in Part I the phenomenon of gender theory and its implications. The theory is obviously a slap in the face of the Creator, and shows the degree to which, like the rebellious society described by Paul in Romans, our contemporary world has been "given over" by God to its own willful devices, with the inevitable results of increasing tension and disharmony at every level of society, ominous symptoms of societal breakdown. The hubristic notion of self-construction, ballyhooed by gender theory, can in fact only lead to self-destruction.

24. Ibid., 59.

25. This essentialist affirmation is in some tension with what was said earlier about gender theory's contention that "sexual orientation" is a cultural construction and that genuine freedom means that we are free to concoct for ourselves whatever sexual orientation or expression we want. Gay persons who have identified themselves as gay do wish to affirm that they are this way by nature, not culture. For them, gender theory—if they accept it—would simply be a way of claiming that they could add on other "sexual orientations" if they wanted, such as bi-sexuality or trans-sexuality. But there is an irony here that should not be missed.

26. Ibid., 106–8.

Family relationships are the arena where the absence or distortion of love has the most powerful effect on children, and it is indisputable that this love-lack often, if not always, lies behind a person's later adoption of a gay lifestyle. But there are other arenas. Goldberg puts his finger on one that most people might never think of: "Whether real or perceived, negative peer or parental reactions to a child's physical attributes can cause great pain leading to low self-esteem and feelings of physical inadequacy. . . . Such feelings of self-disparagement can seriously affect one's gender identification."[27] This should come as no surprise, but people who have never struggled with a negative body-image can have no idea of the power of such self-rejecting feelings.

Along similar lines, there is the matter of "gender nonconformity", when children feel out of place, or "different", with respect to members of their own sex.[28] There is the common case of temperamental characteristics, or gifts, which, if not properly affirmed in the family or school environment, may cause a young person to be excluded or even bullied by his/her peers. In American or British culture this may be especially true for boys who are artistically inclined and aesthetically sensitive, but awkward in sports. The more feminine side of their nature may become dominant, while a hyper-masculine "ideal" male figure corresponding to what they wish they were takes shape in their psyche, to which, in later years, they will try to find—and bond to—a real-life equivalent or equivalents, in a hopeless search for their true gender identity. This true identity, of course, is *in them* all along but has been suppressed and transferred outward onto another. In mating with this other, who, psychologically speaking, is a narcissistic projection of the ideal self they wish to be, they are vainly seeking to affirm their masculinity and become who they were made to be.[29] But they are looking in the wrong place, since the only

27. Goldberg, op. cit., 138.

28. See Gagnon, op. cit., 408.

29. As is well-known, many gay people—persons with a homosexual orientation—find themselves at home in the world of the arts. In addition to natural aesthetic aptitudes that may be present, what could be called an *emotional displacement* might be operative here, with the arts being a medium of emotional fulfillment making up for what was not received normally in early family relationships. Furthermore, the self-projection into an artistic form, as in the fictional creation or the dramatic portrayal of characters other than oneself, or, for example, in musical composition or performance, may undoubtedly be seen as both an escape from a deprived inner self and a thrust outward to find fulfillment in an *other*, be it in other *characters*, as in, say, the theatre, or in other *scenarios* than one's own, as in musical, choreographical, or painterly realizations. This analysis could of

way they can fundamentally affirm their own masculine identity is by coming into healing and establishing non-erotic friendships with men and then close relationships with women, leading ultimately perhaps, but not necessarily, to marriage.

Sexual abuse by an older man (or woman, but this is rarer) is a common cause contributing to the development of same-sex attraction leading later to homoerotic activity. Studies show that a high percentage of boys and girls victimized by older men become practicing homosexuals and lesbians in adolescence and adulthood. Predators are easily able to sense in young persons unmet homo-emotional needs like those discussed above, and their seduction consists in providing male intimacy that then leads to sexual abuse. Needless to say, the societal fragmentation we are experiencing produces more and more emotionally homeless people—emotional vagrants—who turn into predators and produce in turn more and more promiscuous persons, both homosexual and heterosexual.

While there is absolutely no evidence, as I stated above (II.III.5), for the existence of a homosexual gene, no doubt exists that early—even pre-natal—influences may incline a child to experience same-sex attraction from a young age. It is well-known that the fetus is extremely sensitive to what its mother is experiencing during pregnancy. The infant, naturally, will be at least as sensitive as the fetus, so that influences from disorderly relationships in the family, including ones going back a generation or two that would have impacted the parents themselves, cannot fail to affect the baby. Without question, such influences may dispose the child to be sexually attracted in later years to members of its own sex.

Most gay people do not choose to have these same-sex feelings; what they *do* have a choice about, however, is whether to engage in sexual activity with persons of their own sex. They have as much choice about this as heterosexual persons have about engaging in sexual activity before or outside of marriage with persons of the opposite sex. It is ironic that in a society where "freedom of choice" is an idol, the hard-line gay community insists that its members have no choice in their way of life, and in support of this untruth puts forward the patent lie that their behavior is genetically determined. This *choice to have no choice* is a reflection of the perversion in our culture of the meaning of freedom, which has come to be associated entirely with the power to satisfy an immediate desire, even if that desire enslaves the person yielding to it; correlatively, the *choice to*

---

course be applied to many heterosexual artists as well.

have no choice is also a sign of a willful disregard for objective reality in favor of subjective feeling, which induces moral laziness and passivity, deceit, and the abdication of social responsibility. And all this in a culture priding itself on being "scientific"![30]

II.IV.7

The biblical position on sexuality and marriage;
the breakdown of traditional patterns of relationship;
promiscuity and the search for love

The only sector of society that would be in a position today to encourage both the gay and heterosexual parties to refrain from sexual activity that the Bible opposes, is the Church. The Roman Catholic, Orthodox, and Oriental Churches, and the evangelical sectors of the Protestant Churches, including the Pentecostals, are holding the line on traditional Christian positions, even while struggling, often reluctantly, to respond to the new attitudes and sexual behavior in modern society with understanding and imagination. One notes here and there a fear of being mocked and a difficulty in finding the language and arguments to counter radical gay propaganda and defend the Scriptural position coherently. It is also proving a challenge for these Churches to manifest effectively God's love and power on behalf of those in the gay community who want to leave the gay lifestyle. Biblical illiteracy is rampant in our society, and much of the population, including many church-goers, knows practically nothing any longer of the biblical prescriptions in ethical matters, or the reasons

---

30. The almost total disjunction in Western culture between what is still perceived by the majority of the population to be the objective, empirical, factual world of science/technology and what is perceived to be the completely subjective sphere of ethics, aesthetics, and religious faith, is a sign of cultural incoherence that is leading to polarization and disunion at every level of society, with attendant confusion and progressive civil strife and breakdown. The consequence of this in contemporary sexual mores, characterized by frequent and casual sexual coupling with no reference to marriage or permanence or child-bearing, is the effectual divorce of the body from the mind/heart, such that bodies, not persons, come together in sexual encounter, and sexual partners are seen as *objects* for physical gratification rather than as *persons* giving and receiving love. In no way, however, can such encounters be truly satisfying, since human beings are in fact whole persons—spirit, soul, and body—and relationships that break up these personal dimensions into separate parts, and that cut off the body from the mind and heart, can only lead to a profound absence of inner fulfillment and a disintegrated sense of personal identity.

for them, or the means of grace enabling us to obey them. Individuals are thrown back on their own resources and thrash about without sound moral guidance, hearing discordant voices on every hand and following little more than their nose, their "feelings"—or radical lobbies and demagogues!—to make appropriate moral decisions.

The biblical position on sexuality and marriage is based on the anthropological understanding of man/woman created in the image of God and made for companionship with the Creator. From this perspective, a human person has eternal value, and is not to be treated as an object. His or her life is a gift of God and is sacred. Its form is gender-defined, so that the whole life of a person—spirit, soul, and body—is involved in his or her sexuality. It is through his/her sexuality, understood in this comprehensive manner, that a person's *life* is expressed and the *race* perpetuated.

Contemporary culture divorces sexual activity from the deeper meanings of love that presuppose the spiritual and psychic lifelong bonding of two persons through their physical bonding. Similarly, as I observed above, the connection between marriage and procreation is weakening, as is the connection between biological parents and their biological children. One of the chief causes of this is the pressure from the gay community to legalize gay marriage, which would obviously have the effect of transforming the age-long understanding of marriage as being bound up *essentially* with procreation and the welfare of society. Marriage would henceforth be re-defined as "primarily a way in which two adults affirm their emotional commitment to one another," as gay activist Andrew Sullivan has written.[31] For the State to institutionalize as "marriage" a relationship that is determined solely by *feelings* between any two persons and that has nothing to do basically with procreation, the future of the race, and the relation of generations, not to mention gender complementarity, demonstrates the astonishing irrationality and shortsightedness of contemporary ethical and political thought.[32]

31. Quoted in Sider, "Bearing Better Witness," 49. Sider points out the sophistical reasoning of the opponents of traditional marriage who argue that any State supporting such marriage "should not grant a marriage license to sterile couples, those who choose not to have children, or older people who no longer can conceive children" (49). The issue has to do with opposed *conceptions* of the structure and purpose of marriage, not with the particular circumstances of individuals.

32. In the aforementioned article in *Touchstone* (Note 3, above), Douglas Farrow shows that when a State passes a law affirming same-sex "marriage", it usurps natural law and moves in the direction of totalitarian oppression. In attempting, on the one hand, to restrict religious expression to the private sphere, and, on the other hand, to

Christ's teaching on marriage (Matt 19:3–9), based on Gen 1: 27–28 and 2:23–24, assumes the infinite potential and sacred, life-generating meaning of the marriage covenant between a man and a woman, two beings made by God for holiness and everlasting communion with himself.[33] I pointed out earlier that this is echoed ecclesiologically later in St. Paul's teaching, endorsed by two thousand years of tradition, that declares the Church to be the Bride of Christ, and the bride and groom in the covenant of marriage to be an image of this relationship (Eph 5:25–32). This teaching is in continuity with the prophetic teaching of the Old Testament that Israel is the bride of Yahweh, her Lord (cf. Isa 50:1; 54:5–6; Hos 2:16–20). It is by no means incidental to point out that this powerful symbol would be subverted and stripped of much of its meaning if the human "bride" were a man, of the same sex as the groom.

Both Jesus and Paul consider monogamous faithfulness, on the basis of covenanted mutual commitment, to be of the highest value, as being a reflection of God's own covenant faithfulness towards humanity. All through Scripture we are told that God's faithfulness will hold forever. Fulfilled as it is in Christ, this divine faithfulness—which manifests God's righteousness—opens up infinite horizons of communion and joy for mankind. The Bible's commandments about sexual purity have therefore as their objective the recognition of the infinite worth of human beings, as shown through the wonder of gender, of sexuality, and of the covenant love

---

legalize unprocreative "marriage" between persons of the same sex, the State is undermining the two realms that exist prior to and naturally independent of itself. "In attacking 'heterosexual monogamy'," writers Farrow, "same-sex marriage does away with the very institution—the only institution we have—that exists precisely in order to support the natural family and to affirm its independence from the state. In doing so, it effectively makes every citizen a ward of the state, by turning his or her most fundamental human connections into legal constructs at the state's gift and disposal" (Farrow, op. cit., 6). The recent decision by the government of Denmark to make it mandatory for all churches to conduct gay "marriages" is a flagrant infringement of religious freedom that perfectly illustrates Farrow's insight and manifestly points in the direction of totalitarian State oppression carried out under the banner of legal "equality". Same-sex "marriage" has become, in Farrow's words, a "tool of the State" (5), undermining the very democracy its proponents think they are strengthening. Positive law is more and more usurping natural law, in keeping with the human drive to set aside, deny, and finally replace God.

33. Those—and there are many clergy among them—who think that sexual issues such as homosexual practice and gay "marriage" are of minor importance compared with matters to do with sacraments and /or "social action", have clearly never thought through the significance of marriage and the full meaning of sexuality.

and mutual fidelity between a man and a woman that actually provide an image of the plural Being of the Triune God and his love for his creation.

All of this is trodden underfoot today and ignored by our secular culture, to such a degree that many sectors of the Church itself, as we have seen, are blind to these truths and fail to proclaim them with conviction. With respect to homosexuality, cultural influences play an enormous role in the astonishing new acceptance of homosexual behavior in Western society. Modern means of communication enable advertising, the media, and the "entertainment industry" to give free rein to their exploitative greed, of which brazen "in-your-face" sexual imagery and innuendo are the chief selling technique. Literally everything today is commercially driven and sexually saturated. The wild-eyed "whoopee!" of the sexual liberation movement, which by now is mainstream, coupled with the boundless opportunities for deviant behavior offered over the Internet, has opened floodgates for pornography, which is a corrosive poison even more potent than drugs in its capacity to undermine marriage and pervert social behavior. Sex trafficking, sex tourism, pedophilia, and prostitution are everywhere on the rise, as noted earlier. The Gay Lobby's radical agenda, through belligerently propagandistic "sex-education" programs, is penetrating into public schools across the Americas and Europe and being blandly accepted, even touted, by the liberal sectors of the media and the educational establishment, with hardly a protest from the mainline churches or governments, neither of which appears to have any notion of the whirlwind that society will reap—is already reaping—from the normalization of abnormal and pathological behavior. Links between promiscuous homosexuality and pedophilia are well-documented, and the worldwide campaign to lower the legal age of sexual consent is driven by the radical wing of the homosexual community.[34] It is not yet well-known among the general public, but the facts are loud and clear: there is a pedophilia lobby active in European countries and in America that grows stronger every year and that seeks formal legitimization of "intergenerational intimacy" as a lifestyle choice— and the Gay Lobby is one of its most powerful and effective backers.[35] This

34. See Goldberg, op. cit., 68–72, for extensive information about these links. Especially in his footnotes 24, 25, and 26, Goldberg documents a number of websites and journals that discuss or promote sex between male adults and minors, in the name of "sexual liberation for children" and "children's entitlement to pleasure".

35. Ibid. This fact is a horrifying perversion of the fondness many homosexuals have for children, as evidenced in the growing movement for adoption among same-sex couples. Perhaps this fondness also shows a yearning among many homosexuals to give to children the affection that they may not have received when they themselves

should not be overlooked simply by arguing—correctly—that the average gay person is not a pedophile and abhors such behavior as much as the average heterosexual person.

I have discussed in Part I of this essay a number of other social factors and philosophical currents that have led to the degraded condition of modern culture and the increase in homosexual propaganda and practice. Not the least of these, as I have suggested, is the breakdown of traditional marriage and the surge in the divorce rate in the wake of wars, technological and industrial development, the flight from the land, mass urbanization, economic dislocation, capitalist consumerism, addictive pornography, and forced emigration/immigration. The growing acceptance by the general public in the West of homoerotic activity as "normal", and a powerful lobby politicizing such activity and promoting it as equal or even superior to heterosexual activity, is an abnormal epiphenomenon, unprecedented in history, and a clear sign of civilizational crisis. It accompanies, as we have seen, the general increase in sexual promiscuity throughout the population. Traditional family structures and social relationships of every kind are being turned upside down, in the West and across the world. This is one of the most convulsive aspects of modern *de-regulation*—moral, social, and economic; and the radical Gay Liberation movement—which is an *ideology*—is one of its most disturbing fruits.

The hedonistic behavior in our consumerist society, including but certainly not limited to sexual promiscuity, is at bottom a search for love and identity-affirmation by millions of people for whom customary relational patterns traditionally found in family, religion, local customs, or solidarity and continuity at a work-place, have dissolved, through technology and its ripple effects, or become warped or dysfunctional, and who as a consequence have very little sense of who they really are. Identity is to be found in and through *relationship*, through forms of *community*, not through the vain search by isolated individuals for their "inner self", or the "god-within", entities in the pursuit of which huge sums of money and time are wasted annually. Such narcissistic activity is one manifestation of global dislocation and upheaval. Sadly, by running away from God, which is what such behavior amounts to, the people acting this way can find neither peace nor their true identities as men and women created in God's image. God is against such behavior because, as a refusal of him and the creation order he has established, it is—vertically—a

were children. The movement for adoption also reveals, in my view, an inner hunger for traditional family relationships.

manifestation of rebellion and idolatry and—horizontally—evidence of selfishness and socially irresponsible 'me-ism'—narcissism—resulting *from* and *in* communal collapse. The fruitful laws of life and love are being disregarded. For millions of people, the consequences are loneliness, desperation, and despair.

The only real healing for this *sickness-unto-death* is repentance and a return to God's creation ordinances; and the only sources for the proclamation of these ordinances are the communities made up of faithful Jews and Christians, wherever these may be found. The liberal Jewish synagogues and Protestant churches, with the majority of TEC defiantly in the lead, have abandoned their spiritual and ethical calling in this regard and are now actually affirming as good what is manifestly a falling short of the order and love prescribed by the Creator. In light of this, the cheap grace of "inclusivism" and the banal declaration that "God is love", emptied of the theological content that would explain what this means, are travesties and must be understood, from a Scriptural perspective, not as a provocation of God's judgment but as a frightening *manifestation* of it, brought upon us by our own actions. God has *given over* portions of his Church to their own perverse choice to seek *not his will*, but *their own*. (Paul's rebuke of human society in Romans 1:18–32 may legitimately be applied here to the Church itself and not just to the world at large.)

It is a depressing commentary on the blindness of the liberal churches that they are encouraging as normal, even commendable, behavior that displays in a variety of ways the fruit of a lack of love in the past and a search for a reparative love in the present. In the name of the God who is indeed Love and who has both the power and the desire to pour out his grace into those wounded hearts and heal them, these churches propose—often out of fear or misplaced "grace"—a nostrum in the form of a bland approval of the homosexual condition. The reality of God's holiness, and the power of Christ's crucifixion and resurrection to turn lives upside down and right side up and establish in them the order of divine truth, are being willfully ignored by people who *know better*, or ought to, or would, if they had not jettisoned three thousand years of theological tradition and the Rock (Christ) on whom they were standing, himself the Logos, the Word of God.

II.IV.8

*The Creator's high view of the body and of sexuality; integrity of
the person: body, soul, and spirit; washed and sanctified in Christ;
God's call to holiness*

To conclude this section, let us look briefly at one of the other key New
Testament Pauline passages that mentions homosexuality, 1 Cor 6:7–11:

> *The very fact that you have lawsuits among you means you have
> been completely defeated already. Why not rather be wronged?
> Why not rather be cheated? Instead, you yourselves cheat and do
> wrong, and you do this to your brothers. Do you not know that
> the wicked will not inherit the Kingdom of God? Do not be de-
> ceived! Neither the sexually immoral nor idolaters nor adulterers
> nor male prostitutes nor homosexual offenders nor thieves nor the
> greedy nor drunkards nor slanderers nor swindlers will inherit the
> Kingdom of God. And this is what some of you were. But you were
> washed, you were sanctified, you were justified in the name of the
> Lord Jesus Christ and by the Spirit of our God.*

One of the telltale signs of the divine judgment we have brought on
ourselves is the explosive and obsessive nature of the homosexual issue
within the mainline churches and, in TEC, the proliferation of scissions
and lawsuits between bishops and dioceses and between priests and parishes. With few exceptions, dissension and acrimony reign, self-righteous
posturing on both sides is common, and the neo-pagan society round-
about looks on condescendingly and guffaws.

In his First Epistle to the Corinthians, St. Paul rebukes the immature
Christians for their mutual recriminations and hostility. He then goes on
to list some sins that God severely judges. The proximity of this list to his
disapproval of the Corinthians' recourse to courts—even "unbelievers'"
courts—to judge their disputes, is striking in light of what is going on in
The Episcopal Church and other mainline churches today.

Corinth was known for its idolatry and sexual license. In addition, a
case of incest had recently disturbed the young church. It is not surprising
then that Paul's list of unacceptable practices should include a number of
sexual sins, though they do not carry greater opprobrium than the other
sins named. The word *pornoi*—translated 'sexually immoral'—is a general
word for sexual immorality and, like the other words in the passage referring to sexual practices, takes its meaning chiefly from the passages in

the Holiness Code that we looked at earlier. It probably includes the other sexual sins Paul goes on to mention, but clearly, given the problems in the church, the Apostle felt the need to specify these. The term *moichoi* designates adulterers; the word *malakoi*, according to Kevin Scott, is Greek slang for passive partners in homosexual activity; and the word *arsenokoitai*, not attested in ancient literature before its appearance in this passage, means literally *males who lie together* and would seem, again according to Scott, to be a rendering of the language of Lev 18:22 and 20:13.[36]

In the present context, what I wish to underline is v.11, where Paul states clearly that there were among the Corinthian Christians people who had fitted all the categories of sinners enumerated in the previous verses: *"And this is what some of you were."* They are not these things anymore. They have been washed, sanctified, and justified in the name of Jesus Christ and by the Spirit of God. They are new creations. They have come into their true identity. It is not simply that they *do not do* any longer what they used to do, though this is the case; it is that they *are new beings* under the lordship of Christ, sinners who have died to their old self through commitment to Jesus and faith in the Triune God. They have been born again (John 3:3), born of water and Spirit (John 3:5). By grace through faith they have been transformed in a very real sense *ontologically* from within and then baptized; God has given them a new heart and a new spirit, as Ezekiel had prophesied six hundred years before:

> *I will sprinkle clean water upon you, and you will be clean; I will cleanse you from all your impurities and from all your idols. I will give you a new heart and put a new spirit in you; I will remove from you your heart of stone and give you a heart of flesh. And I will put my Spirit in you and move you to follow my decrees and be careful to keep my laws."* (Ezek 36:25–27). The Apostle Paul points to the fulfillment of this prophesy in Rom. 6:4: *"We were therefore buried with him through baptism into death in order that, just as Christ was raised from the dead through the glory of the Father, we too may live a new life.*

In the latter part of chapter 6 of his Epistle to the Corinthians, the Apostle elaborates on the theme of the body. *"The body is not meant for sexual immorality but for the Lord, and the Lord for the body."* (v. 13b). And he goes on: *"Do you not know that your bodies are members of Christ himself? . . . . Do you not know that your body is a temple of the Holy Spirit,*

---

36. Scott, op. cit., 42–43, and Hayes, op. cit., 382–83.

who is in you, whom you have received from God? You are not your own; you were bought at a price. Therefore honor God with your body." (vv. 15a, 19–20). I have already commented on this, but the theme is so important that it merits re-emphasis. Sexual relations outside the covenant commitment of marriage are displeasing to God not because (perish the thought) he despises sexuality and the body, but precisely because he has a very high view of them. He is their Creator—the Creator of our physical being and our sexuality; the body is the physical dimension of the person he has made, who is spirit, soul, and body (1 Thess 5:23). These aspects of our being are inseparable until death, which means that sexual intercourse is a spiritual act. Those who engage in it are bound together, joined psychically and spiritually as well as physically, since the distinct aspects of the human person cannot in fact be dissociated, as contemporary society is presuming to do (see 1 Cor 6:16).

If there is just attraction and physical passion without the mutual commitment that fulfills love; or if there is abuse; or if there is misuse of the natural organs, as in homosexuality, then the body—the whole person—is in varying degrees being treated as a mere object for pleasure and not as a subject. The persons are in effect being broken up into parts and dishonored, and their inner identity is being fragmented. This is a perfect mirror-image of the scientific/technological methodological paradigm that governs modern life. When the pleasure is past, the attraction exhausted, the two who have been joined will separate and look for other partners, leaving parts—one might say 'prints'—of themselves forever lodged in each other's psyches. There will be brokenness and sadness, even if there may also be some nostalgic memories where genuine affection was expressed. If the relation was one of abuse or misuse, there will be an inner sense of dissolution and shame. Feelings like these may be repressed so that the persons are scarcely conscious of them, but only God can actually *remove* them and cleanse the soul and spirit, through the grace of forgiveness and new birth in the Spirit. Otherwise, guilt, self-hatred, and depression can easily follow, or perhaps increasing dissipation or some sort of addiction, sexual or other, in order to forget or drown the inner fragmentation and emptiness. This is not "sexual liberation", but defilement and self-destruction, marked by a coarsening of character and a hardening of the heart. We see this everywhere today in our morally bankrupt society.

God wants better for us—*much better*. He made the body and sexuality for our joy, not our sorrow; for fulfillment, not loss and defilement.

The Son of God became *incarnate* in the person of Jesus Christ. He came in the flesh, in a *body*. As representative Man—the Second Adam—he gave up to death his whole person—spirit, soul and body—so that, by virtue of his *physical* resurrection, the broken person each of us is—the heterosexual as much as the homosexual, but *differently*—might, by faith, be made whole, and at the eschatological resurrection of the dead, be clothed again with a *body*—what St. Paul calls a "spiritual body"—which will somehow resemble the resurrected body of Christ (1 Cor 15:44, 49).

Our bodies are of inestimable value and importance to our Creator. He created them in all their wonderful complexity, and he died for them. Let me quote again from 1 Cor 6:13b–15a; 18–20:

> *The body is not meant for sexual immorality, but for the Lord, and the Lord for the body. By his power God raised the Lord from the dead, and he will raise us also. Do you not know that your bodies are members of Christ himself?. . . . Flee from sexual immorality! All other sins a man commits are outside his body, but he who sins sexually sins against his own body. Do you not know that your body is a temple of the Holy Spirit, who is in you, whom you have received from God? You are not your own; you were bought at a price. Therefore honor God with your body.*

We are to treat our bodies with honor, for we—men and women—are made in God's image. When all is said and done, this is the primary reason why God is opposed to homosexual practice. "*As obedient children, do not conform to the evil desires that you had when you lived in ignorance. But just as he who called you is holy, so be holy in all you do; for it is written: 'Be holy, because I am holy'*" (1 Pet 1:14–16).

II.IV.9

Conclusion

I have been concerned in this essay to approach the complex subject of homosexuality from an unusual angle, in order to provoke more rigorous and far-reaching discussion in the Church, in particular in TEC and other mainline Protestant denominations that are reinterpreting the traditional Judeo-Christian understanding of sexuality in such a way as to sanction the ordination of gay persons and the blessing of same-sex unions, and eventually, in all likelihood, the approval and celebration of same-sex "marriages." For reasons I have tried to set forth clearly, I believe the issue to be of great importance for the future of the Church. Up until now, as far as I am aware, little work has been done to bring to bear on the current debate the context of modern technology in which this reinterpretation of sexuality is taking place. My contention is that analysis of this context is vital if we are to gain a proper perspective on the question of homosexuality as it is being raised in our day. Only thus, I believe, can we have the critical distance on the issue that may allow theological debate about it to advance to a new level.

The ideas I put forth here, especially with respect to technology, will be novel to many people, and undoubtedly controversial. Whatever their value, I trust they will prove fruitful. Many points will need much more analysis and development. My ultimate aim is that this essay may be a stimulus to more mature thinking and pastoral practice within TEC and the wider Church; and my desire and most earnest hope is that, regardless of our conclusions, this will take place in an atmosphere of mutual respect and lead to deeper understanding and a more authentic Christian witness in our society. In this way, as we strive to realize "performative unity," we will please our Lord Jesus Christ and give him glory.

Bibliography

Anatrella, Tony. *Le Règne de Narcisse: les enjeux du déni de la différence sexuelle*. Paris: Presses de la Renaissance, 2005.

Auerbach, Eric. *Mimesis: The Representation of Reality in Western Literature*. Princeton, NJ: Princeton University Press, 1953.

Barrett, William. *The Illusion of Technique*. New York: Anchor Press, Doubleday, 1978.

———. *Death of the Soul: from Descartes to the Computer*. New York: Anchor Books, Doubleday, 1986.

Bauckham, Richard. "Reading Scripture as a Coherent Story". In *The Art of Reading Scripture*, edited by Ellen F. Davis and Richard B. Hays, 38-53. Grand Rapids: Eerdmans, 2003.

———. *The Testimony of the Beloved Disciple: Narrative, History, and Theology in the Gospel of John*. Grand Rapids: Baker Academic, 2007.

Bauman, Zygmunt. *Liquid Modernity*. Malden, MA: Blackwell Ltd., 2000.

Begley, Sharon. "I Can't Think!" *Newsweek* (3/07/2011) 2-27.

Bergner, Mario. *Setting Love in Order: Hope and Healing for the Homosexual*. Grand Rapids: Hamewith, 1995.

Bradshaw, Timothy, editor. *The Way Forward? Christian Voices on Homosexuality and the Church*. Grand Rapids: Eerdmans, 2004.

Breidenthal, Thomas. "The Festal Gathering: Reflections on Open Communion." *Sewanee Theological Review* 54:2 (Easter 2011).

Brown, Terry, editor. *Other Voices, Other Worlds: The Global Church Speaks Out on Homosexuality*. London: Darton, Longman & Todd, 2006.

Brun, Jean. *Philosophie de l'Histoire: les Promesses du Temps*. Paris: Stock, 1990.

Burridge, Richard. *What are the Gospels? A Comparison with Graeco-Roman Biography*. Cambridge University Press, 1992.

Collin, Thibaud. *Le Mariage Gay: Les enjeux d'une revendication*. Paris: Eyrolles, 2005.

Comiskey, Andrew. *Pursuing Sexual Wholeness*. Lake Mary, FL: Creation House, 1989.

Davis, Ellen. *Scripture, Culture, and Agriculture*. Cambridge: Cambridge University Press, GB, 2008.

Davis, Ellen, and Richard B. Hays, editors. *The Art of Reading Scripture*. Grand Rapids: Eerdmans, 2003.

Dawson, Christopher. *Religion and Culture*. London: Sheed & Ward, 1948.

Descartes, René. *The Principles of Philosophy LXVI-LXXII*, in *The Philosophical Works, Vol. I*. London: Constable, Dover Edition, 1955.

Delsol, Chantal. "Non au Mariage Homosexuel." *Le Figaro* (5/21/2012) 18.

Bibliography

Dupré, Louis. *The Enlightenment and the Intellectual Foundations of Modern Culture.* New Haven: Yale University Press, 2005.

Ellul, Jacques. *The Technological Society.* Translated by John Wilkinson. New York: Vintage, 1964.

Farrow, Douglas. "Why Fight Same-Sex Marriage?" *Touchstone* (Jan/Feb 2012). Online: www.touchstonemag.com/archives/article.php?id=25-01-024-f, 1–12.

———. *Nation of Bastards.* Toronto: BPS, 2007.

Feuerbach, Ludwig. *The Essence of Christianity.* Translated by George Eliot, 1881. Mineola, NY: Dover, 2008.

Gagnon, Robert A. J. *The Bible and Homosexual Practice, Texts and Hermeneutics.* Nashville: Abingdon, 2004.

———. "Does Jack Rogers's New Book 'Explode the Myths' about the Bible and Homosexuality and 'Heal the Church'?" Online: http://www.robgagnon.net/articles/RogersBookReviewed.pdf.

Gilson, Etienne. *Études sur le Rôle de la Pensée Médiévale dans la Formation du Système Cartésien.* Paris: Vrin, 1975.

Goldberg, Arthur. *Light in the Closet: Torah, Homosexuality, and the Power to Change.* Beverly Hills, CA: Red Heifer, 2008.

Gray, John. *False Dawn: The Delusions of Global Capitalism.* London: Granta, 1998.

Hart, David Bentley. *Atheist Delusions: The Christian Revolution and its Fashionable Enemies.* New Haven: Yale University Press, 2009.

———. "A Philosopher in the Twilight." *First Things* 210 (2/2011) 44–51.

Hays, Richard B. "Relations Natural and Unnatural: A Response to John Boswell's Exegesis of Romans 1." *Journal of Religious Ethics* 14/1 (1986) 184–215.

———. *The Moral Vision of the New Testament.* New York: HarperCollins, 1996.

Haught, John F. *Is Nature Enough? Meaning and Truth in the Age of Science.* Cambridge: Cambridge University Press, 2006.

Heidegger, Martin. *The Question Concerning Technology and Other Essays.* Translated with an Introduction by William Lovitt. New York: Harper & Row, 1977.

Himmelfarb, Gertrude. *On Looking into the Abyss: Untimely Thoughts on Culture and Society.* New York: Vintage, 1995.

Jenson, Robert. "How the World Lost its Story." *First Things* (10/1993). Reprinted in 201 (3/2010).

Jonas, Hans. *The Phenomenon of Life: Toward a Philosophical Biology.* Evanston, IL: Northwestern University Press, 2001.

Jones, Stanton L. "Same-Sex Science." *First Things* 220 (2/2012) 27–34.

Lacroix, Xavier. *La Confusion des Genres: Réponses à certaines demandes homosexuelles sur le mariage et l'adoption.* Paris: Bayard, 2005.

Lewis, C. S. *Mere Christianity.* 1952. Reprint, London: HarperCollins, 2002.

———. *The Abolition of Man.* 1944. Reprint, New York: HarperCollins, 2001.

MacIntyre, Alasdair. *Whose Justice? Which Rationality?* Notre Dame, IN: University of Notre Dame Press, 1989.

MacNutt, Francis. *Can Homosexuality Be Healed?* Grand Rapids: Chosen, 2006.

Moberly, Elizabeth. *Homosexuality: A New Christian Ethic.* Cambridge, UK: James Clarke, 1983.

Molnar, Thomas. *The Pagan Temptation.* Grand Rapids: Eerdmans, 1987.

Morosov, Evgeny. "Political Repression 2.0." *International Herald Tribune* (9/3-4/2011).

Nicolosi, Joseph. *Reparative Therapy of Male Homosexuality: A New Clinical Approach.* Northvale, NJ: Jason Aronson, 1991.

Bibliography

Nietzsche, Friedrich. *The Portable Nietzsche*. Edited and translated by Walter Kaufmann. New York: Viking Penguin, 1959.

O'Donovan, Oliver. *Church in Crisis: The Gay Controversy and the Anglican Communion*. Eugene, OR: Cascade, 2008.

———. *Begotten or Made?* Oxford: Clarendon, 1984.

Pattison, George. *Thinking about God in an Age of Technology*. Oxford: Oxford University Press, 2005.

Payne, Leanne. *The Broken Image*. Westchester, IL: Crossway, 1981.

———. *Crisis in Masculinity*. Westchester, IL: Crossway, 1985.

———. *The Healing of the Homosexual*. Westchester, IL: Crossway, 1984.

Perera, Rosemary. "Friends or Fish? The Erosion of Privacy in an Online World." *Comment Magazine* (11/5/2010).

Porter, Jean. *Natural and Divine Law: Reclaiming the Tradition for Christian Ethics*. Ottawa, Ontario: Novalis, 1999.

Postman, Neil. *Technopoly*. New York: Vintage, 1993.

Radner, Ephraim, and Philip Turner, editors. *The Fate of Communion: the Agony of Anglicanism and the Future of a Global Church*. Grand Rapids: Eerdmans, 2006.

Rifkin, Jeremy. *The Biotech Century*. New York: Tarcher/Putnam, 1998.

Rolston III, Holmes. *The Three Big Bangs*. New York: Columbia University Press, 2010.

Ruston, Roger. *Human Rights and the Image of God*. London: SCM, 2004.

Satinover, Jeffrey. *Homosexuality and the Politics of Truth*. Grand Rapids: Hamewith, 1996.

———. *The Empty Self: C. G. Jung and the Gnostic Transformation of Modern Identity*. Westport, CT: Hamewith, 1996.

Schenck, Ken. "The Wesleyan View of Communion." Online: http://kenschenck.com/communion.html.

Schneiders, Sandra. *The Revelatory Text: Interpreting the New Testament as Sacred Scripture*. 2nd ed. Collegeville, MN: Liturgical, 1999.

Scott, Kevin. *At Variance*. Edinburgh: Dunedin Academic, 2004.

Scroggs, Robin. *The New Testament and Homosexuality*. Philadelphia: Fortress, 1983.

Scruton, Roger. *An Intelligent Person's Guide to Modern Culture*. South Bend, IN: St. Augustine's, 2000.

Secher, Reynald. *A French Genocide: The Vendée*. Translated by George Holoch. Notre Dame, IN: University of Notre Dame Press, 2003.

Sider, Ron. "Bearing Better Witness." *First Things* 208 (12/2010) 47–50.

Stamm, Mark W. "Open Communion as a United Methodist Exception." *The Quarterly Review* 22:3 (Fall 2002).

Stern, Karl. *The Flight from Women*. New York: Farrar, Strauss & Giroux, 1965.

Thiselton, Anthony. "Can Hermeneutics Ease the Deadlock? Some Biblical Exegesis and Hermeneutical Models." In *The Way Forward?*, edited by Timothy Bradshaw, 145–96. Grand Rapids: Eerdmans, 2004.

Toulmin, Stephen. *Cosmopolis*. Chicago: The University of Chicago Press, 1990.

Turkle, Sherry. "The Flight from Conversation." *International Herald Tribune* (4/24/2011).

———, *Alone Together*. New York: Basic Books, 2011.

Ward, Keith. *The Big Questions in Science and Religion*. West Conshohocken, PA: Templeton Foundation Press, 2008.

Wirzba, Norman. *The Paradise of God*. New York: Oxford University Press, 2003.

Yamahoto, J. Isamu, editor. *The Crisis of Homosexuality*. Wheaton, IL: Victor, 1990.